Domestic Law Goes Global:
Legal Traditions and International Courts

International courts have proliferated in the international system, with over one hundred judicial or quasi-judicial bodies in existence today. This book develops a rational legal design theory of international adjudication in order to explain the variation in state support for international courts. Initial negotiators of new courts, "originators," design international courts in ways that are politically and legally optimal. States joining existing international courts, "joiners," look to the legal rules and procedures to assess the courts' ability to be capable, fair, and unbiased. The authors demonstrate that the characteristics of civil law, common law, and Islamic law influence states' acceptance of the jurisdiction of international courts, the durability of states' commitments to international courts, and the design of states' commitments to the courts. Furthermore, states strike cooperative agreements most effectively in the shadow of an international court that operates according to familiar legal principles and rules.

SARA MCLAUGHLIN MITCHELL is Associate Professor in the Department of Political Science at the University of Iowa.

EMILIA JUSTYNA POWELL is Assistant Professor in the Department of Political Science at the University of Alabama.

Domestic Law Goes Global: Legal Traditions and International Courts

Sara McLaughlin Mitchell

University of Iowa

Emilia Justyna Powell

University of Alabama

CAMBRIDGE
UNIVERSITY PRESS

CAMBRIDGE UNIVERSITY PRESS
Cambridge, New York, Melbourne, Madrid, Cape Town,
Singapore, São Paulo, Delhi, Mexico City

Cambridge University Press
The Edinburgh Building, Cambridge CB2 8RU, UK

Published in the United States of America by Cambridge University Press, New York

www.cambridge.org
Information on this title: www.cambridge.org/9781107661677

© Sara McLaughlin Mitchell and Emilia Justyna Powell 2011

First published 2011
Reprinted 2011
First paperback edition 2013

A catalogue record for this publication is available from the British Library

Library of Congress Cataloguing in Publication Data
Mitchell, Sara McLaughlin.
Domestic law goes global : legal traditions and international courts /
Sara McLaughlin Mitchell, Emilia Justyna Powell.
   p.   cm.
ISBN 978-1-107-00416-0 (hardback)
1. International courts.   2. Arbitration, International.
3. Law–International unification.   4. International law–Sources.
I. Powell, Emilia Justyna.   II. Title.
KZ6250.M58   2011
341.5´5–dc22
2011002698

ISBN 978-1-107-00416-0 Hardback
ISBN 978-1-107-66167-7 Paperback

Contents

Figures

Tables

Boxes

Acknowledgments

The origins of this project stem from a conflict management class that Sara Mitchell taught at Florida State University in the spring 2003 semester. The class discussed a paper by Professor Richard Bilder on international courts, which put forth the interesting argument that countries might be better able to settle interstate disputes peacefully if they could credibly threaten to take each other to the World Court. Sara wrote a paper on this topic for the 2003 Peace Science Society conference that looked at whether states were more likely to reach agreements over geopolitical disputes if they jointly accepted the compulsory jurisdiction of the International Court of Justice, showing that indeed they did. While our fellow Peace Science scholars found these results interesting, they posed a question about selection effects, wondering which countries were more likely to support the World Court in the first place.

Emilia Powell tackled this research question in a follow-up paper in 2004. She argued that in order to understand the variation in countries' support for international courts, it would be fruitful to examine the similarity between countries' domestic legal traditions and the legal rules employed by the courts. Having trained as a lawyer in a civil law country (Poland), she asserted that civil law countries would be more likely to recognize the jurisdiction of the World Court than common law or Islamic law countries due to the similarities between the civil law domestic legal tradition and the principles employed by the Court. This book is the culmination of these initial ideas, which led to several other jointly authored and solo-authored papers looking at other types of interstate cooperation (e.g. trade, military alliances, and conflict management), other international courts, such as the International Criminal Court, and the rational design of states' commitments to international institutions.

Several of these papers laid the groundwork for the theory and empirical analyses in this book. Some components of Chapters 2 and 5 were initially developed in the following paper:

Powell, Emilia Justyna and Sara McLaughlin Mitchell. 2007. "The International Court of Justice and the World's Three Legal Systems." *Journal of Politics* 69(2): 397–415.

Chapter 6 is a modified version of the following paper:

Mitchell, Sara McLaughlin and Emilia Justyna Powell. 2009. "Legal Systems and Variance in the Design of Commitments to the International Court of Justice." *Conflict Management and Peace Science* 26(2): 164–190.

We thank Cambridge University Press and Sage Publications Ltd. for permission to reprint this material.

We are truly grateful for research assistance provided by a number of individuals in the past few years. The initial data on PCIJ/ICJ optional clauses was assembled at Florida State University with the assistance of John Brady, Efthymia Charalampaki, and Jacqueline H. R. DeMerritt. Data on compromissory clauses and World Court cases was collected at the University of Iowa by Karl Burhop, Eashaan Vajpeyi, Amanda Licht, Ross Schoofs, and Clayton Thyne. Beth Simmons graciously shared her data on the ICC with us. We also benefitted from usage of the most recent Issue Correlates of War (ICOW) dataset, Sara's joint project with Paul Hensel. We are grateful to Jacqueline H. R. DeMerritt for her assistance in compiling background information on the World Court, especially for the material discussed in Chapter 5.

Several colleagues gave us useful feedback on our research, including Terry Chapman, Paul Diehl, John King Gamble, Doug Gibler, Michael Greig, Darren Hawkins, Paul Hensel, Tanya Janulewicz, Charlotte Ku, Ashley Leeds, Lorna Lloyd, Ron Mitchell, Monika Nalepa, Brandon Prins, Jeff Staton, Jana von Stein, and Krista Wiegand. We are also grateful to several individuals who helped us maneuver through the book publishing process including Paul Diehl, Gary Goertz, Mike Lewis-Beck, Zeev Maoz, Bill Thompson, and John Vasquez. We are also grateful for the excellent editorial guidance provided by John Haslam and Carrie Parkinson at Cambridge University Press.

Sara is grateful to the University of Iowa for the Faculty Scholar Award that I received which provided three semesters off from teaching between 2008 and 2010, time that was essential for completion of this project. I am also grateful to folks at Rice University, especially Rick Wilson, Ashley Leeds, and Victor Marin, for providing a temporary home in 2009 for three months of solid work on the book and excellent moral support. I appreciate many useful comments provided on various iterations of the book when I presented our research at the following universities: Iowa State University; Oklahoma State University; University of California,

Davis; Cornell University; University of Pittsburgh; and the University of Tennessee. I have truly enjoyed working with Emilia on this project. She stimulated my interest in legal explanations for interstate cooperation, teaching me how to think like a lawyer. She has also been a wonderful friend and co-author. Will Moore deserves special thanks for being such a wonderful mentor. I would also like to thank my husband, Steve, and daughter, Vivian, for providing so much love and support and being very understanding while I was gone for three months working on the book. I also owe a special thanks to my mother, Margaret, who has truly been the inspiration for my entire academic career.

Emilia is grateful for the useful comments provided on the project at the Workshop on Law, Politics, and Human Rights at Emory University, and the University of Alabama. Sara Mitchell deserves a very special "thank you" for continuing to provide truly superb advice throughout my career, including this project. Her work has continued to inspire my interest in international relations and her true dedication as a mentor and friend is absolutely invaluable. Finally, and above all, this project would not be possible without the support and love of my family, especially my husband, Charles Wesley, and our daughter, Scarlett Sophia. I thank God for their endless encouragement and support for my academic endeavors, which allowed me to fully concentrate on this project. Scarlett, who was born during the beginning phases of the book, gave me the greatest gift: motivation. My parents Elżbieta and Jerzy and my brother Tadeusz deserve acknowledgment. They all continue to inspire me, not only with their knowledge of the civil legal tradition but also with their faith in my abilities. Thank you for supporting me all the way through my legal education in Poland. I also dedicate this book to my grandmother Zofia, who has always supported me in innumerable ways.

Acronyms

CCJ	Caribbean Court of Justice
CINC	Composite Index of National Capability
CIRI	Cingranelli-Richards
CIS	Commonwealth of Independent States
COMESA	Common Market for Eastern and Southern Africa
ECHR	European Court of Human Rights
ECJ	European Court of Justice
EFTA	European Free Trade Association
EU	European Union
GATT	General Agreement on Tariffs and Trade
HRC	Human Rights Council
ICC	International Criminal Court
ICJ	International Court of Justice
ICOW	Issue Correlates of War
ICRG	*International Country Risk Guide*
ICSID	International Court for Settlement of Investment Disputes
ICTR	International Criminal Tribunal for Rwanda
ICTY	International Criminal Tribunal for the former Yugoslavia
IICJ	Islamic International Court of Justice
ILC	International Law Commission
INGO	International non-governmental organization
IO	International organization
ITLOS	International Tribunal for the Law of the Sea
MID	Militarized interstate dispute
MTOPS	Multilateral Treaties of Pacific Settlement
NATO	North Atlantic Treaty Organization
NGO	Non-governmental organization
OAS	Organization of American States
OLS	Ordinary least squares
PCA	Permanent Court of Arbitration
PCIJ	Permanent Court of International Justice

PTA	Preferential Trade Agreement
SIPRI	Stockholm International Peace Research Institute
EUGene	Expected Utility Generation
UN	United Nations
UNCLOS	United Nations Convention on the Law of the Sea
WTO	World Trade Organization

1   The creation and expansion of
international courts

International courts have proliferated significantly in the international system, growing from only a handful of courts a century ago, to over 100 judicial or quasi-judicial bodies today.[1] Prominent international courts include the International Court of Justice (ICJ), the International Criminal Court (ICC), the European Court of Justice (ECJ), and the World Trade Organization's (WTO) Dispute Settlement Understanding. International courts operate at the regional and global levels and cover a wide variety of issues such as territorial disputes, human rights, the law of the sea, trade, investments, and the use of military force.

While the number of international courts has increased significantly over time, there is considerable variation across courts. First, some international courts receive much stronger and broader state support than other courts. The Rome Statute, which recognizes the jurisdiction of the ICC, has currently been ratified by 111 countries, or over 55% of all states in the world.[2] The World Trade Organization's adjudication mechanism receives a high level of international support as well, with 153 states (75%) belonging to the organization today.[3] Other courts receive significantly less international support, such as the ICJ, where only one third of states in the world accept the compulsory jurisdiction of the Court (Alexandrov 1995).

Second, there is considerable variation in the design of international courts. Some courts, such as the ECJ, have a limited regional membership scope, while other courts, like the ICJ and the ICC, are more global and universal in their orientation. Some institutions, like the European Union (EU), require membership in the community's judicial body, while other international courts, such as the Permanent Court of International Justice (PCIJ) and the ICJ, create variation in states' commitments to the

---

[1] This information is taken from the Project on International Courts and Tribunals at www.pict-pcti.org/publications/synoptic_chart/synop_c4.pdf.
[2] See www.icc-cpi.int/Menus/ASP/states+parties.
[3] See www.wto.org/english/thewto_e/whatis_e/tif_e/org6_e.htm.

courts by allowing for reservations on states' declarations to the courts. A court's jurisdiction may be qualified by time limits, types of disputes, or application to certain laws or nations, which some have argued hinders an international court's effectiveness (Eyffinger 1996).

Third, there is considerable variation in major power support for international courts. While the creation of new world orders after victory in major wars may include the creation of new international courts (Ikenberry 2001), major power victors may become less willing to support these institutions when they challenge their national interests (Posner 2004). A good example is the United States' tumultuous relationship with international courts. The United States withdrew its ICJ optional clause in 1986 in light of an unfavorable ruling in the *Nicaragua* case, and more recently expressed strong opposition to the creation of the ICC (Bolton 2001). On the other hand, the United States was a fervent supporter of the WTO's adjudication mechanism (Brewster 2006). Even more surprising was President George W. Bush's failed attempt to persuade the US Congress to ratify the Law of the Sea Convention, a move that would have opened up the United States to the jurisdiction of the International Tribunal for the Law of the Sea (ITLOS). Other major powers vary in their support for international courts as well. France withdrew its optional clause declaration to the ICJ in 1974 in opposition to the Court's adjudication of the *Nuclear Tests* cases. And yet, as a founding member of the European Economic Community, France supported the creation of the ECJ, a court with considerable teeth, where judgments rendered at the supranational level have altered the domestic law of EU member states (Burley and Mattli 1993).

How are we to understand this rich variation in state support for international courts? When do states support the creation of new international courts and when do they oppose them? Why do some states agree to recognize the jurisdiction of international courts while other states eschew them? We argue that the key to unpacking this empirical puzzle lies in a better understanding of the two-level legal relationship between domestic law and international law (Koh 1997, 2641). To explain the formation of new courts and the expansion of state support for pre-existing courts, our theoretical argument emphasizes the importance of domestic legal traditions. We argue that characteristics of civil law, common law, and Islamic law influence states' willingness to create new international courts or join pre-existing courts. The initial negotiators of new courts design institutions in ways that are optimal from a legal standpoint. Later joiners to the court are influenced by the court's legal principles and rules as well, viewing some international courts as more capable and fair adjudicators than other courts.

Our theory distinguishes between the motives of states creating a new court, what we call the "originators", and the decisions made by states to join existing international courts, a group we call the "joiners." The originators are able to negotiate the design of an international court's rules, while the joiners must condition their decision to accept the court's jurisdiction based on the existing rules and practices of the court. Originators seek to create international courts in their own legal image to reduce uncertainty in future litigation situations. Joiners find international courts attractive if they are able to use the court as a tool for sending signals to other states about their willingness to resolve disputes peacefully and if they view the court as a fair and unbiased adjudicator.[4]

In the next section, we describe several explanations that have been developed to help understand the puzzle of state support for international courts. This is followed by a summary of our theoretical arguments about how domestic legal traditions influence the decisions made by originators and joiners. We then discuss the influence of domestic legal traditions on the rational design of states' commitments to international courts and the broader significance of our research for the academic and policy communities. The chapter concludes with a road map for the remainder of the book.

Why states create or join international courts

There are a plethora of explanations for the proliferation of international courts, accounts which often mesh well with realist, liberal, rationalist, and constructivist viewpoints on international institutions more broadly. Much like the expansion of international organizations (IOs) and regimes, international courts have grown in number and scope, especially after the end of the Cold War. In this section, we review a variety of answers to our initial puzzle regarding the proliferation of international courts. We also discuss some of the shortcomings of these theories, which we seek to remedy in our theory of international adjudication.

Hegemony/structural change

While a skeptical realist might see international adjudication as an idealist's waste of time (Morgenthau 1948), other scholars examine the orders

---

[4] Other international relations scholars have made similar distinctions. For example, Gruber (2000) argues that the originators of regional trade agreements receive more benefits from cooperation than later joiners. Hawkins and Jacoby (2008) make a distinction between early and late joiners to the European Court of Human Rights (ECHR).

created by global or regional hegemons, which establish a set of rules, principles, and institutions that can further the hegemon's goals (Organski and Kugler 1980; Gilpin 1981; Keohane 1984; Ikenberry 2001; Lemke 2002). International courts are created through lengthy and detailed negotiations and it is not surprising that major powers, such as the United States and the United Kingdom, play a significant role in these processes. States victorious in global wars may view the establishment of new global courts as an essential part of the post-war order construction process, as illustrated by the creation of the PCIJ following World War I and the formation of the ICJ following World War II. A hegemon could bind itself to a new post-war order more credibly by establishing and supporting an effective international court. Powerful states can use international courts to stabilize relationships with weaker powers, pacify weaker states by giving them a voice in the international order, and stabilize the order by locking in the hegemon's preferences (Krisch 2005). One sees a similar logic in arguments that international courts proliferate in the aftermath of significant structural changes because pre-existing norms shift rapidly, creating space for new institutions. Tiba (2006, 215) argues that the erosion of the Westphalia model of state sovereignty following the end of the Cold War gave non-state actors greater standing in international law and helps to explain the recent proliferation of international courts.

However, unlike other international institutions that often provide direct benefits to major powers, such as regional free trade agreements, international courts are distinctive because they can mitigate power asymmetries in interstate bargaining. Weaker countries have more to gain from a system of effective international courts than major powers because international courts help to level the playing field in world politics (Scott and Carr 1987; Bilder 1998). Empirical evidence supports this conjecture: as states' capabilities increase, they are significantly more likely to renege on optional clause declarations to the World Court (PCIJ/ICJ) (Powell and Mitchell 2007). On the other hand, major powers can sometimes benefit from international law and shape it to their power advantage through colonial conquest (imposition of law), by declaring to whom the law applies (civilized vs. uncivilized peoples), promoting legal principles that advantage them in interstate bargaining, and conditioning aid on international legal practices (Krisch 2005).[5]

While we don't doubt that global and regional powers are important players at the negotiating table when new international courts are

---

[5] For example, in the sixteenth century, Spain pushed for a territorial ownership principle based on discovery rather than effective control because their early colonization efforts put them in an advantaged position (Krisch 2005).

established, we think a power-based explanation can only go so far. As noted earlier, major powers support some courts while eschewing others, often at similar points in time, even though state capabilities remain fairly static in the short run. There is also considerable variation among global and regional powers in their enthusiasm for international adjudication. A power-based explanation has difficulties explaining why two major powers with similar capabilities would adopt distinct levels of support for new international courts.[6] Furthermore, not all international courts emerge in the aftermath of system-changing wars. Some are created for functional purposes, as global interactions change in both frequency and form over time.

Functional need

Another story about why international courts are created is that they emerge in situations where they are needed. Human rights courts, for example, emerged as global norms for human rights protection became more entrenched, and as publicity about human rights violations became more prevalent. Similarly, the ECJ was created as a judicial arm of the European Community "to ensure that in the interpretation and application of [the treaties] the law is observed" (Article 220 of the Treaty Establishing the European Community). The WTO's adjudication procedure helped to fill a dispute settlement purpose that was lacking in the prior General Agreement on Tariffs and Trade (GATT) agreement. This theoretical viewpoint sees the creation of new international courts from a functional lens, attributing the proliferation of courts to globalization and increasingly complex and specialized interactions in trade, the environment, human rights, and other issues. One finds a similar story in the literature on IOs, which also links the proliferation of IOs (in part) to expanding functional needs for the institutions (Jacobson et al. 1986). This approach might also explain why certain issue areas have seen much more rapid growth in the number of international courts than others, as states would be wary of ceding significant authority to international courts in certain realms, such as security politics (Alter 2003, 67).

The functional story is a useful one, especially in terms of explaining variance in the frequency of international courts across issue areas. Yet,

---

[6] For example, the British and American governments were extremely reluctant in their support for the creation of the PCIJ in comparison to their French and German counterparts. Interestingly, however, the British and American negotiators, Lord Phillimore and Elihu Root, were much more in favor of a court with compulsory jurisdiction in comparison to the median preference of their respective governments (Lloyd 1985).

even within a single issue area, such as trade, there is considerable variation in the design of international courts. Simply knowing the issues to be covered by a court's jurisdiction does not explain why states decided to create a court at a particular point in time. Moreover, this approach does not help us understand why the court's creators select a particular institutional design. Functional need may help us understand the impetus for negotiations to create new international courts, but it is limited for explaining the variety in institutional design across courts in a single issue area.

Delegation

A series of recent studies focus on the delegation of authority to international courts. One approach by Posner and Yoo (2005) utilizes a principal-agent model to explain why states would cede authority to an international adjudicator. The court can play a useful role by providing new information to the disputants, which reduces uncertainty in the interstate bargaining process. States would only want to cede temporary control to the arbitrator in this situation for the dispute at hand, and would avoid creating long-term commitments to international courts. Yet, this theory is hard pressed to explain the increasing prevalence of adjudication relative to arbitration in world politics (Helfer and Slaughter 2005). It does not consider the varied roles that international courts might play, with administrative authority being ceded more naturally to international courts by states than more sovereignty restricting roles, such as dispute settlement (Alter 2008). This approach also fails to explain why so many states vividly support the ICC by signing and ratifying the Rome Statute, a serious and long-term commitment. Why did the international community resort to the creation of a permanent international criminal adjudicative body? Why not alleviate temporary needs for an international criminal tribunal by continuing to create *ad hoc* courts, such as the International Criminal Tribunal for Rwanda and the International Criminal Tribunal for the former Yugoslavia?

A second delegation story focuses on international courts as mechanisms for states seeking to make credible commitments (Moravcsik 2000; Alter 2003, 2008; Helfer and Slaughter 2005; Mitchell and Hensel 2007; Guzman 2008). States create or join international courts in order to enhance the credibility of interstate commitments. Courts can enhance commitment credibility because they increase the reputation costs for reneging, help identify violations of the law, clarify the law, aid in compliance with international law more broadly, and reduce monitoring and evaluation costs. A good example of the logic of this commitment explanation is found in Simmons and Danner's (2010) study of state ratification of the Rome Statute. They argue that democratizing states with a recent history of civil war can credibly commit to improvements in human rights practices by ratifying the ICC treaty. Because the court's jurisdiction is mandatory and because the independent prosecutor has adequate authority to initiate proceedings (even against the signatory government), this act of ratification sends a credible signal to the rebels about the state's commitment to peace. Moravcsik (2000) makes a similar argument about European states' willingness to join the ECHR as a credible signal about their commitment to democracy.

Yet, if reputation is the driving force in this process, it is not clear why states would need international courts to resolve interstate disputes: "[I]f reputation were strong enough to compel compliance with adjudication, one wonders why it was not also strong enough to resolve the dispute *without* adjudication. Why is reputation too weak to induce compliance before a third party pronounces a nation's legal obligations, but still strong enough to induce compliance after such a pronouncement?" (Ginsburg and McAdams 2004, 1240). We think reputation plays an important role, but that the presence of an international court serves to enhance the efficiency of bargaining. In other words, there must be something about bargaining in the shadow of the court that gives states incentives to create permanent adjudicators. Otherwise they could rely on other non-judicial mechanisms for commitment credibility, such as democracy, past reliability, and IOs. We believe that states signal information to each other through international courts, but the adjudicator need not be present in every dispute settlement procedure in order to exert an influence. By focusing mostly on the practices of international courts, scholars have failed to examine the broader purposes that courts can play. Commitment credibility gets us part of the way in understanding the proliferation of international courts, but as we show later, states have incentives to lock in particular institutional design features in order to enhance the court's efficacy in future dispute situations.

Kantian peace

Another viewpoint is that the proliferation of international courts is part of the broader movement towards a system characterized by Kantian peace (Teson 1992). Over time, the number of democratic states has increased substantially, which has resulted in the creation of numerous IOs and expansive trade networks (Russett and Oneal 2001). Given democracies' preferences for legalized dispute resolution (Raymond 1994, 2004; Slaughter 1995) and given that most system leaders have been democratic, it is only natural that the frequency of international courts would increase in the Kantian system. Democratic states, such as the United States and the United Kingdom, were pioneers in the successful use of arbitration in both the Jay Treaty and the Alabama claims, which spawned further efforts at global arbitration and adjudication at The Hague in 1899 and 1907, culminating in the creation of the Permanent Court of Arbitration and later the PCIJ (Mitchell 2002).

The liberal peace perspective offers important insight into the proliferation of international courts and tribunals. One need only look at the success of legalization and institutionalization efforts in the context of a democratic European region to be convinced of this argument. However, the United States' lack of support for several international courts, such as the ICJ and the ICC, casts some doubt on the liberal story. Whether the United States is merely an outlier among liberal states remains to be seen, yet we think its behavior stems in part from its domestic legal tradition, common law, standing at odds with the civil law nature of the early international court system:

As an initial matter, it is understood for the most part that civil law-trained jurists created modern international law, despite the fact that the term "international law" was coined by a jurist from the common law world, Jeremy Bentham. Of course, theoretically, the jurists responsible for creating the ideas and institutions of international law could have done so in isolation from their domestic legal environments. In fact, however, jurists necessarily borrowed and adopted existing institutions and mechanisms from their existing civil law systems – sometimes subconsciously and perhaps even despite explicit efforts to reject civil law notions. It is only natural that they created international law in the image or shadow of civil law. Thus, from its earliest stage, international law developed among civil law ideas, with the predictable result that it reflected those very ideas. (Picker 2008, 1105)

Early international courts, such as the PCIJ, were created with civil law rules and principles. This led to increased support for this Court among civil law states in comparison to common law and Islamic law states. There is a moderate, positive correlation between common law and democracy, and yet common law countries do not rush to support all international courts equally. Courts created with common law rules in mind, such as the ICC, are much more palatable to the population of common law countries. Democracies may be open to a system of international adjudication, yet they also have many mechanisms in place naturally for successful and credible dispute resolution (Lipson 2003). A fully Kantian system might be one in which courts of last resort exist, but they are rarely utilized (Mitchell et al. 2009).

Contagion

Another perspective focuses on the proliferation of international courts as a process of contagion. Peace activists in the United States and the United Kingdom pushed for their governments to negotiate the Permanent Court of Arbitration (PCA) (Allain 2000). While the PCA was active mostly in the early years, the negotiations at the Hague in 1899 and 1907 played an important role in the creation of the PCIJ after World War I. Negotiators utilized many design principles crafted in those earlier documents. The PCIJ and its successor, the ICJ, subsequently influenced the creation of new courts in the aftermath of World War II. In short, one sees a process of court contagion as new courts partially emulate existing courts and as the increasing number of cases and "sound" judgments leads to further utilization of existing courts and demands for new ones (Tiba 2006). One sees a similar process at the regional level, especially in Europe, as reflected in both the increasing number of regional courts and the rise in caseloads over time (Helfer and Slaughter 2005, 915–916).[7]

It is hard to distinguish the contagion argument from the Kantian peace argument given that both processes have occurred simultaneously in the past century. We think that part of the story of proliferation also stems from states' desire to create effective adjudicators. Given the early reliance on civil law procedures and rules in international courts, it is only natural that states with legal traditions distinct from civil law would seek to create new international courts. The ICC statute adopted several common law features, such as rules regarding disclosure obligations, appeal proceedings, and admission of guilt by the accused. The design of several human rights tribunals, such as the International Criminal Tribunal for former Yugoslavia, was also influenced strongly by common law principles. Similarly, the proposed Islamic International Court of Justice (IICJ) would allow Islamic law states to integrate important religious principles into the process of international adjudication. In short, we believe that contagion is certainly a factor, as courts with good prior records are more likely to be utilized. However, we show theoretically that not all adjudicators are capable of being fair and balanced. Courts that adopt similar legal rules and procedures as those found in the disputants' domestic legal traditions are more capable of helping the parties to strike successful and durable agreements.

---

[7] As Alter (2008, 38) notes, much of this activity is heavily concentrated in the last fifteen years: "[S]eventy-five percent of the total IC [International Courts] output of decisions, opinions, and rulings (24,863 out of 33,057) have come since 1990."

A rational legal design theory of international adjudication

To explain the puzzle of why states create and join international courts, we focus on the intersection of domestic law and international law. After accepting a basic premise that states can benefit from bargaining with the potential assistance of an adjudicator, we contend that not all adjudicators are created equal. States have incentives to create international courts in their own legal image to reduce uncertainty in future bargaining situations. Similarly, states that join standing international courts look to the court's rules and procedures in order to assess the ability of the court to be fair and unbiased. The design put into place by the originators of a new international court influences the level of state support for the court, the design of states' commitments to the court, as well as the ultimate influence of the court on members' behavior. In short, we can understand the emergence and influence of international courts more clearly by focusing on their rational legal design.

The originators: decisions to create a new international court

States have political and legal preferences that they bring to the bargaining table when creating a new court. States that are strongly committed to the court's creation have incentives to lock in their own country's future commitments to the court (Moravcsik 2000). Negotiators may tie their state's future hands by designing a court with sound design principles and enforcement mechanisms. They may also tie their country's hands by raising the reputational costs for reneging on the court's future judgments. If the originators are supportive of the court, they have incentives to create procedures and rules for the court's operation that will benefit their country in future litigation cases, or at a minimum, ensure that the adjudicator's behavior will be reasonably predictable.

If states can anticipate high degrees of future enforcement, they have incentives to negotiate intensely to secure the best deal possible (Fearon 1998). International courts do have not the same types of enforcement mechanisms as domestic courts, although they are able to raise the reputational costs for noncompliance and they have institutional resources at their disposal for helping parties to carry out judgments (Mitchell and Hensel 2007).[8]

---

[8] In this study, we do not problematize the creation of new international courts "all the way down." This might involve a process-tracing of the events leading up to negotiations to form a new court. In the formation of the PCIJ, for example, one might focus on how the

If our basic assumption about a long shadow of the future for international courts is apt, then it is reasonable to argue that states' legal preferences will enter into their calculations as originators of a new international court. There are strong incentives for a state to push for an institutional design that mimics the legal procedures employed domestically inside the state. Uncertainty about how the court will identify cases to be heard and how it will rule on particular cases is mitigated if the court's rules and procedures are familiar. Furthermore, if states have the ability to forum shop in the process of dispute settlement, then the negotiators of a new court have incentives to lock in an institutional design that will benefit their state in the future.

To reduce uncertainty about the interpretation of international law, states attempt to design international courts in a way that resembles their domestic legal systems. As noted earlier, we focus on three major domestic legal traditions in the world: civil law, common law, and Islamic law. Civil law is the Romano–Germanic legal tradition, largely rooted in the laws of the Roman Empire. In this legal tradition, the written letter of law (codes) constitutes the main source of law. Common law, which originated on the British Isles, is based on the *stare decisis* doctrine, according to which judges are bound primarily by precedents established by previous judgments (Opolot 1980). Islamic law, the world's third major legal tradition, arose with the birth of Islam in the seventh century AD, and is based primarily on religious principles of human conduct (Al-Azmeh 1988).

States can use their domestic legal traditions as clues about the court's future proceedings and judgments. Civil lawyers approach drafting and interpretation of multinational agreements as they would a civil code (Koch 2003). Similarly, common law lawyers design international agreements in the spirit of their domestic legal system (Jouannet 2006). This was evident during the negotiations in Rome for the ICC, for example, where civil law and common law negotiators pushed strongly for familiar rules and procedures. States are more comfortable with the role international courts will play in future litigation situations if they are familiar with the court's rules and procedures and confident about the types of decisions the court will render. State support for new international courts will depend on the degree of legal similarity between domestic legal traditions and the rules and procedures established at the negotiating table.

1899 and 1907 Hague Conferences and the events of World War I created a supportive environment for the Court's creation. Thus when we use the term "originators," we are focusing on understanding the design choices states make once they have determined there is a need for the creation of a new international court.

The joiners: decisions to join an existing court

In contrast to the originators of international courts, potential joiners to an international court must accept the court's standing rules and procedures, which are not negotiable. Joiners must weigh the domestic and international costs and benefits of joining an international court. As a general rule, we assume that states prefer working with courts that they view as fair and unbiased. We also assume that states can send signals to other states about their "type" on various international issues through an international court, such as a commitment to the peaceful settlement of interstate disputes or the promotion of ethical human rights standards. While such signals are aptly described as cheap talk, they can be conveyed meaningfully through an adjudicator to other states with similar legal preferences (Powell and Mitchell 2007).

Unbiased adjudicators may be effective at helping parties strike cooperative agreements by correlating strategies, creating focal points, and signaling information (Garrett and Weingast 1993; Ginsburg and McAdams 2004; McAdams 2005, 1049). An adjudicator "uses cheap talk to construct a 'focal point' in a coordination game" (McAdams 2005, 1059) by focusing on particular equilibrium outcomes and conveying this information to the disputants. Adjudicators may also promote cooperation by revealing private information to disputants (Posner and Yoo 2005), such as the players' types, which works best if the adjudicator is unbiased and has strong reputational incentives for being truthful (McAdams 2005).

We build upon this expressive theory of adjudication by considering how linkages between domestic legal systems and the rules and procedures of an international court influence states' willingness to support the court. We argue that states can send cheap talk signals to other states about their types more effectively through an adjudicator that shares its legal principles and rules. We develop the argument in the context of the World Court, a court that has been designed according to civil law principles. Civil law is the most frequent type of domestic legal tradition in the world, with this legal system constituting between 48% and 78% of all states in the world in the past century (Powell and Mitchell 2007). Furthermore, the PCIJ and ICJ have procedures and rules that are extremely similar to civil law, including the lack of precedent in decision-making and recognition of the doctrine of good faith (*bona fides*). This legal similarity between civil law and the World Court's rules reduces the uncertainty that civil law states face when dealing with the Court.

The sizable frequency of civil law states in the world makes it easier for civil law countries to send a cheap talk signal through the PCIJ/ICJ about their willingness to resolve disputes peacefully. The legal similarity between civil law and the principles and rules of the World Court enhances the court's ability to correlate strategies, create focal points, and signal information. This produces an expectation that civil law states are significantly more likely to recognize the jurisdiction of the World Court in comparison to common law and Islamic law states. This suggests that not all courts are fair and unbiased towards all countries. The rational design set in place by the court's originators influences the willingness of later joiners to coordinate their behavior through the court.

The rational design of states' commitments to international courts

In addition to providing leverage for understanding why certain states are more likely to recognize the jurisdiction of an international court than others, domestic legal systems and their prominent characteristics can also give us insight into the rational design of international legal commitments. There is considerable variation in the form and design of contracts in civil law, common law, and Islamic law. These contractual differences in the domestic realm carry over onto the international arena where states make commitments to international courts.

Many international courts, like the PCIJ and the ICJ, allow for flexibility in states' commitments to the courts in the form of reservations, or "restrictions relating to the content of the commitments entered into a particular declaration" (Szafarz 1993, 46). We develop several rational design hypotheses linking the characteristics of domestic legal systems to the number and type of reservations placed by states on their commitments to international courts. We anticipate that civil law states will place the smallest number of reservations on their declarations to an international court, while common law states will have the highest number of reservations. These differences stem from the strength of the *bona fides* and *pacta sunt servanda* principles in civil law systems. Due to the lack of contracting freedom in Islamic law, we also anticipate that Islamic law states will prefer recognition of an international court in a more limited context, such as a bilateral treaty with a clause recognizing a particular court for dispute settlement. In short, the characteristics of domestic legal traditions have substantial effects on the form of states' commitments to international courts.

The effect of international courts on member states' behavior

The originators of new international courts have incentives to lock in familiar legal rules and principles that stem from their domestic legal traditions. Potential joiners find international courts more attractive if they utilize familiar rules and procedures. States' domestic legal principles also influence the design of states' commitments to international courts. Yet, even if all of these rational legal design processes are at work, we are still left wondering if international courts have any efficacy in world politics. The final part of our project considers the influence of international courts on member states' behavior.

We show that states do indeed bargain differently in the shadow of international courts. For example, countries that ratify the Rome Statute show significant improvements in their domestic human rights behavior. However, international courts are not equally effective for all members. States whose domestic legal traditions most closely match the rules and principles utilized by an international court are able to bargain most efficiently in the shadow of the court. Civil law states that recognize the compulsory jurisdiction of the World Court, for instance, are more likely to strike agreements with other civil law states that recognize the court's compulsory jurisdiction. Yet the same bargaining efficiency is not achieved in pairs of states with common law or Islamic law traditions. This implies that we must know something about the legal design of an international court to assess its efficacy. It also implies that we cannot look only at cases that come before a court; the presence of an effective adjudicator implies that countries will bargain more efficiently on their own. This examination of the "dogs that don't bark" has been identified as an avenue of important inquiry in the law literature (Bilder 1998), although it is an empirical proposition that has to date remained untested. Our project fills this gap by showing that international courts have significant out-of-court influences on member states' behavior.

Broader significance of the project

The subject matter of this study is timely and important. We think that the lack of attention to domestic legal systems in the international relations literature is puzzling given that most interstate contracts are governed by a variety of legal principles and are often negotiated by lawyers. By focusing on legal systems, our project contributes to the broader legalization project in international relations (Goldstein *et al.* 2001) and interdisciplinary research integrating insights from international relations and international law (Slaughter *et al.* 1998; Ku *et al.* 2001; Simmons and Steinberg 2007). Our theoretical arguments come from both political science and international law literatures, which helps us to develop a rich explanation for the creation and expansion of international courts.

Several recent books have developed rational choice (and other) theoretical frameworks for understanding international law (Reus-Smit 2004; Goldsmith and Posner 2005; Leonard 2005; Armstrong *et al.* 2007; Guzman 2008). There are also dozens of books on specific international courts, including the PCIJ (e.g. Lloyd 1997), the ICJ (e.g. Rosenne 1962; Gamble and Fischer 1976; Alexandrov 1995; Eyffinger 1996; Oduntan 1999; Gill *et al.* 2003), and the ICC (e.g. Schabas 2007; Schiff 2008; Struett 2008). Yet there is a gap between the general theorizing of the former approaches and the context-specific explanations of particular courts in the latter. Our project fills this lacuna by developing a generalizable theory that can be applied to all international courts. The theory is broad enough to explain the formation of new courts and the expansion of support for existing courts, and thus gives us leverage for understanding variance in states' commitments to international courts across time and space.

It is also crucial to explain the processes by which courts emerge and grow in order to understand their influence in world politics. Our theory makes clear that states make rational choices when designing new courts or joining pre-existing courts. International courts are not necessarily designed in an optimal way for all countries. In fact, the originators of new courts have incentives to design courts in their own legal image, which creates biases in favor of certain types of countries when the court makes judgments. The ICJ, for example, has rules and procedures that mimic those in civil law systems, and not surprisingly, civil law countries have been much more likely to recognize the jurisdiction of this Court than common or Islamic law states (Powell and Mitchell 2007). ICJ justices exhibit these biases in their case decision-making when they show favoritism towards countries that are similar to their home state (Posner and Figueiredo 2004). These same biases make some courts much more appealing to states than other international courts, which helps to account for the proliferation of international courts over time and the desire for forum shopping among new courts.

Our theory also builds upon the important work in international relations relating domestic and international politics (Putnam 1988). We show that these linkages are not simply *political*, but also that the relationships between domestic law and international law are consequential for world politics as well. We show how domestic-international law interrelationships have led to convergences between civil law and common law over time. This process of convergence helps to explain the unique, hybrid nature of the ICC. Furthermore, the proliferation of international courts has resulted in greater cross-fertilization of legal principles across international courts as well (Brown 2007).

Our study also advances research in international relations on the rational design of international institutions (Mitchell 1994; Koremenos *et al.* 2001). Our focus on domestic legal systems adds an interesting new dimension to the rational design project. We show that the characteristics of domestic legal systems influence the design of state commitments to international courts in multiple ways, including the length of declarations to courts (number of words), the number of reservations placed on courts' jurisdictional powers, and the types of reservations employed by states (i.e. *ratione temporis, ratione materiae, ratione personae*). Domestic legal systems impinge on states' rational choices to join international courts, as well as the specific forms of their commitments to these courts.

While states make rational choices when creating new courts or joining pre-existing courts, these decisions may have negative consequences for the coherence of international law as a whole. The impetus for states to create courts in their own legal image leads to the proliferation of international courts because states that are left out of the process have incentives to build their own courts. The proposed IICJ is a good example, as the legal principles of existing international courts (e.g. the ICJ, and ICC) do not mesh well with Islamic law. The expansion of international courts has both positive and negative influences in world politics. On the positive side, international courts can be effective conflict managers for member states who view the courts' rules and procedures with legitimacy. Thus the greater the number of potential adjudicators existing in the international system, the more likely states should be to resolve things on their own outside of court. On the negative side, the proliferation of international courts may create judicial decisions at odds with one another across international courts, which may impede the development of a coherent and robust body of international law.

Road map for the book

In Chapter 2, we provide a detailed description of the history and characteristics of the three major legal traditions that we focus on theoretically: civil law, common law, and Islamic law. We describe a variety of dimensions that differentiate domestic legal systems including:

- doctrine of the precedent (*de jure*)
- law and religion
- *bona fides* (good faith)
- *pacta sunt servanda* (keeping promises)
- freedom of contract

- the design of contracts
- the degree of formalism
- administrative regulation
- approach to litigation
- appeal.

We also discuss the status of these principles in international law more broadly. We conclude the chapter by talking about the temporal convergence between common law and civil law over time and the potential influence of this trend on state support for international courts.

In Chapter 3, we develop the theoretical argument that guides the remainder of the study. As noted above, we focus on how domestic legal traditions influence the decisions of the originators of new international courts and the joiners of pre-existing courts. We also present arguments about the rational design of states' commitments to international courts. The final part of the chapter provides a justification for the two courts selected for our empirical analyses: the World Court and the ICC.

In Chapter 4, we test arguments about the originators of new international courts empirically by examining the international negotiations in Rome in 1998 that resulted in the creation of the ICC. We show how the resulting agreement was a negotiated compromise between negotiators from civil law and common law states. We focus our discussion on four design features of the ICC that illustrate the ultimate hybrid nature of the Court and the legal compromises that were struck in the Rome negotiations: (1) the nature of the trial, (2) the position of the ICC judges during proceedings, (3) admission of guilt of the accused, and (4) appeal proceedings. We also conduct a statistical analysis of ICC signature and ratification (1998–2004) among the set of originator states that were involved in the Rome negotiations. We find that civil law and common law states are significantly more likely to ratify the Rome Statute in comparison to states with mixed law and Islamic law traditions, which fits with our argument that states are more likely to support international courts created in their own legal image.

Chapter 5 focuses on the potential joiners to standing international courts. Illustrating the argument by focusing on the World Court (PCIJ/ICJ) as an important adjudicator, we consider the ability of states to communicate with each other through the PCIJ/ICJ through recognition of the court's compulsory jurisdiction. We argue that civil law states can correlate their bargaining strategies and generate clear focal points for coordination through the PCIJ/ICJ more easily than common law or Islamic law states because the prevalence of civil law states in the international system creates an effective and diffuse cheap talk signal.

Furthermore, the originators of the PCIJ and ICJ created rules and principles that mimic those in domestic civil law systems. This similarity in legal design makes it easier for civil law states to correlate strategies, signal information, and create focal points through the PCIJ/ICJ. The theory is tested with state-year data from 1921–2001. Empirical analyses show strong support for the theoretical claims that civil law states have the highest propensity to recognize the jurisdiction of the World Court.

The next chapter extends the analyses in Chapter 5 by focusing on the *design* of states' commitments to the PCIJ/ICJ. In addition to analyzing the number of PCIJ/ICJ reservations, we also analyze specific forms of reservations made under optional clause declarations: general, *ratione materiae*, *ratione personae*, *ratione temporis*, and other reservations. We also compare the form of states' jurisdictional recognition of the PCIJ/ICJ: compulsory vs. compromissory jurisdiction. Empirical analyses of states' commitments to the PCIJ/ICJ from 1921–2001 show that common law states place more restrictions on their optional clause declarations than civil law or Islamic law states, with the majority of those restrictions relating to specific areas of international law (*ratione materiae*). However, there are notable differences with respect to bilateral and multilateral treaties, with civil law states embedding compromissory clauses more often in multilateral treaties, while common law and Islamic law states prefer bilateral compromissory clause treaties. Interestingly, Islamic law states belong to the highest average number of bilateral compromissory clause treaties. We relate these interesting design differences to the broader literature on the rational design of institutions.

While international courts have proliferated significantly in recent years, whether they have any real influence on interstate politics remains debated. The final empirical segment of our project, Chapter 7, examines the consequences of state support for international courts. The empirical focus is similar to previous chapters, with an emphasis on the ICC and the World Court. To analyze the effect of ICC ratification on state behavior, we evaluate changes in states' human rights practices after joining the ICC, including overall human rights scores and individual components of these indices (frequent torture, extra-judicial killings, political imprisonment, and disappearances). To evaluate the consequences of optional clause declarations to the PCIJ/ICJ, we utilize data from the Issue Correlates of War (ICOW) Project on territorial, maritime, and river issue conflicts. We consider whether two states that recognize the jurisdiction of the PCIJ/ICJ are able to reach peaceful agreements more easily to end contentious issue claims, whether they carry out agreements reached more readily than states that do not recognize the PCIJ/ICJ, and whether they avoid militarization of contentious issues. We also examine a broader sample of all politically relevant dyad years to determine if joint recognition of the jurisdiction of the PCIJ/ICJ significantly decreases the chances for dyadic militarized conflict. These tests are important because they provide some of the first large-N statistical analyses of the out-of-court effects of international courts that law scholars have argued should exist.

The concluding chapter summarizes the primary arguments and empirical findings in the study. We situate the importance of our research in the broader political science and international law literatures and we discuss the policy relevance of the findings in the book. We conclude by talking about the significance of our work for understanding the creation and expansion of other international courts, such as the IICJ and the ITLOS. By considering the life cycle of international courts, from their inception and legal design to their ultimate effect on member states' behavior, our study paints an optimistic viewpoint of the positive role that international courts can play in helping to promote more peaceful and ethical state behavior.

2 Major legal traditions of the world

In this chapter, we lay the groundwork for our theoretical argument about the creation of new international courts and the expansion of state support for pre-existing courts by focusing on the characteristics of the three major domestic legal traditions in the world: civil law, common law, and Islamic law. We provide a brief historical account of the origins of these three legal families and we describe the major distinctions between them, including differences in the source of law, distinctions in the law of contracts, and variations in legal procedures (e.g. litigation). We then discuss how these features of domestic legal traditions influence foreign policy decision-making processes, especially as they impinge upon the creation of new international institutions and the signature and design of interstate commitments. We conclude by describing some of the convergences that have occurred over time between these legal families, especially between civil law and common law, and the significance of this temporal trend for our research.

Introduction to legal systems

Each state in the international system, as a political entity, possesses its own legal system, which is manifested at any point in history by a system of rules, norms, and principles. There are several definitions of the term "legal system." Merryman (1985, 1) defines it as "an operating set of legal institutions, procedures, and rules." He goes further and explains: "In this sense there are one federal and fifty state legal systems in the United States, separate legal systems in each of the other nations, and still other distinct legal systems in such organizations as the European Economic Community and the United Nations." Rene and Brierly (1985, 19) state:

"Each law in fact constitutes a *system*: it has a vocabulary used to express concepts, its rules are arranged into categories, it has techniques for expressing rules and interpreting them, it is linked to a view of the social order itself which determined the way in which the law is applied and shapes the very function of the law in that society."

A legal framework present within each state, in its entirety, is unique as far as its evolution, internal characteristics, and methods of operation. Nevertheless, according to numerous legal scholars, despite the multitude of differences existing between legal orders present in the world today and in the past, we can speak of so-called legal families, or legal traditions (David and Brierley 1985; Glendon *et al.* 1994; Glenn 2007). The concept of "legal tradition" differs substantially from the above-described notion of "legal system." Perhaps the best definition of the term "legal tradition" is provided by Merryman (1985, 1–2):

A legal tradition, as the term implies, is not a set of rules of law about contracts, corporations, and crimes, although such rules will almost always be in some sense a reflection of that tradition. Rather it is a set of deeply rooted, historically conditioned attitudes about the nature of law, about the role of law in society and the polity, about the proper organization and operation of a legal system, and about the way law is or should be made, applied, studied, perfected, and taught. The legal tradition related the legal system to the culture of which it is a partial expression.

In other words, whereas a legal system describes a set of rules and norms functioning within a unit, such as a state or an organization, a legal tradition denotes a basic legal culture that underlies a family of laws. Because the notion of legal tradition has cultural connotations, some authors perceive it in a very broad way. Glenn (2007, 140), for example, asserts that legal traditions exist "as large amounts of detailed and communicable information."

Even if we agree that legal traditions indeed comprise information, this does not preclude us from describing and categorizing legal traditions. We argue that it is not only possible, but also conceptually useful to classify legal traditions into some sort of groupings that share important characteristics. As most scholars agree, this process of classification should be based on identifying fundamental elements of a legal order, through which "the rules to be applied are themselves discovered, interpreted and elaborated" (David and Brierley 1985, 20).[1]

Law scholars have developed several classifications of legal traditions. For example, Glenn (2007) argues that chthonic law, Talmudic law, civil law, Islamic law, common law, Hindu law, and Asian law constitute major, complex, transnational legal traditions. Other legal scholars propose slightly different categorizations, most of which include a different subset

---

[1] For a discussion on whether legal traditions can be compared, see Glenn (2001, 2007).

of Glenn's (2007) categories.[2] Some categorizations, such as that of La Porta *et al.* (1999), include additional categories, such as Scandinavian law or socialist law.[3]

In this book, we focus on major legal traditions. We adopt Badr's (1978) definition of a major legal system, which stipulates that legal systems can be considered to be major if their "application extended far beyond the confines of their original birth places and whose influence, through reception of their principles, techniques or specific provisions has been both widespread in space and enduring in time" (Badr 1978, 187). According to this definition, in order for a legal tradition to be considered major, it has to fulfill two requirements. First, its geographical reach must be substantial. Second, its influence cannot be ephemeral but must be long-lasting. We believe that three domestic legal traditions fulfill the requirements of this definition: civil law, common law, and Islamic law.[4]

All legal scholars, regardless of which categorization of legal traditions they concur with, agree that legal traditions are internally intricate and complex. Just because legal systems of two states belong to the same legal tradition does not automatically mean that they are identical. The legal order of the United Kingdom, which constitutes a prime example of the common law tradition, is somewhat different from the system of the United States or the legal framework present in Ghana and India, which also belong to the common law family. Nevertheless, some degree of external coherence is maintained, which allows us to identify common law as one of the major legal traditions (Glenn 2007, 329). The same is true for the civil law tradition. For example, while there are significant differences between the legal systems of Germany and France, the major civil codifications which regulate civil law in both of these countries,

[2] See also David and Brierley (1985) and Joireman (2001, 2004).
[3] Our categorization of legal traditions is somewhat different from categorizations used by other scholars. In political science and economics, the most commonly used typology is the La Porta *et al.* (1999) "legal origin" variable, which has the following categories: English, Socialist, French, German, and Scandinavian. We believe that the categories introduced by La Porta *et al.* do not adequately reflect the fundamental differences between domestic legal traditions. First, we believe that splitting the civil law family into French and German yields an unnecessary sub-categorization, since both of these legal families are based on highly similar, and often times identical, procedural and substantive concepts. Even La Porta *et al.* (1999, 1131) point to this fact: "French, German, and Scandinavian laws, in contrast, are part of the scholar and legislator made civil law tradition, which dates back to Roman Law." Our categorization combines these three sub-categories into a single civil law category. Another major weakness of the La Porta *et al.* (1999) dataset is its omission of the Islamic legal system, which we believe constitutes one of the major legal traditions of the world.
[4] We also classify some countries as having mixed legal systems because they combine legal rules and principles from more than one major legal family.

Bürgerliches Gesetzbuch (Germany) and *Code Civil* (France), stem from the same source: Roman law.

Another very important characteristic of legal traditions is that their boundaries are far from being impenetrable. Because legal traditions are constituted by information, and because information cannot be fully contained within one territory, legal traditions are not completely detached from one another (Glenn 2001). Throughout history, certain legal norms (e.g. equity), after originating in one legal tradition, become established in another legal system. An extreme example of the merging of legal traditions is embodied in our classification of some domestic legal systems as having a mixed legal system. Several states, such as Thailand, Israel, Niger, and Brunei, have legal systems that constitute an amalgamation of legal institutions, norms, and principles that stem from more than one major legal tradition.[5]

In addition to being porous across borders, legal systems are also quite dynamic. Like any other social construct, law undergoes never-ending changes. The world that we live in constantly evolves. Relations between humans and political and social entities go through continuous transformations, some of which can be abrupt. Because of this steady process, institutions and characteristics of legal traditions can evolve, become established, or cease to exist. The need of a society for law leads to the evolution of legal institutions. Such was the case with the Roman law institution of the consensual contract, or *emptio venditio* (an agreement without formality), which allowed the Romans to form contractual agreements with foreign merchants, who did not understand the intricate contractual formalities of Roman law (Watson 1984; Kolanczyk 1997; Bojarski 1994).

Sometimes particular legal institutions can turn out to be unnecessary and cease to exist. Slavery in the form present under the Roman *ius civile* or the pre-civil war United States constitutes just one example. Historical changes may also affect legal traditions in a more fundamental way. The best example is provided by the hasty dilapidation of the Socialist legal orders in Eastern Europe. After the 1989 fall of the "iron curtain," major principles and concepts underpinning the socialist tradition of law were often removed from the domestic laws of states that belonged to the Soviet block.

Undoubtedly, legal traditions and legal systems continuously change. Domestic legal systems belonging to each legal tradition evolve, allowing

---

[5] Thailand and Israel have legal systems that mix civil law and common law traditions. Niger is a mixture of civil law and Islamic law, while Brunei is a mixture of common law and Islamic law.

for movement within each legal tradition itself and for convergence across legal systems. Yet the defining characteristics of each of the legal traditions sharply delineate them, including distinct procedures (doctrine of precedent (common law) vs. codes as written sources of law (civil law), reliance on religious sources (Islamic law), major concepts (*bona fides*), and principles (*pacta sunt servanda*). The endurance of major legal traditions in the face of many broad and sweeping historical changes attests to their robustness and also allows for a meaningful examination of the interrelationships between domestic law and international law across time and space. Having elaborated on the concept of a major legal tradition, we now turn to a description of the historical evolution and defining characteristics of the three major legal traditions analyzed in this study: civil law, common law, and Islamic law. Table 2.1 provides an overview of these characteristics, while Box 2.1 provides a list of countries in each domestic legal tradition over the past century.

The history of civil, common, and Islamic legal traditions

Civil law

The civil legal tradition has its roots deeply anchored in the Roman legal tradition, one of the most celebrated legal frameworks of all times. Roman law originated, as its name suggests, in Rome, but very quickly established its presence in a large part of continental Europe and beyond. The origins of Roman law can be traced to Roman jurists (*jurisconsulta*) giving advice (*responsa*) with respect to particular cases and disputes between Roman citizens (Glenn 2007). With the growth of the Roman Empire, *responsa* and other forms of law were slowly incorporated into scholarly commentaries and imperial legal pronouncements (Shapiro 1986, 128). After the split of the Roman Empire, Roman law was eventually codified in the eastern part of the Empire governed from Constantinople, where under the rule of the Emperor Justinian (527–565), the famous *Corpus Juris Civilis* was created.

In this way, the legal tradition of Rome developed over time into a mature and well-systematized system of laws, which as a whole became known as Roman law. When the Empire expanded, the Romans took their law with them all over Europe, as the authority of the Roman state stood behind its laws. As a result, people residing in the conquered territories, although familiar with the laws of Rome, always regarded them as the laws of the conqueror. After the fall of the Roman Empire, the influence of Roman law diminished significantly, and the conquered nations came

Table 2.1 *Fundamental differences between civil, common, and Islamic legal traditions*

	Legal characteristics									
Legal tradition	Doctrine of the precedent (de jure)	Law and religion	Bona fides (good faith)	Pacta sunt servanda (keeping promises)	Freedom of contract	Design of contracts	Degree of formalism	Administrative regulation	Approach to litigation	Appeal
Civil law	No	Separate	Yes	Medium	Yes	Not detailed	High	High	Inquisitorial	Yes
Common law	Yes	Separate	No	Medium	Yes	Very detailed	Medium	Medium and increasing	Adversarial	Yes
Islamic law	No	Not separate	Yes	High	No	Detailed	Low	Low	Not formalized	No
International law	No	Separate	Yes	Medium	Yes	Not detailed*	Varies according to substantive areas of law	Increasing; varies according to substantive areas of law	Varies; depends on the court	No; few exceptions

* Here we refer to contracts between states (treaties) and not contracts governed by private international law.

Box 2.1 Classification of domestic legal traditions

Common law countries

Antigua & Barbuda, Australia, Bahamas, Bangladesh, Barbados, Belize, Bhutan, Canada, Cyprus, Dominica, Federated States of Micronesia, Fiji, Ghana, Grenada, Guyana, India, Ireland, Jamaica, Kiribati, Lesotho, Liberia, Malawi, Malaysia, Marshall Islands, Mauritius, Nauru, Nepal, New Zealand, Palau, Papua New Guinea, Philippines, Samoa, Sierra Leone, Singapore, Solomon Islands, St. Kitts-Nevis, St. Lucia, St. Vincent and Grenadines, Tanzania, Tonga, Trinidad and Tobago, Tuvalu, Uganda, United Kingdom, United States of America, Zambia, Zanzibar, Zimbabwe

Civil law countries

Albania, Andorra, Angola, Argentina, Armenia, Austria, Azerbaijan, Belarus, Belgium, Benin, Bolivia, Bosnia-Herzegovina, Brazil, Bulgaria, Burkina Faso, Burundi, Cambodia, Cape Verde, Central African Republic, Chad, Chile, Colombia, Congo, Costa Rica, Croatia, Cuba, Czech Republic, Democratic Republic of the Congo, Denmark, Djibouti, Dominican Republic, East Timor, Ecuador, El Salvador, Equatorial Guinea, Estonia, Ethiopia, Finland, France, Gabon, Georgia, Germany, Greece, Guatemala, Guinea, Guinea-Bissau, Haiti, Honduras, Hungary, Iceland, Indonesia, Italy, Ivory Coast, Kazakhstan, Kyrgyz Republic, Laos, Latvia, Liechtenstein, Lithuania, Luxembourg, Macedonia, Madagascar, Mali, Mexico, Moldova, Monaco, Mongolia, Mozambique, Netherlands, Nicaragua, North Korea, Norway, Panama, Paraguay, Peru, Poland, Portugal, Republic of Vietnam, Romania, Russia, San Marino, Sao Tome and Principe, Slovakia, Slovenia, South Korea, Spain, Surinam, Swaziland, Sweden, Switzerland, Taiwan, Tajikistan, Togo, Turkey, Turkmenistan, Ukraine, Uruguay, Uzbekistan, Venezuela, Vietnam, Yugoslavia

Islamic law countries

Afghanistan, Algeria, Bahrain, Comoros, Egypt, Gambia, Iran, Iraq, Jordan, Kuwait, Lebanon, Libya, Maldives, Morocco, Nigeria, Oman, Pakistan, Qatar, Saudi Arabia, Sudan, Syria, Tunisia, United Arab Emirates, Yemen, Yemen Arab Republic, Yemen People's Republic

| **Countries with mixed legal traditions** |
| Botswana, Brunei, Cameroon, China, Eritrea, Israel, Japan, Kenya, Malta, Myanmar, Namibia, Niger, Rwanda, Senegal, Seychelles, Somalia, South Africa, Sri Lanka, Thailand, Vanuatu |

back to their old chthonic legal practices, which were still engrained in the knowledge of the people (Glenn 2007).

Roman law made a triumphant re-entry to the legal circles of Europe during the eleventh to thirteenth centuries, when legal proof was fundamentally changed and Roman *ius civile* was rejuvenated. The great new universities, which took on law and theology as their principal disciplines, played a vital role in adapting Roman law to the new ways of the times, which produced a new form of Roman law, distinct from its original format (David and Brierley 1985, 44).[6] The reception of Roman law in Europe was extensive. Some countries, such as Italy, accepted principles and institutions of that law in their entirety; other nations, such as Germany and France, acknowledged Roman law only as a subsidiary legal system.

The civil law tradition gave birth to several magnificent legal codifications, such as the Civil Code of Napoleon (*Code Napoléon*, originally called the *Code civil des Français*, or civil code of the French) of 1804, the German Civil Code (*Bürgerliches Gesetzbuch*) of 1900, and the Italian Civil Code (*Codice Civile Italiano*) (David and Brierley 1985). These codifications, by the power of their states and by their sound legal reasoning, influenced the laws of many other states. Colonization contributed greatly to the spreading of the civil legal tradition into several African, American, and Asian states. The civil legal tradition constitutes one of the most important legal traditions in the world. As Badr (1978, 187) notes, "Judged by its geographical scope and its durable influence, Roman law indeed qualifies as the major world legal system *par excellence*." This pattern is evident in Figure 2.1, which plots the frequency of the three major legal traditions in the world since 1920. Civil law states have constituted a majority of states in the world in most years, with 48–78 percent of states having civil law traditions.

Common law

On the territories of the United Kingdom, a quite divergent system of law came to prevail, that of the common law. The birth of this legal tradition

---

[6] The modernized Roman law became known as the *usus modernus Pandectarum*.

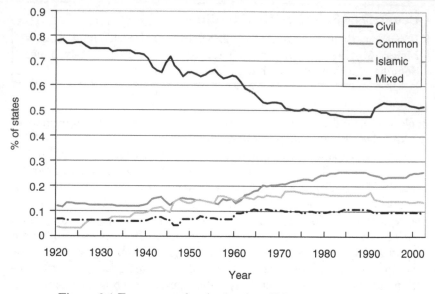

Figure 2.1 Frequency of major legal traditions

is interpreted by some legal scholars as simply the result of a historical accident, the military conquest of England by the Normans (Glenn 2007). The Battle of Hastings in 1066, won by the Norman invaders, had for all practical purposes destroyed the existing feudal system. King Harold and his knights were killed or chased out by the Norman invaders, who put together the basic components of the common law system. The tradition of common law was, through the power of the English kings, able to resist most of the continental influences of Roman law. Through its successful resistance to the civil legal tradition, the British territory became dominated by a unique legal system, where the written letter of law did not play an important role. Because written sources equivalent to the written sources of Roman law were largely absent, the practice of *stare decisis* developed and became stronger over time (Seagle 1946). As a result, English judges, instead of looking at written sources of law, were bound by precedents established by previous judgments.

The Norman conquest created a unique situation where the new lords were culturally and linguistically different from their serfs and peasants. Also, their very understanding of "right" and "wrong" differed from that of the population of the British Isles. In order to effectively administer justice in the British territories, the jury system was created (Glenn 2007). The jury was to present local realities, traditions, and findings of a particular case to a royal judge.

The common law tradition, just as its civil counterpart, expanded far beyond the borders of England. Beginning in the sixteenth century, it impacted the legal development of the United States and Australia. In later times, as British colonial rule flourished, common law was transplanted to numerous African, American, and Asian nations, whose present laws still mirror the common law concepts and principles (Badr 1978). Some authors point to the fact that although both civil and common legal traditions have influenced the legal orders of states other than their place of birth, the way in which this process took place was different: "Whereas the common law migrated through principles of private and public common law and by exporting distinct legal institutions – the jury, the writ of *habeas corpus*, an independent judiciary, and an adversarial procedural system – mainly to other Commonwealth countries, the civil law penetrated other systems through its comprehensive, systematic codes" (Rogowski 2002, 305). Because of its significant impact on legal systems outside the borders of England, the common law tradition qualifies as one of the major legal traditions of the world.

Islamic law

Because Islamic law is inherently bound to the religion of Islam, its development is intertwined with the birth of Islam, which dates back to the revelations of Muhammad. It evolved in the seventh century AD in the Arabian Peninsula and in the lower part of Mesopotamia (Badr 1978, 187). According to Hallaq (2005, 19–20), substantive development of Islamic law came later than the development of Islamic faith. Prior to Muhammad's arrival in Medina, faith and morality constituted his main concern. In 626 AD, however, "Quaranic revelation began to reflect a new development in Muhammad's career, whereby, apparently for the first time, he started thinking of the new Islamic community, the Umma, as capable of possessing a Law that parallels, but is distinct from, other monotheistic laws" (Hallaq 2005, 20). As the Arab empire expanded, and as the Islamic religion continued to reach a growing number of people, the Islamic legal tradition continued to spread. As a result, Islamic law became the law of the land in numerous lands of Central Asia and beyond and became adapted to local customs, ideas, and institutions. Thus, "accretions of local customary laws shaped the variegated character of Islamic law as it adapted to its changing environment producing localized and culturally specific manifestations of Islam and Islamic law" (Moore 2002, 753).

Later, the Islamic legal tradition influenced not only the lands dominated by the Arabs, but also territories in southeast Asia (e.g. Indonesia) and Africa (e.g. Sudan), which were never a part of the Arab empire (Badr 1978, 188). Due to the strong bond between Islam as religion and Islam as law, territories subject to this legal system have successfully resisted the influence of civil and common legal traditions. Given its geographical spread and its unique characteristics, the Islamic legal tradition is the third major legal family in the world.

International law

Some legal scholars describe international law as the "greatest of the empires to be conquered for the reign of law" (Seagle 1946, 349). Its unique history begins with the ancient Greeks, who as a result of their political and economic interdependence, began to use international arbitration to regulate potential conflict between their polis (Seagle 1946, 352). The idea of law among nations grew stronger over time, fueled especially by the development of the doctrine of natural law from the fourteenth century on. In essence, proponents of the natural law theory, such as Saint Thomas Aquinas, Grotius, and Pufendorf, believed that natural law, naturally instilled in men, is superior to laws enacted by humans. According to natural law theorists, there exists an overarching universal ideal system of law that is supreme to all legal orders designed by the hand of man. It is not surprising that natural law was often used as a benchmark supplying moral standards by which positive, human-created legal frameworks could and should be judged, condemned, or legitimized.

Proponents of the natural law doctrine conceived of the international system as a type of society, whose members are bound by the law of nature and rules of *ius gentium*, or international law (Bull 1977, 27). The main purpose for evoking natural law as the basis for international law was to "liberate the law of nations from the constraints of existing practice and develop rules appropriate to the new situation" (Bull 1977, 28). With time, the doctrine of natural law gave ways to positive international law consisting of treaties, principles, practices, and customs. Scholars of international law in the eighteenth and nineteenth centuries turned their attention away from the doctrine of natural law:

In identifying the sources of the rules by which states are bound, theorists of international society in the eighteenth and nineteenth centuries turned away from natural law and towards positive international law; more generally, they took as their guide not abstract theories about what states should do, but the body of custom and treaty law that was accumulating as to what they did do. (Bull 1977, 34).

The transition towards positive law was complete when the term "law of nations" (*droit des gens*) strongly associated with the term "law of nature," gave way to the term "international law," first used by Jeremy Bentham in 1780.

The development of international law relies directly on existing domestic legal traditions. Principles, concepts, and rules present within states are oftentimes transported to the international arena. Some even argue that this process undermines the *sui generis* nature of *jus gentium* (Picker 2008, 1091). The influence of domestic legal systems on substantive and procedural international law has a long history, whereby international jurists have tended to draw from their own legal traditions when creating international law (Picker 2008). Due to the dominance of Roman law in Europe, early developments in the law of nations embraced many of the ideas stemming from the civil legal tradition. A majority of these influences are still present in international law today; examples include *bona fides*, *pacta sunt servanda*, and the lack of *stare decisis*. The influence of common domestic legal traditions on international law is much more recent. Only after the Second World War did common law principles and ideas find their way into international substantive law and international adjudicative bodies (Picker 2008, 1105). The influence of common law on international law has been to a large extent fueled by the dominant position of common law states in the international system. This has been called more recently the "Americanization" of international law (Wiegand 1996; Keleman and Sibbitt 2004).

Differences between civil, common, and Islamic legal traditions

In this section, we explore the major differences between the three major legal families. First, we describe fundamental differences in concepts, principles, and sources of law, such as the doctrine of the precedent, *bona fides*, and *pacta sunt servanda*. Then we focus on procedural differences and distinctions in the law of contracts, including freedom of contract, the design of contracts, formalism in procedures, litigation and trial rules, and avenues for appeal. When discussing each difference, we also describe characteristics of international law. Table 2.1 summarizes the primary differences between the civil, common, and Islamic legal traditions and the main characteristics of international law.[7]

---

[7] Information about domestic legal systems has been gathered using the *CIA Fact Book*, which describes major characteristics of legal traditions of each state in the international system, and several other subsidiary legal sources, including Glendon *et al.* (1994), Opolot (1980), and a website maintained at the University of Ottawa: www.juriglobe.ca/eng/sys-juri/index-syst.php.

Doctrine of the precedent

One of the main differences between civil, common, and Islamic legal traditions relates to the doctrine of precedent. The doctrine of precedent is one of the most distinguishable features of common law and sets it apart from civil and Islamic law. This common law practice is known simply as case law, which is defined as the decisions of judges laying down legal principles derived from the circumstances and characteristics of particular disputes coming before them (Darbyshire 2001). The reason why such a great importance is attached to case decisions is explicated by the doctrine of *stare decisis*, which is also known as the doctrine of judicial precedent. The term *stare decisis* is an abbreviation of the Latin phrase "*stare decisis et not quieta movere*" (to stand by precedents and not to disturb settled points). In its most basic form, the doctrine of *stare decisis* states that when trying a case, a judge is obliged to examine how previous judges have dealt with similar cases (precedents). In the process of looking back, a judge is expected to discover principles of law relevant to a case under consideration. Decisions taken by a judge will be consistent with the existing principles in that branch of law. Stated in a general form, *stare decisis* signifies that when a point of law has been settled by a judicial decision, it forms a precedent, which is not to be departed from afterward (Opolot 1980). The main advantage of the doctrine of judicial precedent is that it leads to consistency in the application and creation of principles in each branch of law. It also enables common law lawyers to forecast with some degree of certainty what kind of judgment may be expected in a particular case.[8]

In contrast to common law, the civil legal tradition lacks formal judicial precedent in the activity of a majority of the courts (Glenn 2007).[9]

---

[8] Prior to 1966, the highest courts of the United Kingdom and the United States took conflicting positions on the question of what a judge should do if confronted with an unreasonable or outdated precedent. The House of Lords decided in 1898 that it was bound by its own decisions. In the United States, on the other hand, the principle of *stare decisis* has never been considered an absolute command, and the duty to follow a precedent is held to be qualified by the right to overrule prior decisions. The highest courts of the states, as well as the Supreme Federal Court, have the right to depart from a rule previously established by them. In the United Kingdom, the situation changed in 1966 when the Practice Statement of the House of Lords established that previous decisions of the House are treated by it "as normally binding," but this is subject to a right "to depart from a previous decision when it appears right to do so" (Shahabuddeen 1996, 106–107).

[9] However, this generalization must be qualified. On the one hand, case law and judicial precedents to some extent appear in some civil law nations, especially in the context of the supreme or constitutional courts. On the other hand, statutes that comprise written legal principles and rules have become an important form of law in common law nations. This is particularly true for the United Kingdom, which is faced with unremitting pressure to introduce new legislation because of its membership of the EU (Rogowski 2002).

According to the Roman *ius civile* tradition represented by civil law systems, law making is a function of the legislature. Contrary to a common law judge, a civil law judge's task is considered to be passive; he or she must implement legal rules contained mainly in various codes and laws of lower status (Pejovic 2001). Civil law judges are to refrain from any creative role; their task is to invoke the written sources of law. This procedure prevents them from relying on previously decided cases. Each case is treated as a separate and unique circumstance without any precedent. As far as the predictability of judgments goes, even though there is no legal rule that would bind a judge to decide according to previously established case law, civil law judges indicate how they will solve similar disputes in the future when justifying their decisions.

Islamic law lacks any operative notion of precedent (Glenn 2007). In fact, the Islamic judicial process, guided by a *qadi* (judge), is understood as a very dynamic process, where "all cases may be seen as different and particular, and for each of which the precisely appropriate law must be carefully sought out" (Glenn 2007, 177). Traditionally, Islamic law states have not had much hierarchy in the judicial system. For example, in Saudi Arabia, "Upon passing judgment against the defendant, the *qadi* must specify the reasons upon which it is based. The judge does not have to follow precedent, not even his own previous rulings, but the decision must have support in the Koran, Sunna, and *ijma*" (Reichel 2008, 261; see also Kingdom of Saudi Arabia, the Code of Law Practice 2001[10]). Thus, each case may be based on a different set of laws stemming from the *Shari'a*, as different *qadi* may apply the law in slightly divergent ways. Actually, during the Umayyad period, "judges were not bound by precedents, even their own, hence the same judge [might] give a different ruling in settling two similar cases if convinced, or at least ... able to convey the conviction, that an error was committed in the first place" (Ford 1995, 527). In addition, in most Islamic law states, there is no established system of case-reporting, without which the concept of *stare decisis* has no practical meaning (Imber 1997). The rejection of *stare decisis* in Islamic law constitutes a consequence of the religious nature of the primary sources of law. If the Word of Allah constitutes a direct source of law, then "jurists can no more change it through the progressive development of case precedents than they could themselves speak on behalf of the Deity" (Ford 1995, 528).[11]

International law is similar to civil and Islamic legal traditions in that it does not officially embrace the principle of *stare decisis*. Formally "in

---

[10] Available at www.saudiembassy.net/about/country-information/law/CodePractice01.aspx.
[11] A partial exception from the no-precedent rule can be found in the case of Pakistan, where the courts have had some ability to modify the *Shari'a* (Ford 1995).

international law it is simply not the case that as a formal matter, case law makes new international law" (Picker 2008, 1101). Article 38(1)(d) of the ICJ Statute lists as one of the sources of international law "judicial decisions and the teachings of the most highly qualified publicists of the various nations, as subsidiary means for the determination of rules of law." This statement, however, must be examined in conjunction with Article 59 of the ICJ Statute, which states: "The decision of the Court has no binding force except between the parties and in respect of that particular case." Accordingly, judicial decisions can only be used as a subsidiary means for determination of rules of international law. As such they do not constitute, as in the common law system, actual sources of law (Shaw 2003, 103). In other words, the Court may take into consideration its previous judgments, but it is not formally bound to follow them (Palmeter and Mavroids 1998, 400). Limitations on international judicial law making are highly similar to the civil law approach: "The role of the international judiciary is more like civil law in its deference to the letter of the law and in its self-imposed restraint" (Picker 2008, 1114).

Despite the fact the *de jure* precedent is generally absent in international law, several adjudicative bodies have embraced *de facto* precedent. The ICJ, for example, has throughout its history endeavored to closely examine its previous decisions and follow its earlier judgments. Furthermore, in several judgments, the Court has *de facto* engaged in law creation, in cases such as the *Reparations* case and the *Anglo–Norwegian Fisheries* case.[12] According to Alvarez (2005, 460), *de facto* precedent is employed by a wide variety of international adjudicative bodies: "[N]either the absence of a hierarchy among these international dispute settlers nor resistance to adopting a clear doctrine of *stare decisis* has prevented what is a routine characteristic of common law decision-making: reliance on prior 'caselaw' or attempts to distinguish prior opinions as if they were precedents requiring differentiation to the extent not followed." Also, the WTO Appellate Body has increasingly emphasized the importance of its previous decisions: "Other than the texts of the WTO Agreements themselves, no source of law is as important in WTO dispute settlement as the reported decisions of prior dispute settlement panels" (Palmeter and Mavroidis 1998, 400).

In addition to *de jure* prohibition of precedent and its *de facto* presence in some of the international adjudicative bodies, there is another theoretical and conceptual issue that should be considered. Some scholars argue that the concept of *stare decisis* stands in sharp contrast with the positivist

---

[12] ICJ Reports 1949, p. 174; 16 AD, p. 318; ICJ Reports 1951, p. 116; 18 ILR, p. 86. Also see Shaw (2003, 104).

notion of international law: "whereby states must explicitly agree to be bound by the law rather than by the legal conclusions of judges or arbitrators involved in extraneous disputes involving other states" (Picker 2008, 1101). The fact that the written letter of law is sometimes different from the actual practice of adjudicative international bodies presents an interesting example of the process through which Western domestic legal systems influence international law. Civil law roots of *jus gentium* theoretically constrain the process of judicial law making, and the more recent common law influences make the *de facto stare decisis* principle increasingly acceptable (Picker 2008, 1112). According to Alvarez (2005, 463–464), most prominent international courts and other adjudicative bodies like the ICJ, the ECJ, the ICTY, the ICTR, the WTO's dispute settlement system, and the ECHR have to some extent attempted to contribute to the development of international law, as "virtually no subject within international law is now immune from at least potential adjudicative law-creation" (Alvarez 2005, 464).

Sources and nature of law

The separation between religion and law in the Western legal traditions (civil and common law) has a long history. It dates back to the eleventh century, when philosophy, law, and theology became independent disciplines in the universities (Powell 2006a). Academic scholarship was based primarily on written texts, and the texts that lawyers and theologists used (*Corpus Juris Civilis* and the Bible, respectively) were different (Mattei 1997a, 24). Thus, both civil and common legal traditions are secular, which entails a relatively strict separation between the law and the religion. Western religious values have undoubtedly provided a basis for fundamental rules and norms of both civil and common legal traditions. However, religious sources do not constitute direct sources of law. For example, murder is prohibited in all Western legal systems. Although "Though shalt not murder" constitutes one of the Ten Commandments, the Bible is not used as a basis of judgment.

Civil and common law traditions are based on secular sources of law. The main feature of a civil legal system is that it is codified in various codes. A code is a "systematic, authoritative, and guiding statute of broad coverage" (Schlesinger *et al.* 1998, 271). As such, civil law is classified, well-structured, and "contains a great number of general rules and principles" (Pejovic 2001, 819). For example, with regards to contractual relationships, all main principles that are to apply to contracts are contained in codes. Usually, these general principles appear in the front sections of the codes, implying their application to all contractual relations enumerated in a code.[13] As such, civil codes meticulously regulate rights and obligations, solutions for any legal complaint, the role of the judge and the parties in the proceedings, and types of remedies. In the spirit of civilian formalism, civil lawyers see interpretation of legal rules and norms as an exercise that is to take place strictly according to pre-existing rules (Koch 2003). Even though case law does not constitute a formal source of law in the civil legal tradition, the practical usefulness of prior judgments should not be understated.[14] Precedent still retains value as a guideline for the parties and also as a benchmark for the court in the process of legal reasoning. The case law of higher courts, although formally non-binding, seems to play an important role in providing a direction for the courts of lower instances. Judges of these courts usually try to avoid the reversal of their judgments by higher courts.

In common law, precedent, or case law, constitutes the primary source of law. Thus, in contrast with civil law, in common law "the case does more than teach judges something; it exists separately as law to be followed, or distinguished" (Gordon 2002, 324). Legislation or statute constitutes another source of law in the common law tradition, although their thoroughness and range vary from country to country. In the United Kingdom, the mother of the common law tradition, statutes have become increasingly important, especially with the deepening of European integration. In the United States, another common law state, statutes play a crucial role, as a relatively large proportion of laws are directly regulated via the written letter of law.

Islamic law, on the other hand, is founded on religious principles: "Islam, probably more than any other religion, has the character of a jural system which regulates the life and thoughts of the believer according to an ideal set of rules regarded as the only correct and valid one. This system, unlike positive law, proceeded from a high divine source embodying God's will and justice" (Khadduri 1956, 359; Al-Azmeh 1988; Lippman *et al.* 1988). The *Shari'a*, the law of Islam, constitutes the path to righteousness. Rather than prescribing a minimum of satisfactory conduct, it points the faithful to an ideally wholesome life (Shapiro 1986). In Islamic legal culture, there exists no sharp division between morals, religion, and legal obligations. As Van Hoecke and Warrington put it, "All law is

---

[13] Of course, there are some differences between the codes of different civil law states, but there are also certain features of all of the codes that set them apart from laws of the other legal families (Pejovic 2001).

[14] Judicial precedent (*la jurisprudence*) constitutes a source in the French legal system (civil law tradition). However, only a small portion of the precedents (decisions of the plenary session of the *Cour de cassation*) is binding. Other judicial decisions have only "a persuasive force" (Owsia 1991, 36).

based on and deduced from the Koran, despite legal doctrine in practice being generally considered a source of law, and sometimes even against the literal wording of the Koran" (Van Hoecke and Warrington 1998, 507). Even though both of the Western legal traditions extracted many important legal principles from religious sources, such as the Bible, the legal systems themselves are separate from religion. In contrast, Islamic law "is intrinsic to Islamic faith and life in Islamic countries" (Reichel 2008, 124).

Even though the concept of divine law in Islam appeared in the eighth and ninth centuries AD, it matured through the process of identifying and defining the key sources of Islamic law, which are of a religious nature (Moore 2002). The four primary sources of Islamic law include the Koran, the Sunna, judicial consensus, and analogical reasoning (Vago 2000). The Koran is the sacred book of the Muslims, and it literally means "the Reading." It comprises guidelines and rules of conduct that God revealed to the Prophet Muhammad through the angel Gabriel. Rules included in the Koran deal with various aspects of Muslim's lives, such as religious, personal, social, economic, and legal matters (Reichel 2008, 125). The number of all the legal verses in Koran, according to the traditional count, is about 500 (Hallaq 2005, 21). The Sunna literally means "the path taken or trodden" by the Prophet Muhammad, and it contains his explanations, deeds, sayings, and conduct (Glenn 2007, 173–174). The Sunna has been reported in *hadiths* – statements including traditions of Muhammad's actions and customs. Initially in an oral form, *hadiths* were eventually recorded in a written form. Each *hadith* consists of two separate parts: (1) the main text of the report that describes the actual narrative (a deed or a saying of Muhammad), and (2) the text that lists the history of the recording of the narrative.

In addition to the two primary sources, the Koran and the Sunna, Islamic law relies on two subsidiary sources: (1) judicial consensus (*ijma*), and (2) analogical reasoning (*qiyas*). Judicial consensus, which limits the discretion of the individual judge, is established by "a common religious conviction" of major traditional legal scholars (Glenn 2007); it regards specific points of Islamic law. After Muhammad's death, leaders of the Muslim community, the *caliphs*, used consultants to aid in interpreting the two primary sources of law in circumstances when it was hard to reach a straightforward legal conclusion (Souryal 2004). Analogical reasoning, the fourth source of Islamic law, is used in circumstances not addressed by the Koran or the other two sources (Vago 2000).[15] According to this

---

[15] The religious nature of Islamic law is enshrined in several Islamic states. For example, Saudi Arabia, Bahrain, Kuwait, Oman, and Yemen declare themselves as "Arab Islamic

method of legal deduction, the ruling of the Koran and Sunna may be applied to a new problem or a legal question directly not covered by either of these sources. This, however, may take place if the set precedent or paradigm and the new problem have a common operative or effective cause. For example, analogical reasoning, or *qiyas*, is applied to the injunction against drinking wine to create an injunction against the use of modern drugs, such as cocaine.

The nature of international law is best expressed by Brierly's (1963, 1) definition: "[T]he Law of Nations, or International Law, may be defined as the body of rules and principles of action which are binding upon civilized states in their relations with one another." This body of rules has developed primarily from the ideas and practices of the Western world, causing the dominant character of international law to be decidedly Western. Numerous underlying principles of international law can be traced to ancient Rome, Greece, and medieval Europe. Although international law in its present form constitutes a secular legal system, the Catholic Church and the Catholic doctrine have had a significant impact on the substance of the law of nations. Canon law and ecclesiastical law, which developed primarily during medieval times, shaped to some extent many basic rules of international law, such as authority over territory and the conclusion and observance of international treaties (von Glahn and Taulbee 2007, 37). Just as within the Western legal systems, international law embraces the view that a distinction between the law and religion must be observed. Thus, in all international adjudicative bodies, such as the ICJ, the ICC, or the WTO Dispute Settlement Body, "politics and morals are not, as a theoretical matter, acceptable bases for a judgment; decisions involving politics and morals are criticized" (Picker 2008, 1096). Sources of international law are exhaustively enumerated in Article 38(1) of the Statute of the ICJ. They include international conventions, treaties, international custom,[16] general principles of law recognized by civilized nations,[17] judicial decisions,

states." This term is meant to convey the inherent bond between *Shari'a*, or Islamic law, and state rule, monarch, and the citizens. This stipulation sets *Shari'a* above all man-made laws, including trade law. Also, property in Islamic law is placed in a broader social context in that "absolute ownership of property is seen as vested ultimately in God" (Glenn 2007, 182).

[16] The material sources of custom include diplomatic correspondence, policy statements, press releases, the opinions of official legal advisers, states' legislation, and the practice of international organs.

[17] Two major opinions exist regarding the meaning and scope of the general principles of law: The first one asserts that general principles of law refer to general principles present in domestic legal systems (fair hearing, *bona fides*). The second view holds that general principles of law pertain to the principles of natural law. The first view "best describes the majority view in contemporary thought (and court use)" (von Glahn and Taulbee 2007, 70).

and the teachings of the most highly qualified publicists. The first three constitute major sources; judicial decisions and scholarly writings are subsidiary sources of international law (von Glahn and Taulbee 2007, 59).

The principle of good faith (bona fides)

Good faith or *bona fides* is very difficult to define. Most scholars agree, however, that it has three constitutive moral elements: (1) honesty, (2) fairness, and (3) reason (Zimmermann and Whittaker 2000). Medieval jurists provided the best description of *bona fides*. According to them, good faith meant that a party "must keep his word, refrain from deceit and overreaching, and honor obligations that are only implicit in his contract" (Zimmermann and Whittaker 2000, 93). In general, the concept of good faith requires that contracting parties abstain from dishonesty and keep their promises. Furthermore, the parties are not only obliged to behave according to standards of fair dealing during contract negotiations, but also to observe the fundamental norm of *pacta sunt servanda* (once signed, contracts must be fulfilled) (Zimmermann and Whittaker 2000, 136). The principle of good faith has strong roots in the civil law and Islamic law traditions, while its influence is considerably weaker in common law.

The concept of good faith originated in Roman law, where it gave the judge an equitable discretion to decide a case brought before him according to what seemed to be reasonable and fair. Thus, *bona fides* associated with trustworthiness and honorable conduct permitted the judge to denounce breaches of good faith by taking into consideration the particularities of each case (O'Connor 1991, 117). As such, *bona fides* has affected the entire civil legal family. Despite the fact that modern civil systems vary to some extent, the general concept of *bona fides* constitutes in this legal family one of the most important abstract rules. In most, if not all civil law states, civil codes classify contracts into types. Each type is governed by a detailed list of overarching principles. References to good faith appear in various civil law codes in both general clauses and specific legal prescriptions, which regulate a particular subject matter.[18] The Swiss Civil Code (*Schweizerisches Zivilgezetzbuch* of 1907), for example, contains a general good faith provision, which states "In exercising his rights and in performing his duties everyone has to act in accordance with good faith."[19]

---

[18] The exact expression of the *bona fides* principles varies somewhat across civil domestic legal systems. Nevertheless, the general rule is to incorporate this concept in both general and particular legal stipulations.

[19] Article 2I. Also quoted in Zimmermann and Whittaker 2000, 51.

Another example is provided by Article 242 of the German Civil Code, which stipulates that the obligor is bound to perform the contract in good faith (*Treu und Glauben*) (O'Connor 1991). Similar regulations appear in almost all civil codifications. Because *bona fides* has been incorporated directly into civil codes, the courts have to interpret the contracts "in the light of the concurring or integrating rules that the legal system had for every type of contract" (Moss 2007a, 11). This directly affects the protection of contracting parties, because the governing law is charged with integrating or correcting the contractual regulations (Moss 2007b, 234). In more general terms, civil law approaches good faith (*bona fides*) as an overarching general principle, which may include the doctrine of unconscionability or frustration (Farnsworth 1995).[20]

The English or common law of contracts, which is based on the liberal ideal of individual autonomy, does not recognize a general duty to negotiate nor to perform contracts in good faith.[21] An extreme version of this liberal approach postulates that one of the privileges of having a right is the freedom of its abuse; an old Latin maxim *neminem laedit qui suo iure utitur* (if you are exercising your right you are not harming anybody) expresses that thought (Zimmermann and Whittaker 2000, 696). While designing their contract, the parties are expected to take care of their own interests; thus, "they do not expect the legal system to protect them and patronize them, but they expect the legal system to give them tools in order to enforce what they have agreed" (Moss 2007a, 4–5).

---

[20] An unconscionable contract is a contract that is so unfair to a party that no informed or reasonable person would agree to it. Usually it results from unequal bargaining positions between the parties. Frustration of a contract occurs when a contract becomes impossible to perform/fulfill or can be performed/fulfilled only in a way significantly different from that originally envisioned.

[21] However, some common law states have gradually introduced the principle of good faith into their legal systems. For example, the United States Uniform Commercial Code in section 1–304 states: "Every contract or duty within this Act imposes an obligation of good faith in its performance." Also, the US Restatement (Second) of Contracts adopted by the American Law Institute in 1979 and published in final form in 1981 provides that individuals have non-waivable duties of good faith. This act stands in a sharp contrast with the first Restatement of Contracts (1932), which did not include a comparable good faith provision (Summerst 1982). In the United Kingdom, the European Consumer Protection Directive of 1994 transplanted good faith directly into the body of British contract law. Despite these developments, we agree with numerous legal scholars that there are still fundamental differences in the status of *bona fides* in civil and common law traditions. Some argue that good faith is a "legal irritant" in the common law tradition and that "the imperatives of a specific Anglo-American economic culture as against a specific Continental one will bring about an even more fundamental reconstruction of good faith under the new conditions" (Teubner 1998, 12).

The words of Lord Ackner (*Walford* v. *Miles*)[22] adequately expressed this philosophy:

The concept of a duty to carry on negotiations in good faith is inherently repugnant to the adversarial position of the parties when involved in negotiations. Each party to the negotiations is entitled to pursue his (or her) own interest, so long as he avoids making misrepresentations. A duty to negotiate in good faith is as unworkable in practice as it is inherently inconsistent with the position of the negotiating parties. (Zimmermann and Whittaker 2000, 40)

Thus, there is no overarching doctrine of *bona fides* in English law regulating contracts. As a general rule, a person who has obtained a right under a contract can exercise it for either good or bad reason.[23] This position differs sharply from the civil law tradition where the doctrine of *bona fides* has been granted a prime position. In the United Kingdom, the birthplace of the common law tradition, the doctrine of good faith has often times been perceived by lawyers as threatening and simply unworkable in the British law system. Some scholars even argue that good faith "could well work practical mischief if ruthlessly implanted into our system of law" (Bridge 1984, 426).[24] Additionally, the common law tradition, in contrast to civil law, embraces a much more restrictive interpretation of the doctrine of good faith, at the same time sharply separating it from the abovementioned principles of frustration and unconscionability or frustration (Farnsworth 1995).

Despite the lack of a general principle of good faith, English common law courts have tried over time to mitigate the negative impact of such a lacuna by developing various legal doctrines that are to put limits on the absoluteness of contractual rights and obligations. Examples include the doctrine of economic duress and the doctrine of frustration (Zimmermann and Whittaker 2000, 47).[25] In that way, common law

---

[22] [1992] 2 AC 128, 138.

[23] An example of a party to a contract exercising its right out of an unjustified reason is provided in the decision of the British Court of Appeal in the case of *Chapman* v. *Honig* ([1963] 2 QB 502). The judge presiding over this case upheld the exercise by a landlord of his contractual right to give notice to his tenant, even though the landlord's decision had been triggered by the tenant giving evidence against the landlord in a dispute with another tenant. The landlord's decision to give notice to his tenant constitutes a good example of how a person can exercise his duty for "a bad reason." Under English law, however, this "unjustified" motive does not hamper the legal right of the landlord to exercise his right (Zimmermann and Whittaker 2000, 40).

[24] Quoted in Zimmermann and Whittaker 2000, 15.

[25] Until the Unfair Contract Terms Act of 1977, the English courts had no general power to monitor against unfair contracts. This act has significantly improved the position of the principle of *bona fides* in the United Kingdom, but it has not, however, changed the basic philosophy of English law (Whincup 1992, 57).

has resorted to patching the legal system with specific institutions and doctrines in order to alleviate the lack of the *bona fides* doctrine. In the United Kingdom, statute law, equity, and the common law have also made contributions, by requiring that several types of contracts require good faith. Nevertheless, "the piecemeal solutions of English law do not necessarily correspond to a general principle" (Moss 2007a, 10).

Good faith constitutes one of the most important principles in Islamic law, as its religious sources, which are of utmost importance to every Muslim, admonish the faithful to keep their agreements.[26] Fraud, dishonesty, and untruthfulness directly contradict the Muslim equitable protection against any type of deception. The Koran stipulates: "Woe to the fraudulent dealers, who extract full measure from others, but give less than due to others in weight and measure, do they not know that they will be called to account?"[27] In general, Islamic jurisprudence perceives of fraud and dishonesty as a "serious moral wrong" (Rayner 1991, 206). The general requirement of *bona fides* is thus strongly anchored in Islamic contract theory, and it applies to contractual relations with believers and non-believers.

Bona fides constitutes one of the general principles of law recognized by civilized nations, and it is, therefore, one of the formal sources of international law (O'Connor 1991, 1). Several scholars of international law consider good faith a cornerstone of international relations because this principle fosters international order and guards against arbitrary behavior (Bull 1977; Virally 1983; Lukashuk 1989). For example, Mann (1973, 162) believes that *bona fides* "unquestionably pervades public international law." One of the first writers on public international law, Alberico Gentili, argued that good faith constitutes a wide ethical and legal principle that should be upheld in international relations. Drawing on the tradition of Roman law, another founding father of international law, Hugo Grotius, granted *bona fides* a place among the universally accepted foundations of the law among nations (O'Connor 1991, 120).

Numerous international law treatises have confirmed the strong position of *bona fides* in international law. Examples include the Declaration on Principles of International Law concerning Friendly Relations and Co-operation among States in Accordance with the Charter of the United Nations (1945), the Final Act of the Conference on Security and Co-operation in Europe (1975), and the Vienna Convention on the Law of the Treaties (1969). In addition, the ICJ in the *Nuclear Tests* cases proclaimed that "one of the basic principles governing the creation and performance

[26] Examples include the Koran, Suras V:1' IV:33; and XVI:91 (quoted in Rosen 2000, 143).
[27] Koran, Sura LXXXIII:1–5.

of legal obligations, whatever their source, is the principle of good faith."[28] In practice, as with any principle of international law, fulfillment of good faith is based on reciprocity, and this underlying standard is often times expressed in states' domestic legislations (Lukashuk 1989, 517).

Pacta sunt servanda

Pacta sunt servanda, as one of the most important expressions of the *bona fides* doctrine, has been granted a prime position in the Western legal traditions. There exists, however, an important difference between the civil and common legal systems. Common law has for a long time accepted that events occurring after a contract had been signed might make the contract impossible or impracticable to fulfill, because the subject matter of the contract has been destroyed, or the obliged party is prevented from fulfilling his obligations due to sickness, or the contract as a whole may have become prohibited by law (*force majeure*) (Rayner 1991; Whincup 1992).[29] In the event of these circumstances, the contract is brought to an end by operation of law and the parties are released from their contractual obligations. Civil law systems view such events as creating only a partial release from a contract until the situation conducive to the fulfillment of contract is restored. On the other hand, civil law systems do not recognize the *parol evidence* rule,[30] which some have argued strengthens the sanctity of contracts in common law states relative to civil law states (Nassar 1995).

In the Islamic legal tradition, the principle of *pacta sunt servanda* is paramount "because it is God Who is the witness of all contracts" (Rayner 1991, 100). Contractual obligations governed by Muslim law require all parties to uphold their commitments. Muslims believe that "this is an order from God to fulfill a promise, whether it be a contract proper ('*aqd*') or an agreement or obligation created by any means other than verbal" (El-Hassan 1985, 54). A contract constitutes not merely secular law between the parties, but also a sacred law, or a "*Shari'a*" (Habachy 1962, 467).[31] This obligation of the faithful to respect their

---

[28] 1974 ICJ Rep. 253, 268, also quoted in Virally, 1983: 130.

[29] *Force majeure* literally means "greater force." These clauses excuse a party from liability if some unforeseen event beyond the control of that party prevents it from performing its contractual obligations. Examples of *force majeure* include natural disasters or other "acts of God," war, or the failure of third parties (e.g. suppliers).

[30] The *parole evidence* rule assumes that a written contract embodies all of the terms of the agreement, and thus that external evidence, such as verbal communication between the parties, could not alter the parties' obligations.

[31] The approach of Islamic law to fulfillment of contracts is fundamentally different from that of common and civil legal systems. Although the Catechism of the Catholic Church

contractual obligations is binding not only in relation to other Muslims, but also towards non-believers. A strict Islamic law interpretation of the *pacta sunt servanda* norm suggests that "a national Islamic state has no vested right to cancel or alter a contract by unilateral action, whether such action takes the form of an administrative, judicial or even legislative act" (Rayner 1991, 87). According to the Koran, even the state of war by itself does not constitute a sufficient justification for contractual violation (Rayner 1991, 87). However, under Islamic law, a contract may be invalidated temporarily by subsequent clauses such as impossibility of performance (*rebus sic stantibus*) and *force majeure*.

The strong commitment to the *pacta sunt servanda* norm is expressed in a 1963 arbitration case between Saudi Arabia and the Arabian-American Oil Company (ARAMCO), where it was declared that:

Moslem Law does not distinguish between a treaty, a contract of public or administrative law and a contract of civil or commercial law. All these types are viewed by Moslem jurists as agreements or pacts which must be observed, since God is a witness to any contract entered into by individuals or by collectivities; under Moslem law, any valid contract is obligatory, in accordance with the principles of Islam and the Law of God, as expressed in the Koran: "Be faithful to your pledge to God, when you enter into a pact. (*Saudi Arabia v. Arabian American Oil Company*).[32]

Pacta sunt servanda, as one of the most important faces of the concepts of *bona fides*, constitutes an important principle of international law. It provides for a necessary foundation for the society of states (Wehberg 1959; Bull 1977). Kegley and Raymond (1990, 87), for example, state: "Against this ever-present reservation of the sovereign right of states to remain unencumbered by moral edicts, there has been a recognition of the need for faithful performance of treaty obligations." The importance of the p*acta sunt servanda* principle in the relations between states is ensured by its status as one of the general principles of law and also as a part of customary law, although the *pacta sunt servanda* rule applies internationally only to treaties in force (Aust 2007).

Of course, under many domestic legal systems, in case of "a radical transformation of the extent of the obligations still to be performed," parties can be released from their obligations.[33] Also, in the event of impossibility of performance, a party to a contract may invoke this reason as grounds for terminating the contract if the impossibility results

instructs in Article 2464 that the eighth commandment forbids misrepresenting the truth in one's relations with others, this article does not constitute a direct source of secular legal obligations.

[32] [1963] 27 ILR 117.

[33] *Fisheries Jurisdiction* case, ICJ Rep. 1973, p. 21.

from the permanent disappearance or destruction of an object indispensable for the fulfillment of the treaty (Vienna Convention). Submergence of an island, an earthquake, or drying up of a river provides examples of such circumstances (Brownlie 2003, 594). Unfortunately, as with many legal rules, the *clausula rebus sic stantibus* is vague and hard to define. On the international arena, states have often invoked this rule in order to free themselves from their contractual commitments. Prussian King Frederick II, for example, justified his termination of a neutrality treaty with Breslau in 1741 on the grounds of *rebus sic stantibus*, which resulted in him occupying the town (Kegley and Raymond 1990, 91).

Freedom of contract

Freedom of contract constitutes another point of divergence between the three major legal traditions. Just like many other principles of contract law, the primary differences across legal traditions arise between the Western legal systems on the one hand, and the Islamic legal tradition on the other. In Western legal thinking, freedom of contracts, coupled with the principle of the autonomy of the will, is considered as one of the major contract-related concepts (Powell 2006a). It states that "one is perfectly free to enter into a contract with whomsoever one wishes" (Mohammed 1988, 126). It stems from the *laissez faire* economic school of thought, which holds that the market performs best when it is left to its own devices. The basic idea dictated by this doctrine is that less governmental intrusion into private economic activities makes for a more efficient system.

In contrast to the Western law of contract, which developed primarily during the eighteenth and nineteenth centuries, Islamic law started taking shape much earlier in the seventh century (Mohammed 1988, 117). In addition, Islamic law, distinct from its Western counterparts, did not have to adjust to the needs of industrial revolution. This strengthened the inherent bond between Islamic religion and Islamic contract law. To this day, Muslim law basically reflects realities of the period in which it originally formed. For example, Islamic law limits the freedom of contract as "no contract which derogates from any principle of the *Shari'a* may be validly concluded" (Rayner 1991, 91).[34] The autonomy of will is

---

[34] It should be noted, however, that quite a few exceptions from this general doctrine do exist in some Muslim nations. The Federal Civil Code of the United Arab Emirates, for example, specifies that a contract may contain certain stipulations that "are not prohibited by a provision of the law" and are "not contrary to public order or morals" (United Arab Emirates Federal Law of Civil Translations, *UAE Official Gazette*, no. 158 (December 1985), also quoted in Rayner 1991, 96, footnote 54).

subject to the Islamic prohibition against certain actions and contracts, such as *riba, gharar,* and others.[35] On this basis, the Islamic approach to economic relations differs sharply from Western-based capitalism since Muslim firms are to operate "under the guidance of norms drawn from the traditional sources of Islam," which prohibit speculation, hoarding, gambling, or destructive competition (Kuran 1995, 159).[36] As we show later, these restrictions on contracting freedom in Islamic law have significant consequences for the (un)willingness of Islamic states to create and join international courts.

The concept of freedom of contract carried over from Western domestic legal systems into the international realm. Here, the basic definition of a treaty adapted by the 1969 Vienna Convention on the Law of the Treaties expresses the importance of this principle in relations between states. For the purposes of the Convention, Article 2(1)(a) defines a treaty as: "an international agreement concluded between states in written form and governed by international law, whether embodied in a single instrument or in two or more related instruments and *whatever its particular designation.*"[37] States are free to choose the subject matter of their agreements. As such, the Vienna Convention "is not so concerned with the substance of a treaty (the rights and obligations created by it), which is known as 'treaty law.' That is a matter for the negotiating states" (Aust 2007, 6). In general, international law in its approach to the freedom of contracting between states is highly similar to the civil law and common law traditions.

Design of contracts

The way that contracts are drafted, including their length and thoroughness, differs considerably in the civil, common, and Islamic legal traditions. Contracts concluded in a civil law system are relatively straightforward due to the presence of civil codes, which contain all main principles that are to apply to contracts. Usually, these general principles

---

[35] *Riba* translates to "usury." *Gharar* refers to an entire range of commercial activities, which involve speculative and aleatory contracts (Mohammed 1988). The Congress of the Week of Islamic Law held in Damascus in 1961 accepted the prohibition against several nominate contracts. It was affirmed that "as the parties are free to make contracts of their own choice, all kinds of contract would be acceptable providing that they do not contradict the basic principles of the *Shari'a* law of contract and the generally acknowledged principles of Islam" (Rayner 1991, 96).

[36] Also see Saleh (2001), who argues that Arab legal systems support a relatively widely understood freedom of contract.

[37] Italics added by the authors; the same definition is given to treaties by the 1986 Convention on Treaties between States and International Organizations.

appear in the front sections of the codes, implying their application to all contractual relations enumerated in a code. For example, the *bona fides* and the *pacta sunt servanda* principles described above are included in civil codes. Codification entails a systematic organization of the contract law and "a scientific recasting of legal concepts," which makes the space-consuming enumeration of legal principles in a contract unnecessary (Langbein 1987, 383).

Common law contracts are much more detailed and meticulous than civil law contracts (Langbein 1987; Lundmark 2001).[38] Scholars identify several factors responsible for the prolixity of common law contracts, including the limitation of remedies for breach of contract to an award of compensatory damages, and the lack of a general overarching legal framework regulating contractual relations (Lundmark 2001). First, in the common law tradition, specific performance as a remedy for breach of contract is an exception. Thus, only in very limited situations, such as those involving a unique object, will a court order this remedy. The parties must be very clear about what performance is expected under the contract, so that when a dispute arises there is no ambiguity concerning performance. This leads to detailed specification of performance contingencies, which makes common law contracts much longer than those written in a civil law tradition.

Second, because there is much less codified law that incorporates overarching general principles, the parties are responsible for including certain stipulations (clauses) in their contract. For example, in common law, *force majeure* is not precisely defined. The parties must enumerate in a contract any events of *force majeure* that will preclude them for being liable on the grounds of non-performance: "This is why the *force majeure* clauses in common law are often very long and comprehensive trying to cover as many *force majeure* events as possible" (Pejovic 2001, 824). Common law grants extensive interpretation powers to the judges; parties want to ensure that their will in a contract is clearly expressed, so that the judge's interpretation will occur within clearly specified limits. Moss (2007b, 234) aptly describes the difference in contract design between civil and common law traditions:

A common law contract is written with the idea of expressing as much as possible and as detailed as possible the whole relationship between the parties, because that document will be, with few exceptions that are not very

---

[38] According to Lundmark (2001), "a typical American purchase agreement of 3,800 words in length devotes only 550 words to business terms, leaving over 3,000 words for standard definitions and boilerplate [recitations of applicable law]" (p. 121). Interestingly, American common law contracts are longer than their British counterparts.

significant in commercial matters, the only basis upon which the judge will render its decision on any dispute. A civil law contract is traditionally written with the idea of regulating the specifics of the case, while leaving the rest to the legal system, which integrates the contract.

Islamic law regulates contractual relationships in a way that is strikingly different from that of common and civil law. The Koran plays a crucial role in establishing the types of contracts admissible to the faithful, their rights, and obligations. Islamic law lacks a general theory of contracts comparable to its Western counterparts. The Koran, however, to some extent, plays the role of a code, in which general principles are included. Parties to a contract are also free, with some limitations, to place stipulations in a contract. These clauses cannot negate the legal purpose of a contract or violate specific laws included in the Koran or the Sunna (Arabi 1998). Contracts under Islamic law are not particularly formal: "Formalism is disregarded to the extent that a contract may also be concluded by conduct alone (*mu atat*) where the offer and acceptance are expressed by an act" (Saleh 2001, 347). Several of the contemporary civil codes in Islamic law states express this commitment to the lack of formalism. For example, Article 65 of Kuwait's Civil Code (1980) stipulates that "for concluding a contract the contented state of mind (*rida*) of the contracting parties needs not take a particular form unless the law specifically states otherwise" (see also Saleh 2001, 347). The Koran expresses a recommendation that contracts should be concluded in writing: "Do not avoid preparation of an agreement whether the stipulates period is short or long, it will be just in sight of God, stronger in evidence and better to rule out doubts."[39] Islamic law directs the faithful to keep their contractual commitments. In fact, terms of an agreement are considered to be the *shari'a* between the parties. Rights and obligations of the parties are usually delineated carefully to ensure compliance with the contract.

The Islamic legal doctrine stipulates that "contracts must be formed in clear terminology reflecting the exact intention of the parties and clarifying all the key terms and provisions of the contract" (Zahraa 1998, 270). The parties must give particular attention to the order of the paragraphs, and group together paragraphs expressing similar ideas. Numbering, indentation, and punctuation also play a crucial role (Zahraa 1998). Islamic law and jurisprudence also permits the contracting parties to include several types of conditions in a contract. However, the contracting parties are not allowed to place any type of special terms as appendages to a contract. Each school of law supports slightly different sets of requisites for the approval of appendages or conditions (Saleh 2001, 354). Some

---

[39] Koran, Sura II:282.

examples include conditions stemming from or not repugnant to the *Shari'a*, conditions that are recognized by valid custom, and conditions that emphasize, strengthen, comply with, or are not repugnant to the crucial components of the contracts (Zahraa 1998). These approaches to the design of contracts place Islamic law states in the middle of the legal spectrum, between common law states on the one end, where parties tend to draft very lengthy contracts, and civil law states on the other end, whose recognition of general principles allows for relatively terse agreements to be concluded.

In international law, a treaty is regarded as the closest legal construct to a contract. In a treaty, states or other legal entities come together to regulate a relationship between them. There are numerous types of international treaties, such as military alliances, trade treaties, and environmental agreements. At the heart of each treaty, however, lies a contractual obligation. In simple terms, a treaty is "basically an agreement between parties on the international scene" (Shaw 2003, 811). In contrast to domestic legal systems, international law establishes very few specific requirements regarding the exact form of treaties. The earlier quoted Article 2(1)(a) of the Vienna Convention on the Law of Treaties establishes that a treaty must be concluded between states in written form, be governed by international law, and can be included in a single instrument or multiple instruments. The International Law Commission's Commentary explains further that the definition of treaty also includes less formal agreements, and agreements contained in a telegram, fax message, or an e-mail. As long as "the text can be reduced to a permanent, readable form (even if this is done by down-loading and printing out from a computer)," a treaty can be regarded as having a written form (Aust 2007, 19).

Degree of formalism

Research in legal history and comparative law shows that legal systems vary in their degree of formalism (Merryman 1985; Damaska 1986; Schlesinger *et al.* 1998; Djankov *et al.* 2002; Koch 2003; Powell and Wiegand 2010). States representing the civil law tradition "generally regulate dispute resolution, including the conduct of the adjudicators, more heavily than do common law countries" (Djankov *et al.* 2002, 7). Civil law scrupulously standardizes the behavior of the disputants and the court through procedural codes, which pertain to judicial powers, procedural rules, and types of remedies. Interpretation of law takes place within a pre-existing framework of law (the codes) (Koch 2003). In civil law, formal rules promote transparency of law; for this reason, judges are constrained in their interpretation of law. Judicial decisions not based on general formal principles seem arbitrary to a civil lawyer. Formalism in civil law reinforces a sharp distinction between law and non-law issues, which can guarantee the predictability of the legal system as a whole (Jouannet 2006).

Common law is more flexible than civil law. Judicial procedure is formalized to a much lesser degree because the political process has granted its judges a very high degree of judicial independence (Djankov *et al.* 2002). Common law judges "often see statutory language as providing a mere springboard from which they create the law for a specific case" (Koch 2003, 43). In comparison with civil law, common law is based on a more freely and dynamic interpretation of rules. Judges actually make law that amends and builds on the pre-existing legal structure. This process often times leads to a gradual evolution of the legal framework. When speaking of the differences between the civil and common law traditions, Jouannet (2006, 309) aptly notes that "Americans [common law] see law as an all-encompassing sociological and political phenomenon, while the French [civil law] see it exclusively as a body of rules and principles."

Procedural law is least formalized in Islamic law (Glenn 2007). Western-style formality of dispute resolution is replaced in Islamic law by the emphasis on acknowledgment, apology, and forgiveness (Irani and Funk 1998, 63). During a trial, reaching a consensus (reconciliation) between the parties is given a priority. During a typical Islamic trial, oral proceedings constitute the main element, and the parties simply present their statements in front of the *qadi* (judge). The in-court proceedings comprise a simple common-sense mechanism, without any documentation, formal procedure, or rules of evidence (Iqbal 2001). Because the *qadi* reaches a decision without any written reason, there is not typically a system of case reporting (Glenn 2007).

Since the Koran promotes simple reconciliation between the disputants, this informal mechanism is given precedence over a formal judgment. In fact, according to Islamic faith, formal adjudication may "breed hatred between parties while reconciliation brings them together" (Iqbal 2001, 1040). The use of informal proceedings leading to a true compromise, *sulh*, is the Prophet Muhammad's preferred method of dispute resolution (Sayen 2003). Unlike the more formalized Western style of in-court proceedings, the major role of a *qadi* is to guide the parties in the process of finding a common understanding and restoring their fellowship. According to Islamic law, "the preferred 'third party' helping the disputants in reaching their agreement is an unbiased insider with strong connections to the aggrieved parties as well as a good sense of the common good and standing within the community" (Irani and Funk 1998, 63).

The degree of formalism in international law resembles civil and common legal systems simultaneously. In some aspects, international law is relatively flexible, even more so than the common law domestic system. There exists no single international body endowed with the power to create international law, nor a single, hierarchical system of courts with the power to interpret the existing law. In addition, states representing different legal traditions often do not view international law the same way. Indeed, "there may be few common reference points among the many international jurists" (Picker 2008, 1086). This state of affairs can arguably create legal uncertainty: "One is therefore faced with the problem of discovering where the law is to be found and how one can tell whether a particular proposition amounts to a legal rule" (Shaw 2003, 66).

This uncertainty is buttressed by the anarchy present in the international system. In addition, several sources listed in Article 38(1) of the Statute of the ICJ are inherently vague in nature. For example, to date no rule has been established that would conclusively determine when an observed repeated practice becomes a custom. Also the exact meaning of "general principles of law recognized by civilized nations" has been the subject of widespread legal debate (von Glahn 1996, 18). As noted earlier, one perspective is that this phrase refers to general principles present in domestic legal systems, while an alternative view holds that general principles of law pertain to the principles of natural law (Shaw 2003, 93–94).

Imprecision of sources and incompleteness of law in several substantive areas give international courts a large discretion in shaping the international legal system. Existing courts, such as the ICJ, "are particularly well positioned to clarify the law for future cases both because the judges remain in place over time and because in each case the tribunal is recognized as the ultimate authority on the interpretation of the relevant laws" (Guzman 2008, 52). International adjudicative bodies are similar to common law courts that are formally endowed with the power to engage in law creation.

International law resemblance to the civil legal system is also noteworthy. Throughout history, it was the Roman legal thought and the civil legal doctrine that have impacted to a large degree the underlying structure of international law. Thus, there exists a considerable degree of formalism in *jus gentium*. Numerous substantive areas of international law are well-structured and highly transparent, embracing the civil law approach to formalism. In general, interpretation of international law takes place within a pre-existing framework of law, with a due emphasis on the sources of law, however vague, enumerated in Article 38(1) of the Statute of the ICJ. Statutes of several international adjudicative bodies, such as the ICJ, the ICC, the ECHR, and the ECJ thoroughly standardize the court's procedure, extent of judicial discretion, and the rights and obligations of the parties involved. The EU, with its enormous body of laws, rules, and regulations, also resembles the civil law commitment to extensive and exhaustive legal regulation.

Administrative regulation

Research in comparative law shows that domestic legal systems differ in their regulation of administrative and regulatory kinds of practices. These differences are fundamentally linked to the degree of formalism characteristic to civil, common, and Islamic legal systems. As with other substantive areas of law, the administrative law in common law systems was initially developed by judges applying law to specific cases, as individuals wronged by administrative actions approached the courts (Singh 2001, 3). Over time, the issue of control of the administration has become one of the main concerns of the law in common law systems. From its inception, the common law model of administrative governance has been fundamentally shaped by distrust in bureaucratic administration. For example, the early US administrative law was based "on common law actions by citizens against regulatory officials as a means for judicial review of administrative legality" (Stewart 2003, 439). Later, when the New Deal Congress established new federal regulatory agencies and bestowed on them relatively broad authority, the dissatisfied public perceived these agencies as an "unconstitutional 'fourth branch' of government" (Stewart 2003, 440).

In common law systems, the final regulatory authority has been placed in the courts as "the proper locus for administrative governance" (Morag-Levine 2007, 604). Judges and juries have the ability to monitor and shape regulatory kinds of practices through overseeing decisions taken by the legislators and the administrative branch. As a result, a large percentage of American administrative law, for example, is judge-made (Duffy 1998). However, the US administrative law is increasingly embracing a more statutory-based nature, as several areas of the law are based on thorough statutory methods (e.g. judicial control of agency procedures, exhaustion, etc.; see Duffy 1998).[40] Stewart (2003, 437) has described

---

[40] The enactment of the Administrative Procedure Act in 1946 constituted an important step in this direction.

this pattern as "a dramatic rise in the scope and intensity of administrative regulation." Similar trends have been taken place in the United Kingdom, where judge-made administrative law has been replaced by statutory provisions, such as the laws of the EU.

In contrast, in civil law systems, administrative law developed as a general scheme of principles and rules established from the "top-down," irrespective of specific cases. As a result, "instead of just concentrating on the legal control of the administration, it has also gone into its other aspects, such as its purpose and responsibilities and how they could be effectively discharged through law" (Singh 2001, 3). The civil law of administration evolved as a body of rules that govern the competences of public authorities. Initially, the common and civil approaches to administrative law were so different that the famous British constitutional lawyer, Albert Venn Dicey, argued that administrative law was a peculiar branch of law present in the continental countries, which was largely unknown to the laws of the British Isles (Dicey 1959, 330).

In general, the civil law model of administrative governance relies on "centralized, agency-based, state administration aimed at the implementation of regulatory standards through expert legislators and bureaucrats" (Morag-Levine 2007, 604). Thus, the decisive power in administrative matters is placed in legislative and administrative authorities. These organs are endowed with the prerogative to enact administrative law. Civil substantive and procedural administrative law is very detailed and meticulously organized in codes and laws of a lower status. It covers matters of a general nature, such as administrative functions, administrative procedure and organization, the relationship between the administration and the citizen, the duties of the citizens in relation to administration, and legal forms of administrative proceedings. In addition to these general issues, administrative law in civil law states encompasses more specific substantive areas, such as building law, traffic law, and civil services, which usually do not fall under the umbrella of administrative law in common law systems (Singh 2001, 6).

Islamic administrative law, as other substantive areas of Islamic law, is closely intertwined with Islamic faith: "The *shari'a* provides the umbrella under which administrative law in Islam, as well as other subsystems, can find relative laws and regulations which are divinely prescribed and humanly interpreted and administered" (Al-Buraey 1985, 351). In the spirit of Islamic faith, the Islamic model of administration places a large emphasis on Islamic values and ethical standards, such as psychological and spiritual well-being of man, freedom, justice, social equity, modesty, simplicity and human dignity (Al-Buraey 1985, 333–353). This stands in relatively sharp contrast with the civil and common law models of administration, both of which place a strong emphasis on material values, such as economy and effectiveness.

Because *Shari'a* overshadows administrative regulation, all important administrative decisions "outside the scope of the daily routine of bureaucratic decisions must not contradict any Islamic principle" (Al-Buraey 1985, 344). Thus, administrative control under Islamic law relies on the obligation to punish any behavior not in accordance with the law (Al-Mutairi 2002). Widely used in the administrative field is the principle of *shura*, or "consultation", which is directly derived from the Koran. Administrative decisions, especially those significantly affecting a larger community of the faithful, must be taken in the spirit of consultation with Islamic experts and qualified jurists. In the process of making an everyday, routine, simple administrative decision, *shura* is interpreted as embracing a more limited meaning of consultation (Al-Buraey 1985).

International law's relation to administrative and regulatory kinds of practices is very unique. Originally free from any administrative regulation, present day international law increasingly embraces mechanisms, rules, practices, and principles that have "a genuinely administrative character" (Kingsbury *et al.* 2005, 17).[41] Similar to domestic settings, administrative practices in international law include "rulemaking, adjudications, and other decisions that are neither treaty-making nor simple dispute settlements between parties" (Kingsbury *et al.* 2005, 17).[42] Some actions of the WTO (the WTO Dispute Settlement Body performs regulatory oversight functions), the International Monetary Fund, the Basle Committee, the United Nations (UN) Security Council, and the World Bank can be understood as constituting administrative action, as many of these bodies are neither adjudicative nor legislative in nature (Krisch and Kingsbury 2006, 3).[43]

These organizations significantly contribute to the increasing institutionalization and performing of regulatory functions on the international arena. Not surprisingly, elements of administrative law tend to appear more often in well-organized, treaty-based, and highly legalized organizations and regimes. The WTO constitutes an excellent example of this phenomenon. As an international regime, the WTO has established rules

---

[41] This view is contested by several scholars. Harlow (2006), for example, argues that it is difficult to find a sufficiently general set of administrative law principles in international law that could potentially form the essence of a global administrative law.

[42] An important contribution to this area of research is the Research Project on Global Administrative Law, NYU School of Law Institute for International Law and Justice (see www.iilj.org/GAL/default.asp).

[43] Alter (2008) notes that international courts are increasingly taking on the role of administrative review.

and decisional procedures that are to be followed by domestic agencies. Also, as within a domestic chain of administrative action, several elements of WTO law require subsequent changes in domestic administrative procedures. The WTO Dispute Settlement Body's function is to ensure that globally established rules are enforced domestically, and that national regulators do not exercise "over-reaching jurisdiction" (Kingsbury *et al.* 2005, 47). Not surprisingly, the number of administrative and regulatory kinds of practices is much more modest in organizations or regimes without definite structures and established administrative organs.

The emergence of an administrative global space challenges the traditional view of international law by blurring the distinction between domestic and international law. Administrative decision makers from domestic and international levels work together in establishing standards applicable to global and domestic levels. Furthermore, administrative decisions made on the international level are often binding on individuals and collective bodies (Krisch and Kingsbury 2006, 11).

Approach to litigation/nature of the trial

The three legal traditions also differ sharply with respect to the nature of the trial. In the common law adversarial approach to litigation, the trial is in essence a contest between two parties who have to prove their case to the court. Litigating parties conduct 'one-sided' investigations, which means *inter alia* that the prosecution has no legal obligation to actively look for exonerating evidence.[44] In general, the adversarial system does not require nor expect the defendant to assist investigators, since the burden of proof rests on the prosecutor (Reichel 2008). In the strictest version of the adversarial approach, "the judge is conceived of as a mere arbiter of the issues raised by the parties and has to form his or her decision exclusively on the basis of evidence and elements submitted by the latter" (Politi and Gioia 2006, 112). In other words, in the adversarial system, judges are considered to be neutral arbiters between the plaintiff and defendant in civil trials, or between the defendant and the state in criminal trials (Carey 2002, 6). During the trial, the opposing sides' goal is to prove their version of the facts and the law. Thus, attorneys develop and present their cases, and then a jury is charged with deciding between the two versions of the facts.

In contrast, in civil law systems, which take an inquisitorial approach to litigation, the trial is not seen as a duel between two adversaries: "[T]he

---

[44] In most common law states, when exonerating evidence is found, it must, however, be presented to the defense.

State has an obligation to investigate both incriminating and exonerating circumstances equally. The defense plays an active role in the State's investigation" (Tochilovsky 2002, 269).[45] The central objective of the inquisitorial trial is to find truth and achieve procedural justice (Reichel 2008). The judge is very active during the proceedings and endeavors to ascertain the facts while concurrently representing the interests of the state in a trial. Far from being a passive recipient of information, a civil law judge bears the primary responsibility of supervising the compilation of necessary evidence. He or she is, therefore, an autonomous power searching for the truth. For example, a civil law judge asks most of the questions during the trial, while the role of the attorneys is to "argue the interpretation that the court should give to those facts" (Reichel 2008, 171).

Due to the unique bond between Islamic law and Muslim faith, trial procedures in Islamic law are truly unique, although some scholars argue that they combine adversarial and inquisitorial characteristics. Stemming from the inquisitorial approach to litigation, in Islamic in-court proceedings there is little division between the judge and the investigator. From the adversarial school of thought comes the right to maintain silence and a modified presumption of innocence (Reichel 2008, 172–173). Because the religious sources do not specify the exact means through which an offender is to be brought to justice, it is difficult to identify a unified body of Islamic procedural law (Reichel 2008). Each Islamic state, therefore, has the freedom to regulate these matters by itself, using the principles of Islamic faith as general guidelines. The trial takes place in front of the *qadi*, who is appointed by the ruler and has to be a "male Muslim (some schools of law allow females to serve as *qadis* in limited circumstances) of recognized intelligence, religious piety, and knowledgeable in *Shari'a*" (Reichel 2008, 173). Criminal convictions are to be founded on certainty. They are often based on criminal evidence, such as testimony, confession, and religious oath, all of which can have a religious significance.

Holy oath that may be required by a court to support a litigating party's statements is oftentimes incorporated into the proceedings if testimonies of the litigating parties are contradictory. The parties simply swear that what they are saying is true in order to support their claims (Powell 2006a). The form of the holy oath draws on its religious importance, in

---

[45] In practice, what this means is that the public prosecutor is obliged to present to the court not only evidence that may lead to the conviction of the defendant but also evidence that may lead to his exculpation. In contrast to the adversarial system, in an effort to make the trial less like a contest between two adversaries, the civil law-based inquisitorial system requires a judge to take an active part in the trial, with a role that is both protective and directive.

that it is commonly taken in the presence of two notaries at a shrine, a mosque, or in the lodge of a religious brotherhood (Rosen 2000). It is believed that false oath will bring severe consequences on judgment day. Thus, "it is not unusual for an individual to maintain a particular testimony right up to the moment of oath-taking and then to stop, refuse the oath, and surrender the case" (Rosen 2000, 11). Trial proceedings take place according to the rules established in the Koran and Sunna, which, for example, regulate the exact number of witnesses and type of oath required in particular cases. For instance, proof of theft requires two witnesses, and proof of adultery requires four witnesses (Lippman *et al.* 1988, 42–45). In general, the witnesses should be "male adult Muslim (some *qadi* allow two women to count as one man) of high moral character who are able to speak clearly, possess a good memory, and be of sound mind" (Reichel 2008, 174).

Because the international system lacks a unified and centralized hierarchy of courts, there are no consistent procedural rules within international law (Shany 2003; Picker 2008, 1128). Over the past several decades, international procedural law has become increasingly similar, as "international courts often adopt common approaches to questions of procedure and remedies" (Brown 2007, 3). This increased similarity, however, has not yet led to the creation of one, integrated system equivalent to that of domestic law. The fact is that several international adjudicative bodies continue to operate according to largely different rules and procedures. This state of international procedural law has been succinctly expressed by the Appeals Chamber of the International Criminal Tribunal for the former Yugoslavia in the case *Prosecutor v. Tadic*: "International law, because it lacks a centralized structure, does not provide for an integrated judicial system operating an orderly division of labour among a number of tribunals, where certain aspects or components of jurisdiction as a power could be centralized or vested in one of them but not the others. In international law, every tribunal is a self-contained system (unless otherwise provided)."[46]

Despite the fact that international courts often show their willingness to draw insights from the practices of other international tribunals (Brown 2007, 4), for the most part different international adjudicative bodies embrace substantially different approaches to litigation.[47] Whether an international court reflects the inquisitorial or adversarial

---

[46] *Prosecutor v. Tadic* (1996) 35 ILM 32, 39, also quoted in Brown (2007, 4).
[47] For example, in international law there is no clear standard regarding the standard of proof, as "the statutes and rules of procedure of international courts are generally silent on the required standard of proof, and international courts apply a degree of flexibility" (Brown 2007, 98).

system is largely dependent on whether continental or common law experts had more say during the process of the court's creation. Several international tribunals, such as the International Criminal Tribunal for the Former Yugoslavia and the International Criminal Tribunal for Rwanda, were designed mainly by common law experts.[48] Consequently, "apart from lacking juries, they are built on common-law blueprints of adversarial proceedings mediated by neutral, 'referee' judges" (Schiff 2008, 48). Several other international courts, such as the ICJ, embrace elements of the inquisitorial model. The influence of the civil law tradition during the creation of the PCIJ was truly unprecedented, despite the fact that representatives from the United Kingdom insisted that the newly created court embody characteristics of common law. In the spirit of *stare decisis*, for example, UK Representative Lord Phillimore and US Representative Elihu Root proposed that one of the sources applied by the Court would be "the authority of judicial decisions and the opinions of writers as a means for the application and development of law."[49]

Appeal

Res judicata constitutes a major principle in numerous domestic legal systems. It poses that "where a final decision has been rendered by a court having jurisdiction over the parties and the subject-matter of the dispute, the parties may not dispute that decision – except on appeal – in subsequent litigation" (Brown 2007, 153). The major legal traditions of the world differ substantially with respect to the right of a litigating party to appeal the verdict of a first instance court. The sharp line of division exists between the Western legal systems on the one hand, and the Islamic legal tradition on the other. In addition, the nature of and the grounds for appeal are different in civil and common legal traditions. Both civil and common legal traditions allow for multiple instances of appeal in a majority of cases (Powell 2006a). Depending on the substantive nature of a case, there are different routes for appeal. Appeals from administrative cases will, for example, take a different appeal route than will civil or criminal cases. In France, a major civil law state, an individual can appeal from the decision of a first instance court to the Court of Appeal, and finally from a decision of that court to the Court of Cassation. A

---

[48] Elements of the civil legal system were also embedded in the structure of both courts; common law elements, however, prevailed.

[49] PCIJ, Advisory Committee of Jurists, *Procés Verbaux of the Proceedings of the Committee, June 16th–July 24th 1920, with Annexes*, p. 301 (The Hague 1920).

similar route of appeal is allowed under British law, where the newly created Supreme Court (October 2009) has assumed the jurisdiction of the Appellate Committee of the House of Lords and the devolution jurisdiction of the Privy Council's Judicial Committee.[50]

The general approach shared by both civil and common legal traditions is that an individual has a full right to appeal to a court of higher instance under certain circumstances: "Appeal is a legal phenomenon that Westerners tend to accept without question" (Shapiro 1980b, 350). One of the major reasons for existence of appellate procedure under both Western legal traditions is to "provide uniform legal rules so that the law will not be one thing in one trial court and quite a different thing in another" (Shapiro 1986, 201). Courts of higher instance are able to provide a degree of verdict standardization through the announcement of general interpretations and definitions, which in the future are able to give direction for the subsequent verdicts of the lower courts (Powell 2006a).

Civil and common law allow appeals on different grounds. Most legal scholars hold that appeal proceedings in general are typical of the inquisitorial (civil law) rather than of the accusatorial systems. In the latter, the right to appeal is allowed only under narrow terms, and "the relevant proceedings are conceived of more as a revision of first instance proceedings, aimed at identifying and remedying failures of the proceedings in first instance, rather than as a 'second' proceeding bearing on the very same facts as examined in the first instance phase" (Politi and Gioia 2006, 115). In other words, in most common law states appeals are limited only to questions of law, as petitioners are not allowed to ask appellate judges to examine facts. Questions of fact are left to the trial judge and the jury (if present) (Shapiro 1980a). Civil law systems approach appeals quite differently, whereby most appellate courts have the authority to review the facts and the appeal is most often achieved via a trial *de novo* (Randazzo and Sheehan 2002). In a trial *de novo*, the appellate court "reexamines all the evidence and legal arguments advanced in the initial trial" (Shapiro 1980a, 645).

Under Islamic law, there is generally no appeal. Islamic judges (*qadi*) work with very specific legal rules provided by the Koran. There is no need for the pronunciation of general principles and interpretations because "only the words of the prophet or the consensus of the community of the faithful can do that" (Shapiro 1986, 202). In addition, Islamic legal culture rejects generalization; thus the need for generating broad laws and

---

[50] The last instance can be resorted to only in case of an appeal with leave on point of law of public importance (Hadfield and Sunkin 2002, 1700).

reinterpreting existing law does not exist. Moreover, standardization and consistency of law, present in civil and common legal traditions, does not play a central role in Islamic law: "Islamic culture regards *both* consensus and diversity among the faithful as gifts from God" (Shapiro 1980b, 361). In addition, the unbreakable link between Islamic law and Muslim religion provides by itself another explanation for the lack of appeal. Islam, in contrast to other world religions, is inherently non-hierarchical. This absence of hierarchy in Islam as religion has been simply carried over to Islam as a legal system (Shapiro 1986, 221).[51] Modern day Islamic law states, however, often allow for appeal. For example, appeals of decisions of lower courts in Saudi Arabia may be filed to the Court of Cassation by either the public prosecutor or the convicted person. In addition, the Court performs an automatic review of the lower courts' judgments if they involve "offences punishable by death, amputation, flogging exceeding 40 lashes, or 10 days' imprisonment, as well as any penalty involving both flogging and imprisonment" (Reichel 2008, 287).

As noted above, a unified set of international procedural rules is non-existent. Moreover, in the international system, there are a host of adjudicative bodies, such as the ICJ, the ECJ, the ECHR, the ICC, the ITLOS, and others. These courts are largely "unconnected with each other and do not form a coherent system comparable to domestic judiciaries" (Pair 2001, 193). Even tribunals that are closely connected to the UN, such as the ICJ, the ICTY, and the ICTR, cannot be arranged in one hierarchical, unified structure. Such a system, where multiple courts and tribunals adjudicate in isolation, does not allow for a sound system of appeal. In fact, in the UN system, "No appeal, *i.e.* no judicial correction is possible" (Pair 2001, 194).[52]

Some international courts do not allow appeal. For example, Article 60 of the Statute of the ICJ provides that: "The judgment is final and without appeal. In the event of dispute as to the meaning or scope of the judgment, the Court shall construe it upon the request of any party." International courts that allow appeal do so in a very limited way, which resembles the common law approach to appeal. For example, the WTO Appellate Body typically hears only appeals of law and not of the facts (Picker 2008, 1129). Interestingly, the ICC, a hybrid of civil and common legal systems, recognizes the right of appeal on a wide basis, as a civil law

---

[51] But see Powers (1992), who argues that Islamic law allows for judicial review under precisely defined and limited conditions.

[52] As Pair (2001, 194) notes, the ICJ "served for a brief period as appellate body to the UNAT [United Nations Adminstrative Tribunal] in special circumstances," and it can serve as "appellate board for ICA [International Commercial Arbitration] decisions if countries agree."

court would. At the same time, however, the ICC appeal proceedings are not considered to be a new trial on the same facts, a rule that stems from the adversarial, common law approach.

Some authors argue that the powers of interpretation and revision that exist before several international courts constitute examples of post-adjudication procedures that limit the principle of *res judicata* (Brown, 2007, 157). The power of interpretation is employed in situations when "one or both parties to a judgment may consider the judgment obscure or contradictory in its reasons and operative provisions" (Brown 2007, 157–158). In such cases, the power of interpretation allows the parties to ask a tribunal for a clarification of the judgment. The second method, revision, can be utilized in order to alter a judgment of a court or an award of a tribunal in cases when a new decisive fact unknown to the party and the court at the time of judgment has been revealed (Brown 2007, 158). Both of these methods are allowed by several international courts, such as the PCIJ/ICJ and the ECJ.

It is clear that the major legal traditions are distinct from one another on a wide variety of dimensions. Yet, what difference does this make in international relations? How do domestic legal system characteristics influence foreign policy making? While some scholars and pundits see a world with a sharp divide between domestic and international law, we argue that there are strong interrelationships between these levels of analysis. These linkages have strong influences on states' willingness to support international courts and international institutions and on the design of any agreements states make in the international sphere.

General attitude towards international law

The nature and structure of civil, common, and Islamic law provide a context within which states shape their attitudes towards international law. Additionally, the inherent nature of *jus gentium* makes some domestic legal systems *a priori* more amenable to the features of international law. International treaties, perhaps the most important source of international law, largely resemble civil law codifications: "Treaties, like civil law codes, are often attempts to create a systemized body of law in anticipation of issues likely to arise in a specific, substantive area" (Picker 2008, 1110). Article 1(1) of the Statute of the International Law Commission explicitly states that the "Commission shall have for its object the promotion of the progressive development of international law and its codification." This trend to codify international law inherently entails methods of law creation present in civil law systems, which naturally makes civil law states more acceptant of international law in general.

There is a straightforward analogy between civil law code and an international law treaty. In the context of international treaties, Simmons (2009, 14) describes this situation in the following way: "Treaties are external political 'deals' that challenge the very concept of organic, bottom-up local law designed to solve specific social problems as they present themselves. They are the philosophical and cultural antithesis of judge-made, socially-adaptive, locally-appropriate *precedent*." Common law states, innately embracing *stare decisis*, may view international law, especially treaties as "foreign substance," not directly stemming from judge-made law (Simmons 2009, 15). Islamic law states view the Islamic law of nations "as derived from the eternal truth and justice that God had bequeathed to humanity through His messenger" (Bsoul 2008, 2–3). *Siyar*, the law that governs relations between Muslims and non-Muslims during war and peace, has its origins in Islamic religious sources. This implies that the actual application of international law should take place within the spirit of Islamic faith. The rules of international law and the judgments of international adjudicative bodies are seen "as being derived ultimately from revelation" (Bsoul 2008, 12). This perception of international law stands in sharp contrast with the actual nature of international law.

The position of the judiciary within each domestic legal system also shapes states' general attitude towards international law. Judges in common law systems have significant powers stemming from the strong position of *stare decisis*, wide discretion in interpretation of law, and a high degree of independence (Simmons 2009). These factors may cause governments of common law states to be more cautious in committing to any international obligations. Incorporating international law directly into the domestic legal system may lead in these states to unexpected results, since the judiciary has the power to interpret international law in an unforeseen way: "As a result, the government in a common law setting faces a wider range of possible treaty effects; a greater range of interpretative possibilities from a highly independent judiciary makes it more difficult to know *ex ante* how any particular treaty will be interpreted" (Simmons 2009, 73–74).

The general lack of *de jure stare decisis* in civil law states, and the limited interpretative powers of the civil law judiciary, should make civil law states more acceptant of international law in general. Governments in these states are not faced with the risk of unpredicted interpretation of international rights and obligations. In general, civil law judges cannot be as creative as their common law counterparts. As Simmons (2009, 17) argues: "The power of the judiciary to interpret the nature of the rights obligation generates uncertainty for governments in common law systems and may create incentives to resist or delay and add reservations at the time of treaty ratification." These differences have a direct effect on the degree of risk that states face when signing onto an international agreement. Of course, there are numerous ways through which a state may minimize the risk inherent to international agreements (Bilder 1981). Unlike general risk-management techniques, however, the risk of unanticipated interpretation of international agreements by an independent domestic judiciary can hardly be minimized.

The position of the judiciary within the Islamic legal tradition is truly unique. In exercising their adjudicative functions, judges are constrained in their interpretation of the sources of law. The following *hadith*, ascribed to the Prophet Muhammad, instructs the *qadi* to use sound reasoning in reaching their decisions in instances when the Koran and the Sunna are silent on an issue:

According to what shalt thou judge? He replied: According to the Book of Allah. *And if thou findest nought therein?* According to the Sunna of the Prophet of Allah. *And if thou findest nought therein?* Then I will exert myself to form my own judgment. *Praise be to God Who has guided the messenger of His Prophet to that which pleases His Prophet.* (Abdal-Haqq 2002, 35).

The fundamental message stemming from this *hadith* is that a *qadi* may formulate his judgment based on his individual opinion only if this opinion can be placed within the sprit of Koran (Abdal-Haqq 2002, 35). This general approach to judicial discretion is interconnected with the belief that the authority of the *qadi* and the jurists is directly derived from Allah; thus, there is no independent authority in a judge himself.

The convergence of civil and common law

Numerous legal scholars argue that the three legal systems, especially the civil and common legal traditions, have become increasingly similar over time (Shapiro 1986; Shahabuddeen 1996; Markesinis 2000). This adaptation pertains to both substantive and procedural laws. For example, in common law states, courts of last resort have come to accept that they are not compelled to follow their previous judgments, but within well-defined boundaries they might depart from them (Shahabuddeen 1996). Both the British House of Lords and the US Supreme Court have distanced themselves from the *stare decisis* doctrine (Funken 2003). Also, the highest courts in some civil law states have started to look more carefully at their previous decisions, although they are not legally bound by the doctrine of *stare decisis* (Shapiro 1986). Judges of highest courts in civil law states do not want to undermine their own authority by overturning their own previous decisions. Lower courts judges, on the other hand, tend to deliver judgments that are consistent with judgments of higher courts, because "a judge's career is negatively affected by too many reversals of his decisions" (Funken 2003, 13). Judge-made law is of growing importance in several major civil law states, to the point that some legal scholars describe the precedents as binding *de facto*, not *de jure* (Peczenik 1997, 465). For example, the rudimentary character of the French code provisions relating to torts has forced the judges to create the law on a case-by-case basis. As a result, although the basic law of torts is contained in the codes, the effective law of torts is expressed in the courts' decisions (Merryman *et al.* 1994). Also, the process of European integration, especially the ECJ case law, has lead to the increased importance of de facto *stare decisis* in all European states.

Statute law has recently become a much more important source of law in certain common law countries. For example, the output of enacted law in the United Kingdom has noticeably increased mostly as a result of the integration of British law with the European legal culture (Markesinis 2000). EU directives oblige the United Kingdom and other member states to pass legislation in accordance with the requirements included in the directives. Also, Australia and the United States have an extensive body of written statutes, especially in the area of bankruptcy law, intellectual property law, tax law, and banking regulation (Mattei 1997b, 101–121). The extensive use of the written letter of law in the United States has led Judge Calabresi to observe that the United States has come into the age of statutes (Calabresi 1985). Codification has also become popular in several developing common law states, who attempt to renovate their legal system speedily – through a written law – rather than implementing the needed changes through time-consuming judge-made law (Funken 2003).

Just as civil law and common law legal traditions borrowed elements of precedent and codification from one another, so too have the adversarial and inquisitorial systems exchanged elements of litigation. Recently, the United Kingdom has introduced some of the features of the inquisitorial system, establishing the Crown Prosecution Service. A public prosecutor can now file criminal charges relying on a grand jury (Reichel 2008). This arrangement, however, "does not enjoy the protection that the legal review exercises by the judge in the inquisitorial systems accorded to the defendant's rights" (Rossetti 2002, 712). In addition, rules of discovery, which require the opposing sides to share evidence, brought the adversarial system closer to its inquisitorial counterpart. Some civil law states have also introduced features of the adversarial system into their trial proceedings. For example, over the past few decades Germany and Italy have changed their judicial system through liquidating *judges d'instruction*, which embodied the pure form of the inquisitorial system. In France, an innovative idea has been introduced which entails increasing the burden of pleading placed on the parties with the goal of alleviating the tasks of the judges (Jolowicz 2003).

The development of the *jus commune* in the context of the EU has led several scholars to conclude that civil and common legal systems will continue to become increasingly similar. For example, Glenn (1993) posits that the process of integration spurred a continual assimilation between the two European legal systems. De Groot (1992, 11) speaks of the possibility that "the legal systems of the European States will form one great legal family with uniform or strongly similar rules in many areas."

Interestingly, the convergence invoked by these scholars revolves around "rules, concepts, substantive and adjectival law, and institutional bodies," which "tell one very little about a given legal system and reveal even less about whether two legal systems are converging or not" (Legrand 1996, 54–56). Thus, despite the "on-face" convergence between civil and common law, there exist several irreconcilable differences between these two legal traditions. According to Legrand (1996, 64–70), civil and common legal systems are substantially different in the following areas:

- the nature of legal reasoning, which is analogical in common law and institutional in civil law
- the significance of systematization: civil law embraces systematization and common law rejects it to some extent
- the character of rules: rules are made, to a large degree, by the judges in common law; codes constitute the main sources of rules in civil law
- the role of facts: common law emphasizes facts, which give birth to rules; in the civil law system, the goal is to establish a concept or an idea in separation from the facts.[53]

The issue of convergence between civil and common legal traditions has been long discussed by scholars of comparative law. We agree that there are several signs of the two legal traditions coming together; nevertheless, convergence does not reach into the very heart of either legal tradition. There exist several important irreconcilable differences between these legal systems of a deep substantive nature, which cannot be disregarded despite the "apparent" convergence of rules and institutions.

---

[53] Legrand also talks about two other dimensions: the meaning of rights and the presence of the past.

Islamic law has been quite successful in resisting the influence of either the common or civil legal tradition. It continues to embrace a very unique approach to law, legal science, and legal reasoning. All branches of law derive from the Koran, God's word, which precludes Islamic law from adapting to the Western legal science. Also, the Muslim view of international law as having basis in the ultimate will of God makes the compromise between the Western legal systems and the Islamic legal system unlikely. According to Bsoul (2008, 2–3), "Muslims jurists view the Islamic law of nations as derived from the eternal truth and justice that God had bequeathed to humanity through His messenger." In reality, this means that Islamic international law is deeply entrenched in religious sources; its relevance and practice must take place within the strict framework of Islam. In addition, throughout the Muslim world there exists nowadays a modernist tendency in understanding and interpreting Islamic law and Islamic jurisprudence, which attempts to rely directly on religious sources: "In general, it may be said that what the modernists desire to produce is a system of modern law based on Islamic jurisprudence (fiqh). It is to be a law where the religious ethos is prominent. This is to be accomplished by drawing heavily on the Koran and Sunna as primary sources" (Salmi et al. 1998, 60).

The recent creation of the ICC constitutes a great example of cooperation and clash between the three major legal traditions. First, the ICC embodies an unprecedented compromise between the civil and common legal traditions. The increasing convergence made the dialogue between these two legal systems possible. The result of the Rome negotiations in 1998 proves that an inter-legal systems exchange of ideas can lead to fruitful results. Also, the support granted to the ICC by civil law and common law states shows that the hybrid court is a success story.

Second, the lack of cooperation on the part of Islamic law states in the process of the ICC negotiations demonstrates the stark differences between the Western and Islamic legal traditions. The low participation of Islamic law states in the Rome negotiations (12.9%) and the low levels of support for the ICC from these states (12.9% signature and 5.1% ratification) reveal the lack of common ground between Islamic law on one hand, and civil and common law on the other. Also, the idea of the IICJ, popular in the Islamic community, further undermines the goals of system-wide international justice. The Statute of the IICJ stipulates that Shari'a is to constitute the fundamental law of the Court. The eventual creation of this Court may result in a grouping of Islamic states under an international judicial system that stands apart from existing courts, such as the ICJ (Lombardini 2001).

Conclusion

In this chapter, we analyzed the procedural and substantive distinctions between the three major legal traditions in the world: civil law, common law, and Islamic law. Next, we apply these characteristics of domestic law to our theoretical arguments about the motives facing the "originators" of new courts and the "joiners" of pre-existing courts. In Chapter 3, we present our rational legal design theory of international adjudication. In Chapter 4, we focus on the "originators" through an in-depth analysis of the negotiations surrounding the creation of the ICC. We show how negotiators pushed for legal rules for the new Court that were similar to rules and procedures from their own domestic legal traditions. The outcome of the negotiations produced a hybrid court which adopted both civil law and common law rules, enhancing the support that the Court received from civil and common law states. In Chapters 5 and 6, we turn our attention to the "joiners" of pre-existing courts, focusing on state support for the World Court. The originators of the PCIJ were successful in establishing a court with civil law rules and procedures. This legal similarity between civil law and the PCIJ/ICJ, combined with the prevalence of the civil law tradition internationally, creates a situation where civil law states coordinate through the World Court more frequently than common or Islamic law states. Distinctions in contract law also influence the form of states' commitments to international courts (Chapter 6), with civil law states having the smallest number of reservations on their optional clause declarations to the PCIJ/ICJ. All three chapters illustrate important linkages between domestic legal traditions and the rational design of interstate cooperation.

3   A rational legal design theory of international adjudication

The proliferation of international courts and tribunals in the international system over the past century poses an interesting puzzle for exploration. Why has the number of international courts and the power that they wield increased despite the significant intrusion such courts can have on state sovereignty? The ICC, for example, requires mandatory jurisdiction for signatories to the Rome Statute and allows for an independent prosecutor to initiate proceedings regarding crimes against humanity when member states are unwilling or unable to do so. The ECJ is similar in that members of the EU are required to accept the court's jurisdiction. Even in situations where states can place reservations on their commitments to international courts, it is difficult to anticipate all future situations that might arise that could disadvantage states, as the United States realized in 1986 in light of the *Nicaragua* case before the ICJ.

The expansion of international adjudication is puzzling from a traditional realist perspective, where the existence of an anarchic system implies that courts might not work well globally because they are not backed by a coercive authority.[1] One possible solution to this quandary is for a global or regional hegemon to step in and help create an international or regional court and then act as an enforcer for the court. For example, the Central American Court of Justice was arguably most effective when regional powers, such as the United States and Mexico, were willing to support the court's rulings (Allain 2000). However, it is not clear that major and regional powers stand to gain from the creation of international courts, especially given the bargaining advantages they face in bilateral negotiations. If states feared the authority that international courts might pose in the future, they would have incentives to limit the courts' role to the provision of information in the dispute

[1] A good domestic analogy to adjudication without coercive sanctions is the system that existed in Iceland for several hundred years, where "Icelandic institutions made law and declared rights, but no governmental institutions existed to enforce those declarations" (Ginsburg and McAdams 2004, 1241). Private parties were left to carry out sanctions in cases where damages went unpaid.

settlement process (Posner and Yoo 2005). Furthermore, the creation of multiple international courts could lead to additional problems, such as overlapping jurisdiction among tribunals and different courts rendering different decisions (Brown 2007, 27), actions which could threaten the coherence of international law more broadly.

In this chapter, we seek to understand why states create new international courts and why states join pre-existing international courts. We argue that an interesting intersection of domestic and international law occurs when international courts are formed. The initial negotiators of new courts design institutions in ways that are optimal from both a political and legal standpoint. Later joiners to the court are influenced by the court's principles and rules as well, viewing some international courts as more capable and fair adjudicators than other international courts. In this chapter, we develop a theoretical argument linking domestic law and international courts.

Our theory distinguishes between the motives of states creating a new court, what we call the "originators," and the decisions made by states to join existing international courts, a group we call the "joiners." The originators are able to negotiate the design of an international court's rules, while the joiners must condition their decision to accept the court's jurisdiction based on the existing rules and practices of the court. We argue that domestic legal traditions influence the decisions of both originator and joiner states, although the theoretical mechanisms operating in the two stages are distinct. We show that domestic legal traditions influence states' acceptance of the jurisdiction of international courts, the durability of states' commitments to international courts, and the design of states' commitments to the courts.

The chapter is organized as follows. We begin by describing the role of adjudicators in world politics. We then present our theoretical arguments to explain the behavior of the originators of new courts and the joiners of pre-existing courts. Our rational legal design theory of international adjudication emphasizes linkages between domestic law and international law. We show not only that states design courts in their own legal image, but that these design choices influence the effectiveness of international courts on the adjudication scene as well. States bargain most effectively in the shadow of an international court that adopts familiar legal principles and rules.

A rational legal design theory of international adjudication

Our theory asserts that states have incentives to lock in institutional legal design features in the negotiation phase of a new international court in order to reduce uncertainty about the adjudicator's role in future bargaining situations. Later potential joiners to pre-existing courts also look to the court's rules and principles for clues about whether the court will be fair and unbiased. International courts will be most effective in helping states to resolve their differences when their expressive functions are maximized, which we argue occurs when states' legal uncertainty before the court is minimized. We begin by describing the general purposes that international courts fulfill in world politics and discuss some of the risks that states face when tying their hands to the courts. We then discuss how the originators of new international courts minimize these risks at the negotiating table by locking in an optimal legal design for the new court. Next, we talk about how later joiners to the court can signal information about their "types" by treating jurisdictional acceptance as a form of cheap talk. This is followed by a discussion about the consequences of these rational legal design decisions on the design, durability, and ultimate effect of states' commitments to international courts. We end the chapter with a justification about the two courts selected for our empirical analyses in the remainder of the book: the World Court (PCIJ/ICJ) and the ICC.

The role of adjudicators

To understand why states create new international courts, we must first consider the benefits and costs of establishing a new adjudicator. In domestic legal systems, courts play multiple roles, including dispute adjudication, administrative review, criminal enforcement, and constitutional review (Alter 2008, 37). One of the primary roles that international courts play is as adjudicators of disputes. Through the process of adjudication, international courts help states resolve contractual disagreements. For example, the United States and Canada took a dispute to the ICJ in 1979 over delimitation of the maritime boundary and fishing rights in the Gulf of Maine. The parties had reached earlier bilateral agreements in the late 1970s to help settle their differences about delimitation of the boundary, but the court was needed to help resolve disagreements about the precise limits of those borders. The Court's predecessor, the PCIJ, played a similar role in the *Legal Status of Eastern Greenland* case of 1933, assessing Denmark's claims to Greenland in light of Norwegian opposition. Much like the *Gulf of Maine* case, the parties had prior contractual agreements over the territory that the Court helped interpret (Ginsburg and McAdams 2004, 1292).

More broadly, courts as dispute adjudicators help to solve multilateral coordination problems, helping the parties converge on equilibrium solutions to conflicts. Many of the cases that come before international courts are aptly described as coordination problems, where multiple solutions to a disputed issue exist, and where the parties must agree on some equilibrium solution (Ginsburg and McAdams 2004). Countries are aware of the multiple coordination problems that may arise in world politics, including disagreements over land borders, maritime zones, and trade. State leaders have incentives to send strong signals to other states about their resolve and strength, yet they also may wish to signal a willingness to bargain peacefully and avoid military contests because they realize that conflict is costly (Fearon 1995). However, signals about peaceful conflict management are hard to convey, because they are often perceived as cheap talk (Crawford and Sobel 1982; Farrell 1987; Farrell and Gibbons 1989; Matthews 1989; Farrell and Rabin 1996; Kim 1996).[2]

It is interesting to consider what role an international court plays in this interstate bargaining process.[3] According to the expressive theory of adjudication, unbiased adjudicators may be effective at helping parties strike cooperative agreements by correlating strategies, creating focal points, and signaling information (Garrett and Weingast 1993; Ginsburg and McAdams 2004; McAdams 2005, 1049). Furthermore, states may be able to transmit information about themselves through the adjudicator by formally recognizing its adjudication powers. Thus interstate bargaining may be influenced both by the presence and behavior of an adjudicator and by the parties' ability to send information to each other through the adjudicator.

Beginning with the adjudicator's own behavior, the court may convince parties to coordinate their behavior by focusing on some random event, or to correlate their equilibrium behavior. For example, a coin flip could be used to select between two equilibrium outcomes; however, this solution is problematic. First, if a randomized process for dispute resolution could be agreed upon by the disputants, then this would preclude the need for a third-party mediator. Second, it would be tempting for the disputants to renege on any agreement reached through a randomized decision-making mechanism (McAdams 2005, 1057). To overcome this problem, the adjudicator "uses cheap talk to construct a 'focal point' in a coordination game" (McAdams 2005, 1059) by focusing on particular equilibrium outcomes and conveying this information to the disputants.

---

[2] Cheap talk can be defined as a "statement that may convey information even though the statement is costless, nonbinding, and nonverifiable" (Baird et al. 1994, 303).

[3] Like McAdams (2005), we treat interstate bargaining as a coordination or mixed-motive game. For an alternative international law perspective that treats interaction as a prisoner's dilemma game, see Goldsmith and Posner (2005).

An equilibrium is considered focal "if it has some feature that, for reasons of psychology, history, or culture, draws attention to itself, making it 'stand out' among all equilibria" (McAdams 2005, 1061). In short, by favoring a particular outcome, an adjudicator using cheap talk makes it stand out from all other possible outcomes or solutions.

International courts create focal points that states can use in coordinating their equilibrium strategies through the process of adjudication and by giving advisory opinions. Thus, adjudicating institutions like the ICJ and ECJ help to "create a shared belief system about cooperation and defection in the context of differential and conflicting sets of individual beliefs that inhibit the decentralized emergence of cooperation" (Garrett and Weingast 1993, 184). The ECJ, for example, has been successful at creating a focal point of mutual recognition, which has created a shared framework about how the common market works (Garrett and Weingast 1993). Under Article 234 of the Treaty Establishing the European Community, lower domestic courts may seek guidance from the ECJ with respect to cases that pertain to Community law, and the highest domestic courts are obliged to do so. Through this procedure, the Court has been able to construct focal points in numerous important issue areas. In fact, "landmark Court judgments have come in response to requests from national courts for preliminary rulings" (Dinan 2005, 294).

The role of the ICJ is to settle disputes between states in accordance with international law. By providing judgment in contentious cases, the Court creates focal points. In a series of cases related to territorial claims, the World Court upheld the principle of *uti possidetis juris*, helping to create a focal point of newly independent states having the same borders they maintained under colonial rule.[4] Another way in which the ICJ can create focal points is via advisory opinions on legal questions that can be referred to the Court by authorized United Nations organs and several specialized agencies. This method allows the ICJ to construct non-binding interpretations of international rules and principles. For example, the advisory opinion in the *Nuclear Weapons* case dealt with an abstract question of whether international law permits the threat or use of nuclear weapons.[5] Similarly, in the advisory opinion in the *Construction of a Wall* case, the UN General Assembly requested that

---

[4] According to Mushkat (2008, 190), relevant cases include: *Frontier Dispute* case (*Burkina Faso* v. *Republic of Mali*), 1986 ICJ. Rep. 554; *Case Concerning the Land, Island, and Maritime Frontier Dispute* (*El Salvador* v. *Honduras, Nicaragua intervening*), 1992 ICJ Rep. 355; and *Case Concerning the Territorial Dispute* (*Libya* v. *Chad*), 1995 ICJ Rep 6.

[5] *Legality of the Threat or Use of Nuclear Weapons*, Advisory Opinion, 1996 ICJ Rep. p.66.

the ICJ assess the legal consequences of the security wall built by Israel in the Occupied Palestinian Territory (Merrills 2005, 146).[6]

Adjudicators may also promote cooperation by revealing private information to disputants, such as the players' types, which works best if the adjudicator is unbiased and has strong reputational incentives for being truthful (McAdams 2005). The *Gulf of Maine* case provides an interesting example, as the ICJ appointed a technical expert to collect new information about the maritime dispute, information which proved crucial in the Court's final judgment.[7] The proceedings in the ICJ *Qatar v. Bahrain Maritime Delimitation and Territorial Questions* case also revealed important information about the players' types, especially their truthfulness. During the proceedings, Bahrain accused Qatar of submitting eighty-two forged documents to the Court (Wiegand 2009, 11).

The expressive theory of adjudication (Ginsburg and McAdams 2004; McAdams 2005) provides a compelling story about why states might turn to adjudication. The unbiased adjudicator is capable of helping disputants resolve coordination problems by creating focal points and bringing new information to light, which mitigates the uncertainty that states face in the process of interstate bargaining. However, states still face a great deal of uncertainty when they resort to international adjudication and when they make long-term commitments to international courts (Bilder 1981). This uncertainty relates to two types of international courts: (1) courts like the ICJ, where only *states* can appear as parties, and (2) courts like the ICC, where *individuals* can be tried for international crimes.[8] In either type of international adjudication, no state can be certain that a court's deliberations will lead to a conclusion that constitutes the state's most preferred outcome.

The uncertainty can be attributed in part to the fact that international adjudication entails applying and interpreting international legal rules and deciphering inconsistencies between rival norms in the context of specific cases (Abbott and Snidal 1998; Alter 2006). In this sense, international courts are no different from domestic courts, because all courts have to face interpretation of legal rules: "[W]hen seeking to overturn all but the most flagrantly illegal state actions, litigants and courts must inevitably

---

[6] *Legal Consequences of the Construction of a Wall in the Occupied Palestinian Territory,* Advisory Opinion, 2004 ICJ Rep. 136.

[7] The United States and Canada jointly nominated retired commander of Her Britannic Majesty's Navy, Peter Bryan Beazley, to act as the technical expert. Beazley assisted with technical matters in the case, helping to analyze boundaries and charts. He wrote the technical report, describing the boundary solution decided by the chamber, as well as the methods used to draw the boundaries.

[8] Keohane *et al.* (2000) identify two ideal types of legalized dispute resolution: interstate and transnational.

appeal to particular interpretations of such ambiguities [ambiguities between norms]" (Keohane *et al.* 2000, 461). For example, sometimes the ICJ has to engage in a relatively creative process of norm interpretation and decide "when new trends in practice, as evidenced in non-binding declaration codes, guidelines and other soft materials, cross the threshold of normativity and merit recognition as law" (Merrills 2005, 160). In fact, international courts engage in the process of rule interpretation more often than domestic courts, as the body of international law is much less precise and contains many loop holes (Powell and Wiegand 2010). Furthermore, by opening themselves up to adjudication, states may lose control over the outcomes of bargaining over highly salient issues, as the costs for reneging on judgments rendered by international courts are extremely high (Bilder 1998; Mitchell and Hensel 2007). The fact that distinct adjudicative bodies interpret international law differently increases states' uncertainty regarding international adjudication (Charney 1998; Spelliscy 2001). The resulting divergence in application of the law has raised several concerns with the quality of an international legal framework: "Such diversity may be seen as contributing to the disintegration of international law because each organ is committed to applying its own views and resolving disputes within its own formally isolated system, thereby thwarting the tendency towards homogeneity and increasing the uncertainty of the standards of behavior to which states are supposed to conform" (Spelliscy 2001, 156).

The expressive theory of adjudication tends to assume the existence of an unbiased adjudicator. Yet, as we show below, states have incentives to negotiate terms when creating international courts that will in fact bias the court in their favor. By creating a court with familiar rules and principles, states will have greater certainty about which cases the court will hear and which rules it will employ in rendering judgments, which will ultimately strengthen their out-of-court bargaining position. We contend that states use their domestic legal systems as clues about the court's future proceedings and judgments. Similarity between a domestic legal tradition and an international court allows a state to better understand the intricate rules of international adjudication, allows a state to predict the outcome of the in-court proceedings better, and causes a state to feel more comfortable with international dispute resolution. In the next section, we provide more detail about how this process of rational legal design unfolds in the negotiation phase to create a new international court.

The originators: decisions to create a new international court

States have political and legal preferences that they bring to the bargaining table when creating a new court. States that are strongly committed to the court's creation have incentives to lock in their own country's future commitments to the court (Moravcsik 2000). Negotiators may tie their country's future hands by designing a court with sound design principles and enforcement mechanisms. They may also tie their country's hands by raising the reputational costs for reneging on the court's future judgments. If the originators are supportive of the court, they have incentives to create procedures and rules for the court's operation that will benefit their country in future litigation cases, or at a minimum, ensure that the adjudicator's behavior will be reasonably predictable.

This lack of certainty about how the court will identify cases to be heard and how it will adjudicate in specific cases is mitigated if the court's rules and procedures are familiar. In other words, to reduce future uncertainty concerning the application of international law by international courts, states that participate in the process of the creation of a new court purposively design it in a way that resembles their domestic legal tradition. As such, domestic legal systems assist states in creating "procedures for the elaboration of norms within an IO," or "supplying missing terms and decision rules" (Abbott and Snidal 1998, 15). When we refer to an international court's procedures, we are adopting a definition similar to Brown (2007, 8): "'[P]rocedure' includes not only the conduct of proceedings, including the power of international courts to rule on preliminary objections, the adduction of evidence, and the exercise of incidental powers, during and after the adjudication on the merits, but also the constitution of international tribunals and questions relating to their jurisdiction." States can be more comfortable with an international court if they are familiar with the court's rules and procedures and more confident about the types of decisions the court will render. Judge Hardy Cross Dillard of the ICJ has directly referred to the issue of familiarity:

[W]hile perhaps regrettable, it does not seem unnatural that those in charge of the foreign affairs of governments should prefer to settle disputes by processes with which they are familiar, that are flexible, and that remain under their control, rather than risk a settlement through processes with which they are less familiar, that appear more rigid, and that entail a loss of control. (Dillard 1978, 228)

States are able to form expectations about the method of interpretation of legal rules and in-court procedures if the two sets of legal rules (domestic law and the legal design of a court) align with one another because "when similar legal language is used, similar legal mechanisms are adapted" (Powell and Wiegand 2010, 11). In other words, we propose that states use their domestic legal systems as clues about the outcome of each case. If states have the ability to forum shop in the process of dispute settlement, then the original negotiators of a new court have incentives to lock in an institutional design that will benefit their state in the future. In the process of negotiations, the originators rationally give a certain design to an international court (Koremenos *et al.* 2001).

Furthermore, if states can anticipate high degrees of future enforcement, they have incentives to negotiate intensely to secure the best deal possible: "[T]hough a long shadow of the future may make *enforcing* an international agreement easier, it can also give states an incentive to *bargain harder*, delaying agreement in hopes of getting a better deal" (Fearon 1998, 270). International courts do have not the same types of enforcement mechanisms as domestic courts, although they are able to raise the reputational costs for non-compliance and they have institutional resources at their disposal for helping parties to carry out judgments. The UN Secretary General, for example, often provides assistance to parties in the process of compliance with ICJ judgments. The UN played a significant role in the process of monitoring the transfer of the Bakassi peninsula from Nigeria to Cameroon following the 2002 ICJ ruling (Mitchell and Hensel 2007).[9] These compliance mechanisms seem to have some teeth as well; 93 percent of PCIJ and ICJ rulings over territorial, maritime, or river issues have been carried out by all disputants (Mitchell and Hensel 2007, 735).

If our basic assumption about a long shadow of the future for international courts is apt, then it is reasonable to argue that states' legal preferences will enter into their calculations as originators of the court. There are strong incentives for a state (or group of states) to push for an institutional design that mimics the legal procedures employed domestically inside the state. As noted above, uncertainty about how the court will identify cases to be heard and how it will rule on particular cases is mitigated if the court's rules and procedures are familiar. This is especially important since international courts have in the past diverged in their interpretation of international law.[10] Discrepancy in interpretation of legal rules, albeit disheartening, is inherently connected with the proliferation of international tribunals. Judge Guillaume of the ICJ has expressed his concern numerous times about the emerging possibility of "forum shopping" that can possibly "generate unwanted confusion" and "distort the operation of justice" (Koskenniemi and Leino 2002, 554). A vivid example is provided by the judgment of the International Criminal Tribunal for the former Yugoslavia (ICTY) in the 1999 *Tadić*

---

[9] The final transfer of Bakassi territory was completed in August 2006.
[10] Bilder (1981, 58) talks about the fact that dispute settlement procedures, especially third-party methods, may involve several risks, such as the risk that "procedures may

case, where the Court deviated from the "effective control" criterion that the ICJ used in the 1986 *Nicaragua* case to determine the responsibility of a state for acts of a military group. If states have the ability to forum shop in the process of dispute settlement, then the original negotiators of a new court have incentives to lock in an institutional design that will benefit their state in the future.[11]

To reduce uncertainty about the interpretation of international law, states attempt to design international courts in a way that resembles their domestic legal traditions. Jouannet calls this a process of "selling ... each national legal model in order to influence the establishment of international norms and institutions" (Jouannet 2006, 300). This is in fact a broader process at work in international law:

An increasingly pronounced factor undermining the *sui generis* character of international law is an increased reliance on existing domestic legal systems for development of substantive international law. This is not, however, an entirely new phenomenon. International law developed over the centuries through the work of jurists who were themselves schooled in their own legal traditions; they were first and foremost products of their own legal systems and only secondarily international jurists. As such, when creating international law they would necessarily resort to concepts and structures with which they were familiar. (Picker 2008, 1091–1092).

Civil lawyers approach drafting and interpretation of multinational agreements as they would a civil code (Koch 2003). Similarly, common law lawyers promote designing of international agreements in the spirit of their domestic legal system (Jouannet 2006).[12] This was evident during the negotiations in Rome for the ICC, where civil law and common law negotiators pushed strongly for familiar rules and procedures relating to

be improperly invoked by the third party or unfairly or unreasonably applied by a third party."

[11] Because international courts have diverged in their interpretation of international law in the past, states' decisions concerning international adjudication may also be shaped by their "perceptions and beliefs concerning the presence of uncertainty and risk" (Bilder 1981, 13).

[12] We should note that there are distinctions in the level of detail given to procedures within domestic legal traditions: "In English law, only the most general definitions of 'procedural law' have been given. The best-known definition was provided in 1881 by Lush LJ in *Poyser v Minors*: "Practice" ... like "procedure" ... denotes the mode of proceeding by which a legal right is enforced, as distinguished from the law which gives or defines the right, and by which means of the proceeding the Court is to administer the machinery as distinguished from its product.' ... In a civil law system, that of France, 'procedure' is defined broadly, to include not only the rules according to which the court is seised, and according to which it conducts the proceedings and delivers judgment, 'but also the rules governing judicial organisation, establishing the composition and operation of the courts, and the rules determining the competence of these various courts'" (Brown 2007, 7).

the nature of the trial, the position of the ICC judges during proceedings, admission of guilt of the accused, and appeal proceedings. It was also evident in the creation of the PCIJ, where the design of the new court reflected many civil law principles, such as the lack of *stare decisis*. States can be more comfortable with the role international courts will play in future litigation situations if they are familiar with the court's rules and procedures and more confident about the types of decisions the court will render.

We should point out, however, that there is a tension the originators face in terms of establishing precise procedural rules for a new international court. There is an idea in international law that courts should be given a certain level of independence, in the sense that the courts have the power to determine their own jurisdiction. Known as *compétence de la compétence*, this principle has been recognized in many international courts including the ICJ,[13] the WTO Appellate Body, the Inter-American Court of Human Rights (IACHR), the ICTY, and the ITLOS (Brown 2007, 62–63). This principle implies that the originators might create a set of loose procedural rules that could evolve over time: "In drafting the PCIJ Statute in 1920, for instance, the Advisory Committee of Jurists did not make any concerted effort to establish the PCIJ's procedure, but merely adopted a few general rules. It recognized that the question of procedure should be left to the PCIJ itself, and that the Court should be allowed a wide freedom in framing its rules" (Brown 2007, 38–39). On the other hand, it is clear that negotiations to create more recent international courts, such as the ICC, have paid a great deal of attention to procedural detail, with one third of the Rome Statute covering the Court's procedures. Even if procedures are somewhat ambiguous, the designers of a new international court still have some sense of how the court will evolve. The founders of the PCIJ, for example, had good reason to believe that the court would be dominated by civil law judges, and thus that it would naturally evolve in the direction of civil law procedures.

The originators of an international court, as its primary designers, invest a lot of effort to mold the structure of the court to their expectations. Much like major powers who seek to lock in an international order following victory in major war (Ikenberry 2001), states who participate in the conception of a new international court invest an incredible amount of sunk costs into the court's creation and design. The high sunk costs

---

[13] "In *Nottebohm*, the ICJ held that: '[A]n international tribunal has the right to decide as to its own jurisdiction and has the power to interpret for this purpose the instruments which govern that jurisdiction'" (Brown 2007, 62).

and fulfilled expectations regarding the structure of a new court imply that these states should be most supportive of the new court. States that do not actively participate in the process of designing a court are much more "neutral" towards it, since they have not invested any costs in its initial creation. For example, many states that became independent from their formal colonizers after World War II were skeptical of the ICJ and viewed it as reflecting the interest of its originators – the Western states. "The great number of newly admitted African and Asian members with some notable exceptions are at least indifferent and not attracted by the Court's procedures, if not outrightly opposed to them" (Rosenne 1957, 1962, 103).

Once the originators of a new international court have locked in a particular institutional design, they face greater costs for reneging in their commitment to the court in comparison with later joiners. The United States' departure from the ICJ in 1986 was viewed along these lines, with international law scholars and pundits describing the broader negative consequences for the entire system of international law that this decision invoked. Thus, the originators of a new court may face greater international and domestic audience costs for failing to support the court at some later date, which creates a system whereby most originators are defenders of the status quo.

The joiners: decisions to join an existing court

In contrast to the originators of international courts, potential joiners to an international court must accept the court's standing rules and procedures, which are not negotiable.[14] Joiners must weigh the domestic and international costs and benefits of joining an international court. As a general rule, we assume that states prefer working with courts that they view as fair and unbiased. This does not imply that an international adjudicator is unbiased towards all disputants, only that states coming before the court have some assurances that they can trust that particular adjudicator to be fair towards them. The proliferation of international courts has created the possibility of forum shopping, where states can be selective about which courts they join and which courts they bring disputes to. As Shany (2003) notes, there is a considerable amount of jurisdictional overlap between general international courts (e.g. the ICJ and PCA (Permanent Court of Arbitration), as well as overlap

---

[14] Some courts, such as the ICJ, allow states to place reservations on their declarations, although the basic procedures and rules governing the court's operation are not negotiable.

between specialized international courts (e.g. ITLOS, WTO, ICC, HRC (Human Rights Council), ICSID (International Court for Settlement of Investment Disputes)). In this sense, potential joiners can be very strategic about which courts they will select for potential adjudication, seeking out courts with familiar legal rules and principles.

We assume that states can send signals to other states about their "type" on various international issues through an international court, such as a commitment to the peaceful settlement of interstate disputes, respect for the international rule of law, or the promotion of ethical human rights standards. These signals will be helpful for resolving the coordination problems that we discussed earlier, especially if the adjudicator is able to facilitate the parties' abilities to correlate strategies by constructing focal points and providing new information about the disputed issue. While such signals are aptly described as cheap talk, we believe they can be conveyed meaningfully through an adjudicator to other states with similar legal preferences (Powell and Mitchell 2007).

Earlier we described the expressive theory of adjudication (Ginsburg and McAdams 2004; McAdams 2005), which contends that adjudicators help to resolve coordination problems by correlating strategies, creating focal points, and providing information. The expressive theory focuses on the adjudicator's influence as a third-party actor,[15] but does not consider the possibility that some states may have stronger incentives than others to resolve interstate disputes with an adjudicator's assistance. First, the theory assumes that the adjudicator is unbiased. And yet, as we argued above, the originators of new international courts have incentives to lock in procedural rules that are familiar to them. As we noted, the procedures and rules of the PCIJ and ICJ are extremely similar to those used in domestic civil law systems, which creates a bias in favor of civil law states.[16] This institutional similarity between the PCIJ/ICJ and civil law systems encourages civil law states to correlate their equilibrium behaviors naturally because the costs of coordination are reduced and because it is easier for the parties and the adjudicator to "agree on what each will regard as cooperative and defective behavior" (McAdams 2005, 1081). Civil law states accept similar legal principles domestically, which makes it easier for them to correlate their behaviors, and the adjudicator (PCIJ/ICJ) and civil law disputants will converge naturally on the same

---

[15] McAdams (2005, 1078) argues that a single adjudicator is important for getting parties to converge on a single outcome, and that *ex post* compliance with the endorsed outcome is enhanced when a *single* actor or institution serves as the adjudicator.

[16] Posner and Figueiredo (2004) find strong evidence for bias in the ICJ at the level of the individual justices, showing that justices tend to vote in favor of their own states and in favor of states that have similar wealth, regimes, and culture to their home states.

outcomes. Civil law states are also more likely to view ICJ judgments with legitimacy due to their recognition of the principles the Court applies in reaching its decisions, which produces high compliance rates with ICJ rulings. Simply put, because civil law principles are embedded in the structure of the ICJ, civil law states tend to gravitate towards this Court, and be more open to its adjudicative powers. "Contemporary attitudes towards the authority of existing international law can best be seen as a function of a state's historical legal tradition and how this legal tradition shapes the legal culture and institutional structures within each state" (Zartner-Falstrom 2006, 344).

In contrast to the World Court, the ICC emerged as a negotiated compromise between civil law and common law states. The explicit inclusion of common law principles in the structure of the ICC demonstrates the increased influence of this legal system on international law: "The influence of common law jurists, not felt as strongly in the early period of modern international law: is noticeable over the last one hundred years, and particularly so during the last sixty years, since the end of the Second World War. In that time, international law has slowly absorbed various common law ideas and institutions, ones that might very well have been antipathetic to its original civil law character" (Picker 2008, 1105–1106). As we show in Chapter 4, the Rome Statute embodies many legal principles from both of the major Western legal traditions. This implies that potential joiners to the Court, or those states that were not present in Rome, will look to the Court's legal design when considering whether the Court can be a fair adjudicator (in this case, prosecuting crimes against humanity). The Court's hybrid design should increase the attractiveness of the Court to civil law and common law states. Empirical analyses for potential joiners in Chapter 4 support this claim, showing that civil law and common law states have similar rates of ICC ratification and that they are more likely to support the Court than Islamic law or mixed law states.

Second, the expressive theory of adjudication considers the role of cheap talk for creating focal points, but does not examine how the similarities of the disputants' preferences influence the effectiveness of cheap talk for promoting coordination.[17] Analyses of domestic courts and their

---

[17] Political scientists have examined a variety of sources of state similarities including institutions (e.g. regime type), economic interactions (e.g. trade), and cultural ties (language, history, etc.). We focus on similarities between legal institutions because our theory focuses on adjudication, but our theory also explains our findings in Chapter 5 that democratic states are more willing to accept the compulsory jurisdiction of the World Court. The similarity of preferences between democracies and the transparency of their regimes enhances the use of optional clause declarations as cheap talk.

indirect role in resolving disputes provide insight into the relationship between cheap talk and bargaining. We believe that states can engage in cheap talk about their willingness to work with a particular international adjudicator. In the United States, many disputes are settled absent of a formal court decision (Bilder 1998). This is most likely to occur when the dispute lies between parties who "have, and expect to continue, long-term relationships with each other [for] such relations might be disrupted by resort to the courts" (Bilder 1998, 235). Most disputes never reach the court, and most of those that do are settled prior to a final decision being made by the court.[18] This process takes place not only domestically; we believe that the existence of an international adjudicator makes the potential disputants (states) more likely to settle out of court. Bilder (1981, 58) talks about this process in a very informative way:

Broadly speaking, the possibility of third-party involvement in dispute settlement influences the parties towards moderate behavior, since each must anticipate that it may have to persuade an impartial third party, or indirectly, the more general international community, that its actions and reactions are reasonable and legitimate. Thus, the availability of dispute settlement procedures serves to limit risk by constraining the possible consequences of agreement within more foreseeable limits.

Several other international law scholars also recognize this important function of international adjudication. In the context of the ICJ, Merrills (2005, 177) states that: "[I]n recent years several disputes have been settled following reference of the matter to the Court, without requiring a decision. Although cases which are settled out of court do not call for judgments, they are, of course, a further illustration of the contribution which availability of adjudication can make to dispute resolution." In this sense, the ICJ plays an important "background role" (Merrills 2005, 177) in the dispute settlement process (see also Fischer 1982).

Bilder's (1998) argument that out-of-court effects are strongest for parties with similar interests and long-term relationships meshes well with the equilibrium findings in cheap talk bargaining models. Crawford and Sobel's (1982) path-breaking model demonstrates that cheap talk promotes cooperation more readily in bargaining settings if the parties have common interests. Theoretical extensions of Crawford and Sobel's model confirm Bilder's beliefs that the shadow of the future matters as well. Kim (1996), for example, shows that reputation effects in infinitely

---

[18] The pattern of judgments for ICJ cases seems to follow a similar pattern, with 61 percent of cases having no judgment, often due to the disputing parties reaching a settlement before a judgment by the Court is rendered (www.icj-cij.org). See also Fischer's (1982) study, which shows how states can reach outside agreements while the Court is deliberating the case.

repeated interactions can enhance the credibility of cheap talk and produce more efficient agreements. Long-term interactions mitigate incentives to lie about one's type because bargaining parties seek to avoid future losses from damaged reputation (Sartori 2005). This corresponds to arguments made in the delegation literature about the reputational costs states face when working with an adjudicator. If states join an international court to help credibly commit to some other policy position, such as democratization or good human rights practices, then they should be less inclined to renege on a judgment rendered by that court.

As mentioned above, states can engage in cheap talk about their willingness to work with the designated adjudicator in the process of bargaining. We can thus extend the expressive theory of adjudication by treating commitments to international courts as a form of cheap talk. In our theory, we capture two separate processes as cheap talk. The first, taken from McAdams (2005, 1059), is that the "adjudicator uses cheap talk to construct a 'focal point' in a coordination game'" In other words, once a dispute goes to a court, the adjudicator can help the parties achieve the same equilibrium solution. Our theory captures yet another process as cheap talk – the fact that states recognize the court's jurisdiction. Through this process, the parties send cheap talk signals to other states about their bargaining types. We believe that both of these processes are crucial to our argument since the jurisdictional acceptance enhances bargaining in the shadow of the court, while the adjudicator's own use of cheap talk helps them be more efficient for helping the disputants reach durable settlements.

In the context of the ICJ, for example (see Chapters 5 and 6), states would like to convince other states that they prefer to settle interstate disputes peacefully and facilitate agreed-upon solutions to existing coordination problems. Recognition of the ICJ's jurisdiction sends information about a state's willingness to view the adjudicator as a legitimate third-party conflict manager. The similarities between civil law states and the practices of the ICJ produce great benefits for civil law states' use of jurisdictional cheap talk. Civil law systems are the most frequent domestic legal systems in the world. From 1920 to 2002, civil law states constituted 48–78 percent of all states in the world. The predominance of civil law states creates high probabilities that any two states in a coordination game in international politics will both have civil law systems. Thus for any civil law state, its dyadic interactions are most likely to be with other civil law states.

There are several important implications that stem from the global distribution of domestic legal systems. First, as noted above, cheap talk works best when sent to similar states. Second, we know that the largest legal tradition is the civil law tradition. Both of these factors suggest that civil law countries are most likely to benefit from acceptance of the ICJ's jurisdiction when compared with states representing common, Islamic, or mixed legal traditions. The large number of civil law states globally causes the recognition of the Court's jurisdiction to have very diffuse benefits. Civil law states are better equipped than common or Islamic law states to use optional clause declarations as cheap talk, and thus in this sense the adjudicator plays a more *passive* role in the interstate bargaining process (Mitchell and Hensel 2007).

The adjudicator's role as a signaler of private information also works more efficiently in dyads that have legal principles and rules in common with the court. As we demonstrate in Chapter 5, the underlying rules and procedures of the ICJ are highly similar to the basic principles of civil law, which increases civil law states' perception of the impartiality and fairness of the ICJ as an adjudicator. Additionally, similar principles that civil law states apply to interstate bargaining, such as *bona fides*, help to reduce each side's private information. Legal rules that govern contracts and their enforcement are clear; hence uncertainties surrounding future compliance are reduced, making it easier to strike an accord. The high probability for civil law states to interact with other civil law states opens up more opportunities for the adjudicator to signal private information effectively.[19] In short, the expressive power of the World Court in the form of correlated strategies, focal points, and information signaling is enhanced when the disputing parties are civil law states. Our expectation, which is supported empirically in Chapter 5, is that civil law states will be most likely to recognize the jurisdiction of the PCIJ/ICJ in comparison to common law, Islamic law, and mixed law states.

The broader point is that rational legal design matters. If it did not, then states would not try to project their domestic institutions onto international adjudicative bodies. Moreover, if rational legal design did not matter, then common law states would acquiesce to civil law-based international courts, which is certainly not the case. As Picker (2008, 1108) explains when discussing the "Americanization" of international law: "[I]t is almost as though the civil law tradition imbued throughout traditional international law is under attack by the legal imperialism of the common law countries – primarily the United States and the United Kingdom" (see also Wiegand 1996; Keleman and Sibbitt 2004). The originators of new international courts pursue their legal self-interest, which in turn influences potential joiners' views about the fairness and

---

[19] This is similar to Kydd's (2003) claim that biased mediators are more likely to be trusted by disputants.

efficacy of the court once it exists. The cheap talk signal of commitment to an international court works most efficiently for dyads that share legal principles with the court. As we show in Chapter 7, this has important consequences for the adjudicator's efficacy as well. For example, civil law dyads are the only pairs of states that are significantly more likely to avoid militarization and reach and comply with agreements when bargaining in the shadow of the World Court. This accords with our contention that an adjudicator is best able to correlate strategies, create focal points, and provide information to disputants when they view the court as unbiased, a situation that is most likely to emerge when the disputants' domestic legal traditions mesh with the court's legal design. It implies also that states are more likely to have durable commitments to international courts with familiar legal principles.

Design of state commitments to international courts

In addition to providing leverage for understanding why certain states are more likely to recognize the jurisdiction of international courts than others, domestic legal traditions and their prominent characteristics can also give us insight into the design and success of international legal commitments. There is considerable variation in the form and design of contracts in civil law, common law, and Islamic law systems. Contracts signed in these legal traditions differ in terms of their attention to detail, their length, and their inclusion of general principles. We assert that these contractual differences in the domestic realm carry over into the international arena. International negotiators bring their legal backgrounds to the negotiating table, which influences both their willingness to sign treaties and the design of the resulting agreements. Negotiators are forward-looking in the sense that they consider how commitments to international courts will affect future interstate bargaining situations.

There is quite a bit of variance in the degree to which states' commitments to international courts can be flexible. Many courts created in the past two decades have some degree of compulsory jurisdiction (WTO, EFTA (European Free Trade Association), CCJ (Caribbean Court of Justice), CIS (Commonwealth of Independent States), COMESA (Common Market for Eastern and Sourthern Africa), and ICC) (Shany 2003, 5). Other courts allow for flexibility in states' commitments. The ICJ, for example, allows for states to recognize the compulsory jurisdiction of the Court via the optional clause, although this is not required for all UN members. The IACHR and the ITLOS similarly employ optional clauses (Alter 2008). Furthermore, states can place reservations on their commitments to some international courts (e.g. the World Court) and

not others (e.g. the ICC and the ECJ). In some senses, it is not surprising that international courts have moved in the direction of compulsory jurisdiction. Negotiations are long and detailed up front, which
allows for the originators to lock in favorable institutional design features. Furthermore, the typical court created in the post Cold-War era
brings a lot more relevant states to the bargaining table, whereas many
earlier courts were created mostly by the major powers and European
regional powers. The movements towards the Kantian system and contagion effects of successful courts also push in the direction of courts with
stronger authority.[20]

The fact that several international courts constitute part of a larger
institutional network can also influence levels of state support for a court
and the freedom that states have in designing their individual commitments to the court. For example, all members of the EU have to accept
the jurisdiction of the ECJ. The Court has been instrumental in the
process of shaping the law of the EU into a fully developed legal regime
and in establishing several fundamental doctrines of European law, such
as the doctrine of direct effect and the supremacy doctrine (Cichowski
2007, 27).[21] Since its inception, the ECJ has engaged in very extensive
and authoritative interpretation of existing EU law, through clarification,
expansion, and construction of new rules. Through this process, EU law
has developed immensely, often-times in a direction not foreseen by its
creators – the member states. "Member states intended to create a court
that could not significantly compromise national sovereignty or national
interest, but the ECJ changed the EU legal system, fundamentally undermining member state control over the Court" (Alter 1998, 122).

The position of the ECJ within the EU structure is very strong because
all EU members have to accept the jurisdiction of the ECJ and there
is no room for bargaining or structuring a "better deal" for individual
members. There are no reservations on the Court's jurisdiction. Each
member state is subject to the adjudicative powers of the ECJ. Moreover,
the Court is empowered to examine in a routine matter "the compatibility of measures adopted by EU members with their obligations under
the EU law, notwithstanding the existence of parallel constitutional law,

---

[20] The move away from flexibility is quite interesting in a broader theoretical sense, given
recent work in political science on institutional design. Koremenos (2005), for example,
shows that in situations of uncertainty and risk aversion, states will prefer to sign agreements with renegotiation provisions. And yet, in the arena of international law, less
flexibility in the design of new courts is resulting in broader state support for many international courts, as the burgeoning support for the ICC and WTO illustrates.

[21] Direct effect (1963) gives individuals directly enforceable rights protected by the EU law,
and the supremacy doctrine (1964) obliges national judges to give precedence to the EU
law over national laws that come in conflict with the EU law (Cichowski 2007, 27).

administrative law, or other legal forms of challenge under the domestic law of these same states" (Shany 2007, 11). Decisions of the ECJ may also have very direct consequences for the member states, including imposition of new responsibilities on a state, holding a government liable for the violation of EU law, and imposition of sanctions (Garrett *et al.* 1998, 159). Additionally, the ECJ is backed up by a strong enforcement mechanism, where independent and autonomous domestic courts can enforce the ECJ's judgments against their own national governments (Keohane *et al.* 2000, 467). To sum up, the EU accepts the superiority of a supranational court, the ECJ, over national courts. The position of the ECJ is also strengthened by the overall goals of the EU, in particular the goal to build a union of states in Europe.

The situation of the ECJ stands in marked contrast to the ICJ and the ICC. The predecessor of the ICJ, the PCIJ, was established under the auspices of the League of Nations. The Statute of the PCIJ, however, was in its entirety independent of the Covenant. Despite this formal and legal autonomy of the League and the Court, "functionally the Court was a part of the machinery for the settlement of international disputes envisaged in the very conception of the League of Nations" (Gamble and Fischer 1976, 4). The ICJ, established by the UN Charter, constitutes the principal judicial organ of the UN, and is thus embedded in the overall structure of the UN. For example, the UN Charter addresses the general position of the ICJ in Article 93, which declares that all member states of the UN are *ipso facto* parties to the Court's Statute. Regarding the issue of compliance with the ICJ's judgments, Article 94 of the UN Charter declares that: "Each Member of the United Nations undertakes to comply with the decision of the ICJ in any case to which it is a party." The Statute of the International Court of Justice is annexed to the UN Charter, of which it forms an integral part.

The basic source of the jurisdiction of the ICJ is the consent of the states that parties to a given dispute (Szafarz 1993, 3). The PCIJ has very clearly reiterated this principle in the *Eastern Carelia* case, where it stated that: "No State can, without its consent, be compelled to submit its disputes with other States either to mediation or to arbitration or to any other kind of pacific settlement" (Szafarz 1993, 3). Consequently, when a state makes a decision to become a party to the ICJ Statute, it simply accepts that the Court will operate in accordance with the Statute. In order for the ICJ "to have jurisdiction with respect to a given case further acts of will on the part of states involved are required" (Szafarz 1993, 5). Furthermore, states may restrict the jurisdiction of the ICJ by placing reservations on their declarations accepting the compulsory jurisdiction of the Court. In general, even though the ICJ constitutes the principal judicial organ of the UN, states can draft "special arrangements" when they accept the general jurisdiction of the Court. In addition, enforcement of the ICJ's judgments is not as straightforward as it is in the case of the ECJ. Similar to several other international courts and tribunals, states are bound to comply with the judgments of the ICJ, but "no domestic legal mechanism assures legal implementation" (Keohane *et al.* 2000, 466). Furthermore, there is no international mechanism for ensuring compliance either. In Article 94(2), the ICJ Statute allows for a loose type of appeal to the UN Security Council following a judgment, but this option has never been employed in practice (Rosenne 1957/1962).

In contrast to the ICJ, the ICC constitutes an independent IO and does not constitute part of the UN structure. However, the Rome Statute endows the UN Security Council with several powers, such as the power to refer to the ICC situations that would not otherwise fall under the Court's jurisdiction (Article 13 of the Rome Statute). The ICC also cooperates with the UN in several other areas, such as logistical support and exchange of information. Additionally, each year the ICC presents to the UN a report on its activities. The adjudicative powers of the ICC are much more extensive than those of the ICJ, as Article 120 of the Rome Statute provides that no reservations may be made to the Statute. Thus, states do not have an option of drafting their own commitments to the Court. The issue of reservations at the Rome Conference was very intense. In fact, the Preparatory Committee considered several options, such as one permitting any reservations except those specifically prohibited, and no article on reservations (Lee 1999, 431). The ultimate solution – no reservations – received the broadest support. States that strongly supported the compulsory jurisdiction of the Court were also more likely to support the prohibition of reservations (Lee 1999, 432), a similar pattern observed in the negotiations over the proposed compulsory jurisdiction of the PCIJ.[22]

Although an international court's position in a larger institutional network may influence the design of states' commitments to the court, we believe that domestic legal systems can give us purchase for

---

[22] Interesting is the situation of the IACHR, whose track record is spotty as to its influence within the Inter-American system, despite the fact that the Court has repeatedly demonstrated its full potential in some important issue-areas, such as torture and disappearances. According to Article 1 of the Court's Statute, "The Inter-American Court of Human Rights is an autonomous judicial institution whose purpose is the application and interpretation of the American Convention on Human Rights." The Court, although independent, has important ties to the Organization of American States (OAS). For example, it submits its budget for approval to the General Assembly of the OAS (Article 26 of the Court's Statute), and submits a report on its work of the previous year to each regular session of the OAS General Assembly (Article 30 of the Court's Statute).

understanding why *within* a particular structure there is considerable variability in the design of these commitments. We argue that the manner in which contracts are concluded domestically will give us clues about how states will design their commitments to international courts, where such flexibility provisions are available. The legal backgrounds of international negotiators will influence the manner in which they design international agreements. This reality is closely linked to the fact that international law does not exist in a legal vacuum. Instead, the law of nations is based "on conceptions of law found in the legal traditions around the world" (Zartner-Falstrom 2006, 374).

Negotiators from civil law countries bring to the table their experience with civil contract law, and thus they will be more amenable to signing and designing international commitments that reflect the principles governing domestic contracts in civil law systems. Contracts concluded in a civil law system are relatively straightforward, due primarily to the structure of the civil legal tradition. As noted in Chapter 2, the main feature of a civil legal system is a system of law codified in various codes, which establishes many general rules and principles for contractual relations. Usually, these general principles appear in the front sections of the codes, implying their application to all contractual relations enumerated in a code. This results in much shorter contracts in civil law systems relative to common law and Islamic law systems, because it is not necessary to identify all the unforeseen events beyond the control of a contracting party that prevents him/her from fulfilling contractual obligations. This property derives from the strength of the *bona fides* and *pacta sunt servanda* principles in the civil law tradition. We argue in Chapter 6 that the brevity of civil law contracts should carry over into commitments to international courts. For example, civil law states' optional clause declarations signed with the PCIJ/ICJ should be straightforward, with relatively few reservations. Civil law states should also be amenable to signing treaties with compromissory clauses, viewing these choices as complements rather than substitutes (Powell and Mitchell 2007).

International commitments of common law states should reflect characteristics of common law contracts. Contracts in this legal tradition are much more detailed and meticulous than civil law contracts. Because there is much less codified law that incorporates overarching general principles, such as *bona fides* and *pacta sunt servanda*, the parties are responsible for including certain stipulations or clauses in their contract. For example, in common law, *force majeure* is not precisely defined. The parties must enumerate in a contract any events of *force majeure* that will preclude them for being liable on the grounds of non-performance (Pejovic 2001). Such *force majeure* circumstances in the common law tradition usually release all parties from their contractual obligations (Rayner 1991; Whincup 1992).

In the context of state commitments to international courts, these characteristics of common law contracts lead us to expect that common law states will place a higher number of reservations on their declarations to international courts. These restrictions ensure that all of the states' rights and obligations are clearly specified, which resembles the "all-inclusive" approach of domestic common law contracts. For example, when common law countries recognize the compulsory jurisdiction of the World Court through optional clause declarations, they should be more likely to embed reservations in their declarations than civil law or Islamic law states. Common law states should also find the use of compromissory clauses attractive because they limit the World Court's jurisdiction to the subject matter negotiated in a specific treaty.

Islamic law regulates contractual relationships in a way that is strikingly different from that of common law and civil law. The Koran plays a crucial role in establishing the types of contracts admissible to the faithful, their rights, and obligations. Islamic law lacks a general theory of contracts comparable to its Western counterparts. The Koran, however, to some extent, plays the role of a code, in which general principles are included. Parties to a contract are also free, with some limitations, to place stipulations in a contract. These clauses cannot negate the legal purpose of a contract, or violate specific laws included in the Koran or the Sunna (Arabi 1998). The design of contracts under Islamic law is closely connected to its treatment of the *bona fides* and *pacta sunt servanda* principles. Good faith is very firmly established in the Islamic legal tradition. Both the Koran and Sunna permit cooperative interstate agreements as long as they are conducted according to the principles of good faith and honesty. Islamic law identifies fraud and dishonesty as a "serious moral wrong" (Rayner 1991, 206). Because Islamic law expects the faithful to keep their contractual obligations, agreements concluded under Islamic law are relatively meticulous. The rights and obligations of the parties are cautiously drafted to guarantee certainty as to fulfillment of the agreement.

We anticipate that Islamic law states' international agreements will directly reflect the general design of contracts in Islamic law. Islamic states will be very careful in signing agreements with any international institutions, especially international courts. If a state knows that it has to keep its commitments, it will deliberately pay close attention to the way that its rights and obligations are stipulated; clarity and thoroughness are of utmost importance. The fact that Islamic law embraces *bona fides* and *pacta sunt servanda* principles, both of which promote compliance with agreements, should make these states hesitant to recognize the jurisdiction of international courts.[23] Additionally, cultural differences between Western and Islamic civilizations play a big role in shaping the latter's negative perception of Western international institutions. However, when Islamic law states decide to support an international court via recognition of its jurisdiction, their commitments should be long-lasting and relatively specific. In the context of commitments to the ICJ, for example, the number of restrictions placed on Islamic countries' optional clause declarations should be rather substantial, although not as large as for common law states. Islamic law states should be more willing to recognize the jurisdiction of international courts through bilateral rather than multilateral compromissory clause treaties. Islamic law limits to some extent states' ability to make international agreements freely. Thus, there are strong theoretical reasons to expect that Islamic law states will prefer bilateral bargains, which are easier to strike on average. Religious principles directly embedded in Islamic legal systems limit these states' contracting freedom, which results in a smaller number of interstate agreements. However, a strong *pacta sunt servanda* norm produces expectations that contracts negotiated under Islamic law will be upheld, even as circumstances change.

Effect of states' commitments to international courts

The skeptical realist might argue that creating or joining a court does not imply that it will have any serious effect on a state's behavior. For example, while many states sign and ratify human rights treaties, the empirical record suggests that they have little effect on subsequent human rights practices, often resulting in worsened human rights records (Hathaway 2002). One might wonder if a similar process operates when states join human rights courts such as the ICC or the ECHR. Similarly, does the ICJ help member states resolve coordination problems? Many international law scholars paint skeptical views about the World Court, viewing it as a court with little state support and a weak record of judgments (Elkind 1984; Gross 1987; Scott and Csajko 1988; Singh 1989; Oduntan 1999; Allain 2000). On the other hand, scholars tend to focus on situations where the PCIJ or ICJ actually intervened, which may omit important out-of-court effects that the courts may create (Bilder 1981, 1998; Merrills 2005).

---

[23] A good example is the fact that only six Islamic law countries have ever recognized the compulsory jurisdiction of the PCIJ/ICJ.

Our rational legal design theory of adjudication suggests that courts are not created to be identical and are not meant to perform their functions via identical sets of procedural rules. The originators of new courts design them in legally optimal ways, which implies that the courts' efficacy will vary as well, depending on which states come before the courts. As we argued above, international courts should best be able to resolve coordination problems when they share legal principles with the disputing states. In these instances, the cheap talk signal of recognizing the court's jurisdiction is more credible and the adjudicator is better positioned to help the parties reach similar focal points in interstate bargaining. In Chapter 7, we examine the effects of the two courts examined in this book, the World Court and the ICC. We show that both courts have significant effects on member states' behavior.

Because the World Court is designed as a civil law institution, it has the strongest out-of-court effect for civil law dyads. Two civil law countries that recognize the compulsory jurisdiction of the PCIJ or ICJ are better able to avoid militarized disputes. They are also more likely to reach and comply with agreements to resolve coordination issues related to territorial, maritime, and cross-border river issues. On the other hand, common law and Islamic law states do not get similar boosts from bargaining in the shadow of the World Court.

The ICC is a hybrid court that enjoys similar levels of support from civil law and common law countries. We show empirically that ratification of the Rome Statute is consequential; states' human rights records show improvement on multiple dimensions (torture, systematic torture, political imprisonments, and disappearances) when they join the ICC. There is some degree of endogeneity in this relationship, as states with better human rights records are more likely to ratify the treaty, although states also show subsequent improvements in human rights practices as well. In short, our analyses of both courts show that they are significant players in world politics. For the states that create these courts and for joiners that view the courts as unbiased, international adjudicators can be effective at helping states to resolve coordination problems.

Case selection

As noted above, we analyze two prominent international courts in this project: the World Court, which includes the PCIJ and the ICJ, and the ICC. While many regional courts, such as the ECJ and the ECHR, are significant players in world politics, we decided to focus our attention on international courts that offer membership to all interested states. This avoids the problem that might arise in determining the set of potential joiner states to regional courts, as we would need specific ideas about which states belong to the regions in question. It also broadens the number of cases for analyses, especially when we analyze a court like the PCIJ/ICJ, which has been in existence for close to ninety years.

Our focus on the World Court is driven by a variety of factors. The Court has been in existence for a long time, which creates rich variation in state support. Only one-third of countries accept the compulsory jurisdiction of the Court today, which also makes it a more difficult test case for predicting state support for the Court. Most countries that joined the Court were not at the negotiating table when the Court was formed after World War I, which gives us a large set of potential joining states for evaluating our rational legal design theory of adjudication. Additionally, this is one of the few international courts where countries have left after originally joining the Court (e.g. the United States in 1986), which also creates interesting variance in the durability of state support for the PCIJ/ICJ. States' commitments to the World Court can also vary over time. Optional clause declarations can be amended across time, which provides us with interesting and variable information about the rational design of states' commitments to the Court. States can also recognize the jurisdiction of the World Court through more than one mechanism (e.g. optional clause declarations, compromissory clause treaties), which gives us additional leverage for testing rational design hypotheses. In short, the long-term existence of the PCIJ and ICJ, as well as the evolving level of state commitments to these courts, makes them optimal cases for empirical analysis.

We selected the ICC for analysis because we have access to rich information about the negotiations in Rome that led to the legal design of the ICC's Statute. This allows us to evaluate our theory about the originators of new international courts through multiple methods, such as historical process tracing and quantitative analysis of state signature and ratification of the treaty. Furthermore, 160 countries were represented at the negotiations in Rome, which gives us a large number of originator states to include in our empirical analyses. The ICC, as a civil/common law hybrid court, also has a distinct legal design from the World Court (a civil law court), which creates some interesting comparisons across the courts. We are able to show, for example, that common law countries are much more supportive of the ICC than the ICJ, an empirical pattern predicted by our theory.

Another reason that we selected the World Court and ICC for analysis is that we are able to assess the efficacy of both of these international courts to some degree. The World Court has been in existence for a long time, which gives us ample opportunities to assess its effect on bargaining successes and failures in interstate politics. The World Court also deals with many coordination issues, such as territorial disputes, which meshes well with our underlying theoretical framework. The ICC, on the other hand, while a relatively recent court, still provides us with several years' worth of data for analysis. We are able to examine the effect of the Court on states' human rights practices, which allows us to compare the efficacy of this institution in the human rights arena relative to other instruments, such as human rights treaties.

Conclusion

In this chapter, we developed a rational legal design theory of adjudication, which shows how the characteristics of domestic legal traditions influence the creation and expansion of state support for international courts. States lock in favorable legal institutional design features at the negotiating table when creating a new international court. These design features then impinge on other potential joiners' decisions. States are more likely to join pre-existing courts that utilize familiar legal rules and principles because they can bargain more efficiently in the shadow of the court. The adjudicator correlates strategies, constructs focal points, and reduces information asymmetries more easily when it adopts similar legal frameworks to the disputants. Contractual features of domestic legal traditions also help to explain the rich variation in states' commitments to courts, such as the number and types of reservations employed.

Our theory produces a number of general hypotheses. First, countries will seek to lock in their legal preferences when they are involved in the negotiations to create a new international court. The rules put in place should reflect the composition of negotiating states with respect to their predominant legal traditions. Second, states will be more inclined to join pre-existing international courts if the courts employ familiar legal rules and principles. This similarity also influences the efficacy of international courts, as the adjudicator is better positioned to resolve interstate bargaining problems between pairs of countries with legal traditions similar to the court's traditions. Third, states' domestic legal traditions will also influence the design and durability of their commitments to international courts. Civil law countries will employ fewer reservations on their commitments to courts than common law or Islamic law countries. However, the sanctity of contracts in Islamic law will enhance the durability of these states' commitments to international courts. In short, understanding the variation in domestic legal traditions gives us greater purchase for understanding the life cycle of states' commitments to international courts and institutions.[24]

[24] While our theory focuses on the legal design that states may prefer in negotiations to create new international courts, we do not develop a fully fledged theory of interstate bargaining in these situations, which makes it difficult to predict whose preferences will win out in the negotiations. We treat these processes that influence the aggregation of preferences in multilateral negotiations as exogenous. It would be interesting in future work to examine more carefully how factors such as states' capabilities or coalitions/non-governmental organizations (NGOs) influence the ultimate design of new international courts.

4   Domestic legal traditions and the creation of the International Criminal Court

The ICC, created by the Rome Statute in 1998, constitutes a truly unique international adjudicative body. It exemplifies the process of global legalization, it points to the strong connection between domestic and international law, and it embodies a true compromise between two domestic legal traditions. During the Rome negotiations, state representatives pushed for rules and procedures that were familiar to them based on their domestic legal backgrounds, which resulted in the creation of a *sui generis* international court, an interesting hybrid between common law and civil law principles. This design process was not only rational from the perspective of the Court's supporters, it also had unintended consequences in that states considering whether to join the ICC at a later date would be influenced by the original design of the court.

In this chapter, we apply the theory articulated in Chapter 3, which contends that states' domestic legal traditions influence their preferences regarding the legal design of international courts. States involved in creating a new international adjudicative body seek to design a court with familiar legal rules and principles, anticipating that an initial commitment to the court will be durable and have long-term consequences. We argue that the ICC originators pushed for rules and procedures that mimicked those of their domestic legal systems to help reduce uncertainty regarding the Court's future decision-making processes. The hybrid nature of the Court's design that emerged enhanced the attractiveness of the Court to civil and common law states, making them significantly more likely to sign and ratify the Rome Statute. Empirical analyses suggest that common and civil law states were fervent supporters of the ICC in preliminary negotiations and that they have shown higher levels of support for the Court since the ICC's inception in comparison to Islamic law or mixed law states.

The first section of this chapter summarizes the theoretical argument for originators of new international courts, as explicated in Chapter 3. The next two sections provide a brief summary of international criminal law, a short historical overview of the creation of the ICC, and a historical tracing of the creation and design principles of the ICC. This is followed by a summary of the testable hypotheses linking domestic legal system types to ICC signature and ratification decisions. After describing the research design, the hypotheses are evaluated with quantitative evidence through a large-N empirical analysis of state-level signature and ratification of the ICC (1998–2004). The empirical evidence demonstrates that originators do in fact seek to lock in favorable legal institutional designs when creating international courts and that these choices are influential on states' decisions to join the courts once they are established.

The originators of new international courts

As we show in this chapter, negotiating states were influenced by their domestic legal backgrounds and their training in criminal legal procedures when negotiating the design of the ICC. This interesting intersection of domestic and international law occurs frequently when international courts are formed. The initial negotiators of new courts design institutions in ways that are optimal from both a political and legal standpoint.

States face a great degree of uncertainty when engaging in the process of international adjudication because they cannot be certain that a court's deliberations will lead to a conclusion that constitutes the state's most preferred outcome. This uncertainty can be contributed in part to the fact that international adjudication entails applying and interpreting international legal rules, and deciphering inconsistencies between rival norms in the context of specific cases (Abbott and Snidal 1998; Alter 2006). In this sense, international courts are no different from domestic courts, because all courts have to face interpretation of legal rules: "[W]hen seeking to overturn all but the most flagrantly illegal state actions, litigants and courts must inevitably appeal to particular interpretations of such ambiguities [ambiguities between norms]" (Keohane et al. 2000, 461). In an arena like international criminal law, international courts engage in the process of rule interpretation more often than domestic courts, especially given the numerous discrepancies that arise between domestic and international criminal law. The fact that distinct adjudicative bodies interpret international law differently additionally increases states' uncertainty regarding international adjudication (Charney 1998; Spelliscy 2001).

As we argued earlier, this lack of certainty about how the court will identify cases to be heard and how it will adjudicate in specific cases is mitigated if the court's rules and procedures are familiar. In other words, to reduce future uncertainty concerning the application of international criminal law by international courts, states that participate in the process of the creation of a new criminal court have incentives to design it in a way that resembles their domestic legal systems. States are able to form expectations about the method of interpretation of legal rules and in-court procedures if the two sets of legal rules (domestic law and the legal design of a court) align with one another because "when similar legal language is used, similar legal mechanisms are adapted" (Powell and Wiegand 2010, 11). This will reduce uncertainty about what types of crimes the court will punish, as well as the procedures it will employ in the process of prosecuting crimes against humanity.

International criminal law

Usually, international law governs the rights and obligations of states, while criminal law is inherently concerned with prohibitions addressed to individuals, which if violated are subject to state-imposed penal sanctions (Cryer *et al.* 2007, 1). International criminal law, as a branch of public international law, is based on an underlying logic of combining these two concepts. Thus, international criminal law as a substantive branch of international law is inescapably linked to the fundamental character of the latter. Additionally, however, the nature of criminal liability requires that the rules of international criminal law must be clearer and more precise when compared to other domains of international law due to the fact that they deal with individual criminal responsibility. Additionally, courts that operate within the domain of international criminal law must be endowed with explicit and proper procedures which take into consideration basic rights of the accused (Cryer *et al.* 2007, 12).

Under the rule of old, *jus gentium*, individuals were not of direct concern to international law, as states' domestic legal systems regulated the status of an individual. One of the most well-known exceptions from this rule was piracy. Every state in the system was endowed with a right to search and punish pirates regardless of nationality or territoriality link (Cassese 2005, 435).[1] There are numerous definitions of international criminal law, but perhaps the best one is provided by Cassese (2008, 3): "International criminal law is a body of international rules designed both to proscribe certain categories of conduct (war crimes, crimes against humanity, genocide, torture, aggression, terrorism) and to make those persons who engage in such conduct criminally liable." International criminal law constitutes a relatively new and rudimentary branch of international law. Other than war crimes which were punishable starting

---

[1] According to Cassese (2008, 28), war crimes constituted another exception.

in the nineteenth century, the remaining categories of international crimes have developed much more recently. For example, crimes against humanity and genocide were included as international law crimes shortly after World War II, while torture was defined in international law in 1980. Most recently, international terrorism has been added to the list of crimes. Before that, only international custom and treaties prohibited certain acts, such as killing prisoners of war. They did so, however, by addressing the actions of states and not individuals (Cassese 2008, 4).

Additionally, until international criminal courts came into existence, domestic courts were responsible for prosecuting individuals engaging in these internationally illegal activities. The repercussions of this state of affairs were grave: "As a consequence, municipal courts of each state applied their procedural rules (legal provisions on jurisdiction and on the conduct of criminal proceedings) and rules on 'the general part' of substantive criminal law; that is, on the definition and character of the objective and subjective elements of crimes, on defenses, etc." (Cassese 2008, 5). The situation changed when international criminal courts came into existence, because their statutes directly stipulated types of criminal acts that a particular court was to have jurisdiction over. Put differently, international criminal law has not been structured as some other substantive areas of *jus gentium*, which are based on a more coherent and unified set of general principles. In addition, a large number of customary norms dealing with international crimes have developed from domestic law. This reliance on domestic concepts of crime has further contributed to a significant fragmentation of international criminal law. Cassese (2008, 7) describes this situation in the following way:

The grafting of municipal law notions and rules on to international law has not, however, been a smooth process. National legal orders do not contain a uniform regulation of criminal law. On the contrary, they are split into many different systems, from among which two principal ones emerge: that prevailing in common law countries (the UK, the USA, Australia, Canada, many African and Asian countries), and that obtaining in civil law countries, chiefly based on a legal system of Romano-Germanic origin (they include states of continental Europe, such as France, Germany, Italy, Belgium, the countries of Northern Europe such as Norway, Sweden, Denmark, as well as Latin American countries, many Arab countries, as well as Asian states including, for instance, China).

In the following section, we describe how these competing views of criminal law were reconciled in the Rome negotiations. The ICC provides a great example of how domestic legal traditions impact not only the structure of substantive international law, but also the underlying rules and procedures of an international adjudicative body.

Negotiating the international criminal court

The thought of creating an international criminal court had been present in the minds of international law scholars ever since the aftermath of World War I. Scholars and policy makers regarded the idea of punishing individual violators of international law as worth pursuing. Unfortunately, all of the early attempts at creating such an international body ended in failure. For example, the Advisory Committee of Jurists, charged with preparing the project for the PCIJ, recommended that the "High Court of International Justice" be set up with jurisdiction covering "crimes constituting a breach of international public order or against the universal law of nations" (Phillimore 1922–1923, 80). According to Cassese (2008, 319), the failures of these early attempts to create an international criminal court can be contributed to the fact that "state sovereignty was nevertheless still very much the bedrock of the international community." The atrocities of World War II led to renewed efforts, culminating in the successful establishment of the Nuremberg and Tokyo Tribunals, both of which proved that international criminal justice can be effective if backed up by the necessary political will and appropriate resources (Cassese 2008).

The "third wave" of efforts to establish a more permanent international criminal court came after the end of the Cold War. Clear improvements in "East-West" relations, coupled with the increasing relevance of human rights and increasing violations of international humanitarian law, led to the establishment of the ICC. The creation of the ICC was the culmination of years of preparatory work that began in 1989 with a request by the UN General Assembly to the International Law Commission (ILC) to address the issue of a permanent international criminal court. The 1990s provided a favorable era for establishing an international adjudicative body because the end of the Cold War constituted at the same time the finale of an international impasse and the start of an epoch of invigorated multilateralism. There were concerns about the need for a universal human rights court, spurred in part by the emerging use of *ad hoc* tribunals in the post-Cold War era, most notably the ICTY and the ICTR.[2]

---

[2] In 1948, the UN General Assembly adopted the Convention for the Prevention and Punishment of the Crime of Genocide. The UN created a body of legal experts called the ILC to assist in the further development of international criminal law (Schabas 2004, 8–9). The process for creating a new criminal court was jump-started in the late 1980s by several Caribbean states that were seeking assistance to combat drug-trafficking crimes. It was also spurred on by a concern that the proliferation of new *ad hoc* tribunals would lead to divergent interpretations in international law and potentially led to inefficient forum shopping.

The ILC, composed of legal scholars who studied the issue of an international court during the previous decades, submitted the working text for the Court to the Rome Conference. Representatives from 160 countries convened in Rome in June 1998 to excogitate the procedural and substantive details of the ICC (Schabas 2004). Some states, including some of the world's healthiest economies (Germany, Canada, Sweden) and regional powers (Argentina, Chile) stalwartly favored the creation of a strong ICC (Goodliffe and Hawkins 2009). Other states, including China and Israel, openly opposed an autonomous and powerful international criminal court. The process of lengthy and meticulous negotiations resulted in the final text of the Rome Statute, which was approved by 120 states voting in favor, 7 states voting against the treaty, and 21 states abstaining from the vote (Schabas 2004, 18).[3] The ICC came into existence as an independent, permanent court with the ability to try persons accused of the most serious crimes against humanity. The ICC Statute requires that all state parties accept the Court's jurisdiction over all crimes: genocide, crimes against humanity, war crimes, and aggression.[4] The Statute came into force on July 1, 2002, when sixty state parties had ratified the treaty, a figure that has grown to over 50 percent (105 countries) of all states today.

The level of state support for the ICC is an interesting puzzle given that joining the ICC has relatively high consequences in comparison with other international adjudicative bodies, and given that states have not shown such extensive support for other international courts. As noted earlier, only one third of countries recognize the compulsory jurisdiction of the ICJ (Powell and Mitchell 2007). In contrast to the ICJ, reservations are not permitted when states join the ICC.[5] Unlike other international courts that give standing to states only, the ICC allows for an independent prosecutor and the UN Security Council to initiate the Court's proceedings.[6] The scope of the ICC's jurisdiction is also quite large in comparison with other international courts.[7]

[3] The final vote in Rome was confidential. As a result, there exists uncertainty as to which states voted against the treaty. Nevertheless, the United States, Israel, China, Iraq, Libya, and Yemen are widely reported to have voted against the treaty.
[4] Article 5 of the Rome Statute.
[5] This stipulation is, of course, subject to the seven year opt-out for war crimes (Article 124 of the Rome Statute).
[6] Article 15 of the Rome Statute provides that the prosecutor "may initiate investigations *proprio motu* on the basis of information on crimes within the jurisdiction of the Court." Thus, the prosecutor may investigate crimes within the scope of the ICC jurisdiction based on the referral of state parties, victims, the UN Security Council, NGOs or any other reliable source.
[7] If the UN Security Council refers a situation to the ICC, its jurisdiction covers the territory of all states in the world, both state parties and non-parties to the Rome Statute.

States brought a variety of political, economic, institutional, and legal preferences to the ICC bargaining table. The process of establishing international-level rules in Rome was in part a *political* process. Issues such as the role of the UN Security Council, the nature and level of independence granted to the Court's prosecutor, and the scope of the Court's jurisdiction continued to provide a cause of disquiet and incessant disagreement between the negotiating states (Goodliffe and Hawkins 2009). However, because the ICC is a court of law, *legal* factors were equally as important as political factors. Many of the states' representatives during negotiations were lawyers, not only international lawyers but also individuals practicing domestic law as well.[8] For example, the US government administration lawyers "subjected the ILC (*International Law Commission*) drafts to extensive internal review and analysis" (Scheffer 1999, 12). As a result, legal arguments shaped the discussion: "In Rome, where many of the delegates were lawyers (many of the decision-makers in national governments were also lawyers), legal argument dominated most issues; even when law manifestly could not dictate a particular resolution, ideas about law shaped the arguments raised" (Wippman 2004, 159).

Many of the existing explanations for the creation of the ICC focus on how *political* factors, such as the power and regime type of the negotiating states, influenced the creation and ultimate design of the Court. The most powerful state present at the negotiating table, the United States, is often portrayed as a spoiler in the negotiations due to its staunch opposition to a strong, independent criminal court. Initially, according to David Scheffer, former US Ambassador at Large for War Crimes Issues, the Clinton administration was in support of an international criminal court (Schiff 2008, 170). The United States was willing to provide support for the ICC if the UN Security Council was able to overshadow the Court's actions. After the Rome negotiators decided that the ICC would have a strong prosecutor, one independent from the Security Council's veto powers, the United States started to increasingly withdraw its support (Schiff 2008, 170). "Bolton and others fear[ed] that the ICC represents a dangerous attempt to substitute law for politics in international affairs" (Wippman 2004, 179). In the negotiations in Rome, the United States objected to the ICC on multiple grounds:

If the situation is referred by a state party or initiated by the prosecutor, the ICC jurisdiction can cover the territory of a non-state party if that state consents to the ICC's adjudicative powers.

[8] As Schiff (2008, 167) describes: "Because of the need for legal expertise to deal with ICC matters, states' representatives to the ICC in The Hague tend to be people with backgrounds in law, often seconded to foreign ministries from justice ministries and sometimes with some background in criminal law."

(1) the ICC could expose US citizens to being sanctioned for crimes not recognized by US law
(2) the ICC threatens US sovereignty to prosecute its own criminals
(3) the ICC undermines the ability of the US government to fight the war on terror
(4) the ICC is subject to abuse because it is not controlled by a system of careful checks and balances (Weller 2002, 697–698).[9]

In response to American and permanent Security Council member opposition, a group of "like-minded states" formed a coalition in support of the ICC. By the start of the Rome negotiations, the like-minded coalition constituted over 37 percent of the 160 participating states (Schabas 2004, 15–16). An explanation of ICC formation viewed through the lens of relative power would focus on the balance of power that emerged primarily between the United States and members of the like-minded group, and the compromises that were ultimately struck between these groups.

Insight into the domestic characteristics of the negotiating states provides another compelling *political* explanation of the emergence of the ICC. Simmons and Danner (2010) develop an interesting credible commitment theory to explain state decisions to join the ICC. They argue that two factors interact to produce high or low levels of support for the ICC: (1) the level of domestic accountability and (2) the recent history of domestic violence (e.g. civil war). Governments that have recently committed atrocities against domestic civilians may find the ICC an attractive commitment because it can tie their hands in the future. Whether this hand-tying strategy works is dependent on the level of domestic accountability inside the state, where a high level of accountability implies freedom of press, functioning democratic institutions, and a commitment to the rule of law. High credibility states without violent histories can commit to the ICC fairly easily because they anticipate that criminal cases are not likely to go to the international court. Low credibility states with recent domestic violence also find a commitment to the ICC attractive because it allows these governments to send a credible signal about their future commitment to civil peace. The theoretical argument and empirical findings produce a surprising expectation: "Peaceful democracies and civil-strife ridden non-democracies tend to display similar ratification propensities" (Simmons and Danner 2010, 240).

[9] Interestingly, the United States played a crucial role during the Rome negotiations: "The delegation from the United States was the largest at the Conference. Its legal experts contributed key elements to the Statute and, subsequently, to the Court's Rules of Procedure and Evidence" (Schiff 2008, 71).

While an emphasis on political factors, such as domestic accountability, gives us quite a bit of leverage for understanding the creation and expansion of the ICC, we think scholars have given short shrift to *legal* factors, especially the interaction between domestic and international law in the ICC negotiations. The degree of legal regulation enclosed in the procedural provisions of the Rome Statute reflects the legalistic character of negotiations. The amount of procedures outlined in the Rome Statute is truly unprecedented: "The ICC statute contains a full procedural scheme devoting three of its 13 parts to purely procedural issues" (MacCarrick 2005, 39).[10] Although some states may attempt to use it to further their political goals, the ICC constitutes an inherently *legal* institution. It has been called "a treaty-based inter-national legal institution of last resort" (Bassiouni 2006, 422), a "milestone in international criminal justice" (Kelley 2007), and "a legal institution – a court – that would apply binding law regulating the conduct of individuals" (Wippman 2004, 178).

In character, the Rome Treaty resembles to a large degree national laws establishing domestic criminal courts, replete in detailed legal rules. It not only establishes a novel international adjudicative body, but "it is also a criminal code, embodying a highly articulated set of rules on criminal procedure" (Arsanjani and Reisman 2005, 389). These rules are not unique; they have been drawn from domestic legal traditions. When examining the creation of an international legal institution, it is crucial to consider that international law making does not take place in a vacuum but "against a backdrop of existing legal norms and institutions, which condition and limit the range of options viewed by the participants in the process as possible, and which simultaneously shape the process itself" (Wippman 2004, 158).

Thus, not all bargaining outcomes expressed in the Rome Statute came into being as a result of political determinants. The structure and procedures of the ICC were to a large extent determined by pre-existing laws, which reflect criminal codes of domestic legal traditions. Lawyers who were negotiating the Rome Treaty came to the bargaining table with specific ideas about international law, criminal law, and legal institutions stemming from their domestic legal training as civil, common, or Islamic lawyers.

Legal training within each domestic legal tradition determines in part lawyers' understanding of basic legal concepts. It is only natural to expect legal experts to draw upon their legal background in drafting a state's international commitments:

---

[10] This fact distinguishes the ICC from the *ad hoc* tribunals established for the former Yugoslavia and Rwanda.

In comparative law, there are many situations where the same legal term has different meanings, or where different legal terms have the same legal effect. This can often cause confusion to both lawyers and their clients. This confusion most often occurs when civil lawyers have to deal with common law, or *vice versa*, when common law lawyers deal with civil law issues. (Pejovic 2001, 817)

Because of a unique blend of legal traditions present at the Rome negotiations, the ICC was given an unprecedented legal structure, one that reconciles domestic legal traditions. In the next section, we discuss the hybrid features of the ICC that emerged in negotiations between states with very distinctive political and legal preferences.

The legal structure of the International Criminal Court

In order to find a common ground between a majority of the negotiating states, the ICC drafters included provisions in the Rome Statute characteristic to both common law and civil law. Several legal scholars describe the ICC as a genuine compromise between common and civil legal traditions, which makes the Court truly unique (Christensen 2002; Tochilovsky 2002; Kress 2003; Hunt 2004; Politi and Gioa 2006). Prior to the establishment of the ICC, the procedural rules of most international adjudicative bodies resembled either common law or civil law. For example, the Nuremberg and Tokyo tribunals, the ICTY and the ICTR were heavily reliant on the adversarial procedure present in common law states. The ICJ, on the other hand, clearly follows the legal logic of the civil law tradition (Powell and Mitchell 2007). The drafters of the Rome Statute tried to avoid jargon specific to either legal family, which resulted in a set of procedural laws that reflect a compromise between the two legal traditions (Kress 2003). However, this compromise was not easy to achieve: "The pace of work at the Ad Hoc and the Preparatory Committees was extremely slow, as delegates engaged in lengthy descriptions of the benefits and advantages of each national system, apparently having lost sight of the purpose and the negotiating nature of the meetings" (Fernández de Gurmendi 1999, 220).

Because the structure of the ICC successfully incorporates elements of both civil and common law, the Court is able to garner support from states representing both civil and common legal traditions. Many of the features of the ICC have been adopted as the result of critical analysis of its two predecessors, the ICTY and the ICTR. The legal structure of the ICC incorporates several features embedded in both of these tribunals, including some of their strengths and shortcomings. Even though major lessons from both the ICTY and ICTR were embedded into the structure of the ICC, several crucial differences remain. The ICC is complementary to domestic jurisdictions, embraces novel jurisdictional definitions, and has been established under the Rome Statute, not under the UN Charter (Schiff 2008, 45). Additionally, the hybrid civil-common law nature of the ICC, the product of lengthy negotiations between representatives from both of these domestic legal systems, stands in sharp contrast with the mostly adversarial nature of the *ad hoc* tribunals.[11] Schiff (2008, 48–49) describes the nature of the latter courts in the following way:

> The ad hoc tribunals' rules were devised hurriedly primarily by experts from the United States and Great Britain. As a consequence, apart from lacking juries, they are built on common-law blueprints of adversarial proceedings mediated by neutral, "referee" judges. The pattern of prosecutorial initiative in bringing and shaping cases in the tribunals reflect the dominance of common-law concepts in their creation.

The UN Security Council decided that the tribunal judges should be vested with the rights to develop the tribunal's rules of procedure. Judge Antonio Cassese, who has been elected as the ICTY's first President, pressed for a very quick creation and promulgation of these rules. Williams and Scharf (2002, 106) aptly describe the consequences of this decision: "The United States quickly prepared a lengthy draft set of rules for the judges' consideration, along with a detailed commentary explaining the purpose and application of each proposed rule. With the short timeframe, and no other detailed proposals to draw from, the judges agreed to the U.S. draft as their starting point." The resulting set of the tribunal's procedural rules embraced the adversarial approach to litigation, characteristic to the common law system (Bassiouni 1996; Tochilovsky 2002; Williams and Scharf 2002). The ICTY's rules of procedure embrace very few inquisitorial elements such as no jury, no rule against hearsay evidence, and verdicts and sentences that can be appealed by the defendant and the prosecution (Schiff 2008, 59). Subsequently, the ICTR adopted the ICTY's rules. In both of these courts, trials were largely adversarial, "pitting prosecution against defense in front of a panel of judges that would serve as referees, occasional inquisitors, and determiners of guilt" (Schiff 2008, 59). Both *ad hoc* tribunals embraced the adversarial approach to litigation because lawyers with a common

---

[11] The Nuremberg and Tokyo tribunals were also based on the Anglo-American adversarial system. Some of the adversarial features of these two tribunals included "the defendant's right to a detailed indictment, to conduct his own defence or to have assistance of counsel, as well as to present evidence and cross-examine witnesses" (Cryer *et al.* 2007, 351).

law background had the "prevailing influence among the draftsmen" (Cassese 2008, 369).[12]

Numerous times at the ICC bargaining table, it became clear that the negotiated criminal court would not follow the adversarial path of its two *ad hoc* predecessors. Civil law representatives insisted that elements of an inquisitorial approach to litigation be incorporated into the ICC structure. Schiff (2008, 128–129) aptly describes this situation:

The dominance of common-law traditions, and their perpetrator focus, in the ICTY and ICTR grated especially upon representatives of European civil-law states, most notably France, in which the turn toward victims was particularly strong. France generally wanted the Rome Statute to include more of its civil-law tradition than had the tribunals, flowing from genuine conviction of the value of victim representation at court and perhaps as well from national pride considerations.

We describe these negotiations in more detail below. We focus our discussion on four design features of the ICC that illustrate the ultimate hybrid nature of the court: (1) the nature of the trial, (2) the position of the ICC judges during proceedings, (3) admission of guilt of the accused, and (4) appeal proceedings.

The nature of the trial

Civil law and common law systems differ sharply with respect to the nature of the trial. In the common law adversarial approach to litigation, the trial constitutes a contest between two parties who have to prove their case to the court. Litigating parties conduct "one-sided" investigations, which means *inter alia* that the prosecution has no legal obligation to actively look for exonerating evidence. In contrast, in civil law systems, which take an inquisitorial approach to litigation, the trial is not seen as a duel between two adversaries: "[T]he State has an obligation to investigate both incriminating and exonerating circumstances equally. The defense plays an active role in the State's investigation" (Tochilovsky 2002, 269).

The Preparatory Committee helped to reconcile competing civil law and common law perspectives on the nature of the trial: "At the final session of the Preparatory Committee in April 1998, a group of delegations from both civil and common law traditions achieved a major breakthrough. The group met informally and managed to simplify and restructure in a substantial way articles pertaining to proceedings of

---

[12] Cassese (2008, 369) also observes that to expedite the proceedings, over time it became necessary to depart in some sense from the adversarial model.

the pretrial" (Fernández de Gurmendi 1999, 223). Some features of the Court, such as disclosure obligations, stem directly from common law. Disclosure obligations refer to a process that may constitute a part of legal proceedings, whereby parties inform (disclose) to other parties the existence of any relevant documents that are, or have been, in their control. There are also features adapted from the civil law, such as the duty of the prosecutor to investigate both incriminating and exonerating circumstances equally in order to find the truth, which mirrors inquisitorial procedures in civil law systems (Article 54 of the Rome Statute). In general, the Court's prosecutor is designed according to a common law model. However, the civil-law-based Pre-Trial Chamber of the Court tilts its structure back to a "more even balance between the two traditions" (Schiff 2008, 11).

Position of the judges during proceedings

Civil (inquisitorial) and common (adversarial) approaches to litigation differ sharply in the way that they regulate the position of a judge during the proceedings. In the strictest version of the adversarial approach, "the judge is conceived of as a mere arbiter of the issues raised by the parties and has to form his or her decision exclusively on the basis of evidence and elements submitted by the latter" (Politi and Gioia 2006, 112). In an inquisitorial system, the judge is very active during the proceedings and endeavors to ascertain the facts while concurrently representing the interests of the state in a trial. Far from being a passive recipient of information, a civil law judge bears the primary responsibility of supervising the assembly of necessary evidence. The "proper" position of the judge during proceedings was a source of strong contention between civil and common law negotiators in Rome.

Delegations coming from the common law traditions felt that any judicial intervention during an investigation, apart from the traditional warrant issuance function, could affect the independence of the Prosecutor. The contrary position was argued by delegates from countries with a civil law tradition who claimed that justice required the existence of at least some degree of judicial supervision and intervention so that the accused was guaranteed sufficient means to prepare his or her defense and that power was not abused by the Prosecutor. (Guariglia 1999, 228)

The ultimate compromise created a position for ICC judges that is very similar to civil law judges: they are "vested with autonomous powers, most notably relating to the collection of evidence, namely in the exercise of their function and responsibility to protect the rights and interests of the defense" (Politi and Gioia 2006, 112). ICC judges have the power to request evidence in addition to that already collected prior to the trial (Article 64(6)(d) of the Rome Statute), and the Trial Chamber can require "a more complete presentation of the alleged facts" (rule 69 of the Rules of Procedure).

Admission of guilt of the accused

The ICC rules governing an admission of guilt by the accused provide another example of a truly hybrid civil-common regulation. In common law, admission of guilt by the accused leads to conviction and the end of the trial if it was voluntary, unequivocal, and informed. In civil law, such a situation does not necessarily mean that the accused will be convicted; the judge can always decide not to convict the accused based on different or additional evidence (Bosly 2004). This was another point of contention between the common and civil law delegates in Rome. During the lengthy process of ICC negotiations, "it soon became evident that the concept of the guilty plea was the 'test case' for the Preparatory Committee's ability and willingness to arrive at solutions which accommodated concepts from both the common law and the civil law legal systems" (Behrens 1999, 241). Civil and common law delegations worked out a solution that avoided using the familiar terminology of both common or civil legal traditions, and thus "the proposal achieved immediate support" (Behrens 1999, 242). Article 65(2) of the Rome Statute reflects this ultimate compromise: the Chamber may convict the accused based on his/her admission of guilt and end the trial; however, the Chamber is not required to do so.

Appeal proceedings

A unique solution was adopted by the Rome Statute in the context of appeal proceedings. Most legal scholars hold that appeal proceedings are typical of the inquisitorial rather than of the accusatorial systems. In the latter, the right to appeal is allowed only under narrow terms, and "the relevant proceedings are conceived of more as a revision of first instance proceedings, aimed at identifying and remedying failures of the proceedings in first instance, rather than as a 'second' proceeding bearing on the very same facts as examined in the first instance phase" (Politi and Gioia 2006, 115). The ICC again embodies solutions promoted by both common and civil legal traditions. Similar to the civil law approach to appeal, the right of appeal in the ICC is recognized on a wide basis, although the appeal proceedings are not considered to be a new trial on the same facts, a rule that stems from the adversarial, common law approach.

Islamic law and the International Criminal Court

As the above section shows, the writers of the Rome Statute relied on both civil (inquisitorial) and common (adversarial) approaches to litigation. What about the third major legal tradition of the world, Islamic law? The acute differences between Islamic law and Western legal systems constituted a large obstacle at the Rome conference. Much like in the bargaining processes that created other international judicial bodies, Islamic law was largely neglected in the ICC negotiations. First of all, since the Islamic legal tradition is the least widespread among the three major legal systems of the world, Islamic law states constituted by far the smallest group amongst the negotiators.[13] Thus, their bargaining power was much smaller in comparison with civil or common law states.

Furthermore, relations between Islamic law states and international institutions, especially international courts, have been on shaky ground due to the inherent link between Islamic law and the Islamic faith (Brower and Sharpe 2003; Roach 2005). Wippman (2004, 162) describes the attitude of the Arab states towards the Court as "hostile," arguing that Islamic states "feared that the ICC would be used as a tool of Western interests and that their nationals and government officials might some day be subject to ICC investigation and prosecution." The fact that Muslim judges are unlikely to sit on the Court further complicates matters for Islamic law states, who fear that non-Islamic judges "may not be familiar with or sensitive to the *Shari'a* principles and that, consequently, justice may not be carried out as it should be" (Abtahi 2005, 646). Also problematic is the reality that under strict Islamic principles, a Muslim may not be judged by non-Muslim judges (Abtahi 2005). As described in Chapter 2, the renewed interest in religious sources, which characterizes the "modernist tendency" in Islamic law, further separates the Western legal science from the Islamic legal science.

Moreover, some Islamic law states, such as Saudi Arabia, Bahrain, Kuwait, Oman, and Yemen, self-identify as "Arab Islamic states." This term is meant to convey the inherent bond between *Shari'a*, or Islamic law, state rule, the monarch, and citizens. The direct incorporation of *Shari'a* into a state's political affairs is expressed, for example, in the constitution of Sudan, where Article 4 asserts that God holds supreme authority "over both sovereignty and the state" (Roach 2005, 146). This stipulation sets *Shari'a* above all man-made laws, including international

---

[13] In 1998, the year that the Rome Statute was signed, the distribution of domestic legal families was as follows: 53% civil law states, 24% common law states, 13% Islamic law states, and 10% mixed law states. See Table 4.3.

law. Unlike Western legal systems, there is no division between state-level decision-making and the Islamic religion in Islamic law. This implies that judges operating in Islamic domestic legal systems use *Shari'a* to "determine which criminal penalties to impose on Muslims accused of violating *shari'a* codes" (Roach 2005, 153). The ICC would have the power to subject citizens of an Islamic state to secular international laws, which gives the ICC jurisdictional power that goes directly against the Islamic faith.

Generally speaking, domestic criminal laws in most Islamic states stand in sharp contrast to international criminal law. M. Cherif Bassiouni, the Chairman of the drafting Committee at the Rome Conference, described Islamic criminal law in the following way: "Arab Islamic states have generally failed to adopt a 'progressive codification of Islamic criminal justice (procedure and administration), which could sift through and distill the law and practices of Islam and adapt it to a contemporary framework which would keep faith with the past, while setting the foundations for the future.'" (Bassiouni 1982, 42; cited in Roach 2005, 154) In short, Islamic criminal law is fundamentally different from Western legal traditions and international criminal law, and these stark differences ultimately minimized the impact of the Islamic legal tradition on the structure and procedures of the ICC.

Testable implications

The process of purposefully implanting domestic legal rules and procedures into a new international court was evident during the ICC negotiations, where civil law and common law negotiators pushed strongly for familiar rules and procedures relating to the nature of the trial, the position of the ICC judges during proceedings, admission of guilt of the accused, and appeal proceedings. States' representatives present in Rome, who oftentimes had an extensive legal background, naturally gravitated towards institutions present in their own state's legal system. Professor James Crawford, who chaired the Working Group for an International Criminal Court, has described how the Commission "had also to contend with the tendency of each duly socialized lawyer to prefer his own criminal justice system's values and institutions" (Crawford 1995, 404).

As our discussion of the ICC structure shows, the Court constitutes a true hybrid of civil and common legal procedures. States representing these two domestic legal systems were represented in large numbers throughout the negotiating process. As the primary designers of the ICC, civil and common law states have invested a lot of effort to mold the structure of the Court to their expectations. The high sunk costs and fulfilled expectations regarding the structure of the ICC imply that civil law and common law states will be most supportive of the Court. Islamic law states were largely underrepresented throughout the negotiating process, thus their investment in the ICC is much smaller than that of "Western" law states. The unfriendly relationship between Islamic law and international criminal law reduces Islamic law states' support for the ICC.

Once the originators of a new international court have locked in a particular institutional design, they face greater costs for reneging in their commitment to the court in comparison with later joiners. The originators of a new court may face greater international and domestic audience costs for failing to support the court at some later date, which creates a system whereby most originators are defenders of the status quo. We expect that civil and common law states are more likely to sign and ratify the Rome Statute than states with Islamic or mixed legal traditions. These states were the main designers of the Court. Thus, the structure of the ICC, a true hybrid of these two domestic legal systems, gives civil and common law states a greater advantage in knowing the rules and procedures of the Court. The mixture of common and civil law elements of litigation provides these states with clues about the outcomes of future cases. It also reduces uncertainty about the procedures the Court will apply for initiating criminal proceedings. Islamic law did not influence the legal structure of the ICC. Consequently, signature and ratification of the Rome Statute does not benefit these states in the same way that it does civil and common law states. Islamic law states face greater uncertainty when dealing with the ICC. Of course, all states – civil, common, and Islamic – stand behind a veil of uncertainty with regard to potential outcomes of the settlement. The degree of uncertainty, however, is smaller for the Western legal systems. States with mixed law systems should also be less accepting of the ICC given the difficulties they have reconciling their domestic legal traditions with the rules and procedures of the criminal court. This leads to two primary testable hypotheses:[14]

> *Hypothesis 4.1: States with Western legal systems (civil and common) are more likely to sign the Rome Statute than states with Islamic and mixed law systems.*

> *Hypothesis 4.2: States with Western legal systems (civil and common) are more likely to ratify the Rome Statute than states with Islamic and mixed law systems.*

---

[14] Below we discuss the distinctions between treaty signature and treaty ratification. We view ratification as a stronger legal commitment.

Table 4.1 *Descriptive statistics for Chapter 4*

Variable	N	Mean	Std. dev.	Min.	Max.
ICC signature	1,353	0.650	0.477	0	1
ICC ratification	1,353	0.265	0.442	0	1
Civil law	1,353	0.530	0.499	0	1
Common law	1,353	0.241	0.428	0	1
Islamic law	1,353	0.131	0.337	0	1
Mixed law	1,353	0.098	0.298	0	1
Rule of law	968	3.856	1.390	0.5	6
Democracy	1,042	0.569	0.495	0	1
Military expenditures	1,123	5,659.4	31,109.9	0	480,451
Recent civil war	1,353	0.239	0.427	0	1

Empirical evidence: signature and ratification of the International Criminal Court

The temporal domain of this study is 1998–2004, since the Rome Statute was opened for signature and ratification in 1998. The end year reflects restrictions on some of the variables we employ as control variables. The basic unit of analysis in our empirical models is the state-year.[15] The ICC Statute allows state parties to withdraw from the Court if they provide a one-year notice (Article 127(1)), but so far no state has done so. Our main goal is to explain the variation in states' decisions to sign or ratify the Rome Statute, which is why we employ logit models for signature and ratification. To distinguish between the decisions of the Court's originators and states that signed or ratified the Rome Statute at a later date (the joiners), we coded the 161 states involved in the Rome negotiations as originators. Descriptive statistics for all variables employed in our analyses can be found in Table 4.1.

Signature/ratification of the Rome Statute

We code two dependent variables: signature and ratification (or accession) to the Rome Statute. Signature is not legally binding, but it indicates a state's readiness to participate in discussions relating to the formation of the ICC and a pledge not to actively undercut the ICC (Simmons and Danner 2010; Swaine 2003). As such, the act of signing

---

[15] States are defined according to the Correlates of War Project's definition for system membership (Small and Singer 1982). For a list of system members, see www.correlatesofwar.org.

the Rome Statute alone does not commit a state to the ICC's jurisdiction. Signature, although not legally binding, carries an important message to the international community, and shapes other states' perception of the signing state; it has an "expressive value" (Simmons and Danner 2010, 21). Ratification (or accession) carries more weight, since it is legally binding, which makes the commitment more difficult and costly to reverse. We expect common and civil law states to sign and ratify the Rome Statute more frequently than Islamic or mixed law states, although the relationship should be strongest in the ratification stage given the legal ramifications of this act.

Domestic legal traditions

In order to capture the impact of divergent domestic legal families on the propensity of states to sign and ratify the Rome Statute, we utilize the four mutually exclusive domestic legal-tradition categories discussed in Chapter 2: (1) civil law, (2) common law, (3) Islamic law, and mixed law (see Box 2.1). The analyses are estimated with Islamic law as the (omitted) reference category. In this sample, the breakdown of state-years by legal tradition is as follows: civil law (53%), common law (24%), Islamic law (13%), and mixed law (10%). Box 4.1 provides a list of countries grouped by domestic legal type, as well as the dates of their signature and/or ratification of the Rome Statute, where applicable (see also Kritzer 2002).

Control variables

We include three control variables in our analyses: rule of law, military expenditures, and regime type.[16] The first variable, rule of law, captures an additional dimension of the *legal* aspects of support for the ICC, while the latter variables (capabilities, regime type) capture the *political* aspects of the process. The structural and procedural features of the ICC reflect a strong commitment to the rule of law. The independence of the Court and its prosecutor from any type of direct political control reflects the outlook of highly legitimate domestic legal systems where the rule of law abides. Danner (2003, 515) rightly noticed that the legal features of the newly established Court transform the Court "from a political body festooned with the trappings of law to a legal institution with strong political undertones."

---

[16] Two of these measures, capabilities and regime type, are also employed in Chapters 5, 6 and 7. We do not utilize the rule-of-law measure in all chapters due to the temporal restrictions that it imposes. In robustness checks in this chapter, we also include measures found in other analyses of ICC ratification, including domestic threat, civil war, previous instances of torture, and membership in pacific settlement treaties.

Box 4.1 Domestic legal traditions and signature/ratification of the Rome Statute*

Common law countries

Antigua & Barbuda (1998/2001), Australia (1998/2002), Bahamas (2000/no), Bangladesh (1999/no), Barbados (2000/2002), Belize, Bhutan, Canada (1998/2000), Cyprus, Dominica (2001a)**, Federated States of Micronesia, Fiji (1999/1999), Ghana (1998/1999), Grenada, Guyana (2000/2004), India, Ireland (1998/2002), Jamaica (2000/no), Kenya (1998/2005), Kiribati, Lesotho (1998/2000), Liberia (1998/2004), Malawi (1999/2002), Malaysia, Marshall Islands (2000/2000), Myanmar, Nauru (2000/2001), Nepal, New Zealand (1998/2000), Palau, Papua New Guinea, Philippines (2000/no), Samoa (1998/2002), Sierra Leone (1998/2000), Singapore, Solomon Islands (1998/no), St. Kitts-Nevis (2006a), St. Lucia (1999/no), St. Vincent and Grenadines (2002a), Tanzania (2000/2002), Tonga, Trinidad and Tobago (1999/1999), Tuvalu, Uganda (1999/2002), United Kingdom (1998/2001),United States of America (2000/no), Zambia (1998/2002), Zimbabwe (1998/no)

Civil law countries

Albania (1998/2003), Andorra (1998/2001), Argentina (1999/2001), Austria (1999/2000), Belgium (1998/2000), Bolivia (1998/2002), Bosnia-Herzegovina (2000/2002), Brazil (2000/2002), Bulgaria (1999/2002), Chile (1998/no), Colombia (1998/2002), Costa Rica (1998/2001), Croatia (1998/2001), Cuba, Czech Republic (1999/no), Dominican Republic (2000/2005), Ecuador (1998/2002), El Salvador, France (1998/2000), Germany (1998/2000), Greece (1998/2002), Guatemala, Haiti (1999/no), Honduras (1998/2002), Hungary (1999/2001), Italy (1998/1999), Liechtenstein (1998/2001), Luxembourg (1998/2000), Macedonia (1998/2002), Mexico (2000/2005), Moldova (2000/no), Monaco (1998/no), Netherlands (1998/2001), Nicaragua, Panama (1998/2002), Paraguay (1998/2001), Peru (2000/2001), Poland (1999/2001), Portugal (1998/2002), San Marino (1998/1999), Slovakia (1998/2002), Slovenia (1998/2001), Spain (1998/2000), Suriname, Switzerland (1998/2001), Uruguay (2000/2002), Venezuela (1998/2000), Yugoslavia (2000/2001)

Islamic law countries

Afghanistan (2003a), Algeria (2000/no), Bahrain (2000/no), Comoros (2000/2006), Egypt (2000/no),Gambia (1998/2002), Iran (2000/no),

Iraq, Jordan (1998/2002), Kuwait (2000/no), Lebanon, Libya, Maldives, Mauritania, Morocco (2000/no), Namibia (1998/2002), Nigeria (2000/2001), Oman (2000/no), Pakistan, Qatar, Saudi Arabia, Sudan (2000/no), Syria (2000/no), Tunisia, United Arab Emirates (2000/no), Yemen (2000/no)

Mixed law countries

Botswana (2000/2000), Brunei, Cameroon (1998/no), China, Eritrea (1998/no), Israel (2000/no), Japan (2007a), Kenya (1999/2005), Malta (1998/2002), Myanmar, Niger (1998/2002), Rwanda, Senegal (1998/1999), Seychelles (2000/no), Somalia, South Africa (1998/2000), Sri Lanka, Thailand (2000/no), Vanuatu

* The first number in the parentheses is the date of signature; the second number is the date of ratification.
** "a" indicates accession to the Rome Treaty.

The existing literature provides two opposing arguments regarding the relationship between domestic rule of law and states' international behavior towards international courts. Some scholars suggest that states with a high degree of respect for the rule of law domestically should be less likely to sign on to binding international agreements. Because states with high internal respect for the rule of law are more likely to comply with their international agreements, they enter only into international commitments that they can keep (Slaughter 1995; Simmons 1998; Simmons 2000; Goldsmith and Posner 2005; Powell 2006a; Kelley 2007). Citizens in countries where the rule of law is respected internally expect the government to abide by the rule of law internationally. Defection from international commitments can damage states' reputation both internationally and domestically, which makes high rule-of-law states cautious about their international commitments.

An opposing argument suggests that high respect for the rule of law domestically should encourage a state to support legitimate adjudicative institutions and regimes internationally (Powell 2006a). The Rome Statute rests on the principle of complementarity, which allows states who have jurisdiction over a case to first investigate the case themselves; in other words, the ICC is permitted to act only if a state fails to act. More specifically, according to Article 17 of the Statute, the ICC can exercise its jurisdiction over a case if "the state is unwilling or unable genuinely to carry out the investigation or prosecution." It is reasonable to imagine that states with highly legitimate domestic legal systems do not foresee the ICC to ever exercise its jurisdiction over them. They probably think of themselves as never becoming "unwilling" or "unable" to handle a case domestically because they already have strong domestic adjudicative structures.[17] States with low internal respect for the rule of law, on the other hand, are plagued with highly deficient and corrupt judicial structures, making them more susceptible to Article 17. This perspective suggests that states with high internal respect for the rule of law should be more likely to support the ICC.[18]

We measure domestic rule of law using the *International Country Risk Guide (ICRG)* "Law and Order" measure, which provides quantitative expert assessments of the strength of the law and order tradition in various countries. This variable ranges from 0.5 to 6. Low scores indicate deficient legal systems with recurrent use of extralegal activities, such as illegal means for settling disputes. High scores describe states with sound and legitimate legal systems. Several scholars have used ICRG scores to measure legal system quality and the rule of law (e.g. Kelley 2007), and to measure the domestic costs of legal enforcement of international human rights commitments (Goodliffe and Hawkins 2009; Powell and Staton 2009).

In addition to the rule of law, we also consider states' capabilities as an important factor predicting commitments to international courts. As noted earlier, some powerful states like the United States and China feared a strong ICC. One of the goals of the ICC is to curtail atrocities that oftentimes result from war. Strong states are more likely than weak states to be subject to the ICC's investigations and judgments since they are more likely to engage in activities that fall under the ICC's jurisdiction. Strong states are likely to view the ICC as a threat to their sovereignty, while less powerful states see the ICC's impartial adjudication as a protection from human rights abuses and a supplement to their own judicial system, especially if they have insufficient resources to prosecute criminal behavior. For example, several Caribbean states lobbied the UN to move forward in the creation of an international criminal court because they had difficulties policing drug trafficking in their domestic courts. Weak states are also likely to support international courts because they are disadvantaged in interstate bargaining (Struett and Weldon 2006). To measure states' capabilities, we employ the SIPRI (Stockholm International Peace Research Institute) data on military expenditures in

[17] Report of the Ad Hoc Committee on the Establishment of an International Criminal Court, UN GAOR, 50th Session, Supp. No. 22, para. 47, UN Doc. A/50/22 (1995).
[18] This argument contrasts with the theory advanced by Simmons and Danner (2010), who show that the support for the ICC is very strong among states with violent conflict in their past but without domestic accountability systems.

millions of US dollars, at constant (2005) prices and exchange rates.[19] This data covers a wide time span, coded through 2005.[20]

The final control variable that we employ captures the democratic legalist perspective, which asserts that democracies' respect for judicial processes, the rule of law, and consideration for constitutional constraints carries over into international relations (Simmons 1999). Democracies are likely to engage third parties in the resolution of disputes in binding ways such as adjudication or arbitration due to their trust in legal procedures (Raymond 1994; Mitchell 2002). In the context of the ICC, as Kelley (2007, 577) suggests, democracies should be more likely to support the Court since it has been created "to punish offenders of democracy itself: those who dictate viciously and who violently oppress the freedom of their people." Democracies should be more likely to ratify the ICC once they have signed the treaty because they are more likely to keep the promises they make (Dixon 1994; Leeds 1999) due to their accountability to domestic audiences (Fearon 1994; Schultz 2001) and their ability to anchor international obligations in domestic law more firmly (Slaughter 1995; Morrow 2007). To measure each state's democracy level in a given year, we use the Polity IV dataset (Jaggers and Gurr 1995), which combines information from four institutional characteristics into a single democracy score ranging from 0 (least democratic) to 10 (most democratic).[21] We create a dummy variable to delineate democratic states (6 or higher) and non-democratic states (5 or lower).[22]

Empirical analyses

Table 4.2A reports the percentage of states representing each of the legal traditions for 1998, the year that the Rome Statute came up for signature, as well as the percentage of states that comprised the "like-minded" states that openly supported the creation of the ICC (Schabas 2007). Table 4.2B

---

[19] Data available at www.sipri.org/research/armaments/milex.

[20] The national capabilities index as developed by Singer *et al.* (1972) (Composite Index of National Capability – CINC) is presently available only until 2001, which would significantly limit the time span of our analyses. However, when we estimate models with CINC scores, we get virtually identical empirical results.

[21] This includes the competitiveness of political participation, the level of constraints on the chief executive, and the openness and competitiveness of chief executive recruitment.

[22] We tried other democracy measures as well, including the interval level Polity IV democracy score, the democracy minus autocracy scale from Polity IV, and the Freedom House scale of democracy. The results for the multivariate model are sensitive to the particular measure of regime type employed due to the multicollinearity between democracy, rule of law, and civil legal type. The results we present are fairly typical, whereby the inclusion of democracy diminishes the effect of legal variables in the signature but not the ratification stage.

Table 4.2 *Rome Statute ratification and signature rates (N = 192)*
A: legal tradition frequency at Rome negotiations

Legal system	% of all states 1998	% of all "like-minded" states 1998
Civil law	53.1	65.1
Common law	24.0	23.8
Islamic law	13.0	4.8
Mixed law	9.9	6.3

B: legal tradition frequency for states signing and ratifying the Rome Statute (2004)

Legal system	% total	% signature All	Originators	Joiners	% ratification All	Originators	Joiners
Civil law	53.1	56.2	60.3	20.0	63.3	68.2	20.0
Common law	24.0	23.3	19.1	60.0	26.5	21.6	70.0
Islamic law	13.0	12.3	13.0	6.7	5.1	4.6	10.0
Mixed law	9.9	8.2	7.6	13.3	5.1	5.7	0.0

reports the percentages of states signing and ratifying the Rome Statute as of 2004, broken down into the originator and joiner groups of states.

Our theoretical hypotheses find preliminary support; the percentage of civil law states that have signed (56%) or ratified (63%) the Rome Statute as of 2004 is higher than the percentage of civil law states in the system (53%). In addition, civil law states constitute by far the largest group of states that have signed and ratified the Rome Statute. Similarly, the percentage of common law ratifying states (26.5%) is higher than the percentage of common law states in the system (24%). Islamic law states constitute a much smaller group among the signatories (12%) and the ratifying states (5%).

The group of like-minded states was led by civil law (65.1%) and common law (23.8%) states, which helps to explain the *sui generis* design that emerged in the negotiations at Rome.[23] When we separate the originator states from states that joined the ICC at a later date (joiners), we see that

[23] The chi-square test for independence linking legal system type to like-minded status is highly significant: F = 60.57, p < 0.001.

Table 4.3 *Signature and ratification of the Rome Statute, 1998–2004*

Variable	Model 1: signature, all states	Model 2: ratification, all states	Model 3: signature, all states	Model 4: ratification, all states	Model 5: signature, originators	Model 6: ratification, originators
Civil law	0.90**	1.69**	0.18	0.97**	0.15	1.18**
system	(0.17)	(0.28)	(0.27)	(0.37)	(0.27)	(0.41)
Common	0.43**	1.54**	0.07	0.96**	0.32	1.24**
law system	(0.19)	(0.30)	(0.28)	(0.39)	(0.29)	(0.42)
Mixed legal	0.22	0.76**	−0.32	0.65	−0.41	0.81*
system	(0.23)	(0.36)	(0.34)	(0.44)	(0.35)	(0.48)
Rule of law	—	—	0.03	0.13**	−0.04	0.12*
			(0.06)	(0.06)	(0.06)	(0.06)
Democracy	—	—	0.91**	1.01**	1.17**	1.12**
			(0.22)	(0.24)	(0.23)	(0.24)
Military	—	—	−(0.00)	−0.00**	−(0.00)	−0.00**
expenditures			(0.00)	(0.00)	(0.00)	(0.00)
Constant	0.03	−2.38**	0.23	−2.90**	0.41	−3.10**
	(0.15)	(0.27)	(0.30)	(0.42)	(0.31)	(0.46)
Sample size	1,353	1,353	806	806	777	777
Chi-square	35.83**	40.99**	43.81**	61.09**	56.00**	69.00**

Entries are coefficients followed by robust standard errors: *p < 0.10; ** p < 0.05.

civil law states provided the strongest signature support at the court's inception stage (60.3%), while common law states comprised the largest group of later joiners (60%); a similar pattern emerges for ratification as well (civil law states are 68% of the originator ratifying states, common law states are 70% of the joiner ratifying states). While the court's design was well-suited to both civil and common law countries, civil law states were more supportive at the creation stage.

Turning to multivariate analyses, Table 4.3 presents logit models (with robust standard errors) for ICC signature and ICC ratification. In Models 1 and 2, we examine the effects of states' domestic legal traditions on their signature and ratification decisions. We estimate a simplified model due to the loss of 40 percent of the cases (via list-wise case deletion) when control variables are added. Models 3 and 4 report the baseline models for all states with the control variables included, while Models 5 and 6 estimate the multivariate models for the group of originator (negotiating) states at Rome. The substantive effects for all variables are presented in Table 4.4; the predicted probabilities are generated with

Table 4.4 *Substantive effects*

Variable	Predicted probability (signature)*			Predicted probability (ratification)		
	All states (#1)	All states (#3)	Originators (#5)	All states (#2)	All states (#4)	Originators (#6)
Civil law system	0.72	0.81	0.82	0.31	0.39	0.41
Common law system	0.61	0.78	0.84	0.30	0.39	0.42
Islamic law system	0.51	0.77	0.80	0.09	0.20	0.18
Mixed law system	0.56	0.71	0.73	0.17	0.32	0.32
Rule of law (0.5 to 6)		0.79, 0.81	0.84, 0.81		0.29, 0.46	0.31, 0.47
Democracy (0 to 1)		0.63, 0.81	0.59, 0.82		0.19, 0.39	0.19, 0.41
Military expenditures (0–480,451)		0.81, 0.64	0.82, 0.61		0.40, 0.05	0.41, 0.04

* The numbers in parentheses refers to the model numbers in Table 4.3.

Clarify[24] (King *et al.* 2000), setting each variable at its mean or mode while varying the variable of interest.

Hypotheses 4.1 and 4.2 find empirical support, as the coefficients for the civil law and common law dummy variables in Table 4.3 are both positive and highly significant in the signature (Model 1) and ratification equations (Models 2 and 4).[25] This bolsters our expectation that states with common or civil law domestic legal systems would be more likely to sign onto and commit fully to the ICC. The results are weaker for ICC signature when we add the control variables due to the loss of cases, as well as a fairly high level of correlation between democracy, rule of law, and domestic legal systems (civil law, common law) in the set of reduced cases. When we take into account states' regime type, rule of law, and military expenditures, the signature and ratification rates are very

[24] Clarify: Software for interpreting and presenting statistical results, available at: http://gking.harvard.edu/clarify/docs/clarify.html.
[25] We also estimated a more recent model using ratification and domestic legal tradition data up through to 2008. The results are virtually identical to the coefficients reported in Table 4.4.

similar for both civil and common law states. As we see in Table 4.4, the predicted probability of signature is 0.81 for civil law states and 0.78 for common law states, while the ratification rates are 0.31 (civil) and 0.30 (common) accordingly. This fits with our argument that the Court was established as a civil law-common law hybrid court, enhancing its appeal to states with these domestic legal systems.

Interestingly, the predicted probabilities for signature are much higher for all legal types when compared with ratification. States realize that signature of the ICC treaty can improve their image on the international arena, even if the initial commitment is not legally binding. We should also note that the predicted probabilities for civil law and common law states are considerably higher than the probabilities for Islamic law states (0.77 signature, 0.09 ratification) and mixed law states (0.71 signature, 0.17 ratification), more than three times as large in the case of ratification.[26]

The true civil-common hybrid nature of the ICC makes both civil and common law states equally likely to support the Court. The ICC's procedural underpinnings provide these states with clues about how the Court will identify and rule on particular cases. Similarity between domestic structures of civil and common law states and the ICC also reduces uncertainty concerning interpretation of international norms. States with civil and common domestic legal systems are more likely to understand the legal structure of the ICC. At the same time, these states are better able to predict the outcome of an ICC case. Since Islamic law is largely ignored in the ICC Statute, Islamic law states are indeed less likely to sign and ratify the Statute. For these states, uncertainty concerning interpretation of legal rules and the overall legal structure of the ICC is much greater when compared with Western law states.

The ratification models produce a fairly strong fit overall. First, the chi-square values are all significant at the $< .05$ level. Second, the values for the area beneath the receiver operating characteristic curve range from 0.65 to 0.68, which indicates that the models produce a fair model fit.[27] More important than the fit for the entire model, however, is the

---

[26] We also estimated Cox proportional hazard models, which capture the time until a state signs and/or ratifies the Rome Statute. The results are extremely similar to the logit model results. We also considered the possibility for a selection effect in the signature and ratification process, estimating a Heckman selection model with the democracy variable in signature model (only) and the rule of law variable in the ratification stage (only). The Heckman model produced results identical to the separate logit models and the rho parameter was not statistically significant ($p = 0.74$).

[27] The receiver operating characterstic curve is a plot of the true positive rate against the false positive rate for the different possible cut points of a diagnostic test. The traditional academic system rates receiver operating characterstic curves on the following scale: 0.90–1 = excellent; 0.80–0.90 = good; 0.70–0.80 = fair; 0.60–0.70 = poor;

potential improvement of fit after adding the variables for domestic legal systems. This is done with a chi-square test comparing the difference between the baseline model (excluding all variables for legal systems) with the models including legal systems. Addition of these legal variables provides a significant improvement to the ratification model's (Table 4.3, Model 4) predictive power (chi-square = 5.17, p = 0.02). This suggests that domestic legal system variables are giving us purchase for predicting states' decisions to ratify the Rome Statute.

Because in this chapter we focus mainly on the originators of the ICC (Models 5 and 6 in Table 4.3), we estimate the model for only those states that were present at the 1998 Rome negotiations. The results for the originators are very similar to the estimates for all states, although mixed law is now positive and significant (p < 0.10) in the ratification stage (Model 6). In general, though, we find robust support for hypotheses 4.1 and 4.2: the originators of new courts make rational legal choices about the rules and procedures the courts will employ. If states are successful in pushing their desired legal rules in these negotiations, they are more likely to lend support to the court once it becomes established. The behavior of civil and common law states towards the ICC certainly fits this rational design story.

The control variables produce results that are mostly in line with what we expect theoretically. States with high internal respect for the rule of law are more likely to ratify the Rome Statute (Models 4 and 6), although the signature results of the logit model are not statistically significant (Models 3 and 5). States with high domestic levels of respect for the principle of the rule of law are 2.5% more likely to sign the Rome Statute (Model 3) and 58.6% more likely to ratify the Statute (Model 4). These results show that states with a significant rule of law domestically do not foresee the ICC to ever exercise its jurisdiction over them, since they are very unlikely to become unwilling or unable to handle a case domestically. States with low internal respect for the rule of law, with their deficient and corrupt judicatures, are less likely to ratify the ICC treaty. It is ratification of the Statute, not the act of signing that exposes their vulnerability to external jurisdiction for crimes against humanity.

Our results for regime type, an important political factor, demonstrate that democratic states are significantly more likely to sign (Models 3 and 5) and ratify (Models 4 and 6) the Rome Statute than non-democratic countries. Democratic states are 28.6% more likely to sign the Rome Statute than non-democratic states (Model 3) and 105% more likely

0.50–0.60 = fail. See Tape (2005) for an excellent elementary discussion of the receiver operating characterstic curve.

to ratify the Rome Statute (Model 4). Our findings sit well with the democratic legalist perspective that emphasizes that democratic nations' respect for judicial processes and the rule of law carries over into the international arena (Slaughter 1995; Simmons 1999).

Our models also show that strong states are less likely to ratify the Rome Statute than weak states (Model 4 and Model 6), although power seems to have no significant effect on the initial decision to accept the ICC. This meshes with empirical findings for the PCIJ/ICJ, which will be presented in chapter 5, where state capabilities do not influence the initial decision to recognize the Court's jurisdiction but influence the likelihood of states pulling out of the Court. The substantive effects of military expenditures in the ICC ratification model are quite large. The state in the sample with the highest military spending, the United States, had only a 0.04 probability of ratifying the ICC. States with the lowest level of military expenditures in the sample were 925 percent more likely to ratify the Rome Statute. This supports our claim that weak states have more to gain from international courts than strong states.[28]

The lack of major power commitment to the ICC is perhaps best illustrated by the United States' world-wide campaign against the Court, where countries are encouraged, if not pressured, to sign agreements not to surrender Americans to the Court. Furthermore, the United States conditioned its peacekeeping missions and military aid on the conclusion of these bilateral non-surrender agreements (Krisch 2005). In 2004, the US Congress passed the Nethercutt Amendment, which authorizes the loss of economic support funds to all countries who have ratified the ICC treaty but who have not signed a bilateral non-surrender agreement with the US. This act poses a significant threat of cuts in foreign assistance, including funds for cooperation in international security, terrorism, economic development, and human rights.

To check the robustness of our findings, a series of other control variables were added to Models 3 and 4 in Table 4.3, including membership in pacific settlement treaties, threat, and previous torture levels.[29] To ensure that state support for the ICC is unique and not simply part of a broader willingness to join IOs, we controlled for the number of institutions that states belong to that call for pacific dispute settlement. This is taken from the Multilateral Treaties of Pacific Settlement (MTOPS)

---

[28] We also examined models that interacted domestic legal system type with military capabilities. In the signature model, there is a negative interaction, such that more powerful states are less inclined to sign the Rome Statute; this holds for all types of legal systems. In the ratification model, the interaction terms are positive, suggesting that increasing capabilities leads to a stronger inclination to ratify the Rome Statute.

[29] These models are available from the authors by request.

data as coded by Paul Hensel.[30] This variable ranges from membership in 0 to 14 regional and global organizations, with an average of 5.6 institutional memberships. As the number of memberships in these organizations increases, states are somewhat more likely to ratify the Rome Statute (p = 0.077), although this variable has no effect on ICC signature (p = 0.700). The civil and common law variables retain their original sign and significance, with p-values equal to 0.01 (civil law) and 0.011 (common law) in the ratification model. We also included a measure of threat as coded by the Armed Conflict Dataset (International Peace Research Institute 2009). This variable is binary, taking a value of 1 if the state faced any form of conflict identified by the Armed Conflict Dataset and 0 otherwise (mean = 0.24, standard deviation = 0.43). This variable is not significant in the signature and ratification models and does not alter our primary findings. We included a measure of previous human rights behavior as well, as captured by the Cingranelli-Richards (CIRI) Human Right Database (Cingranelli and Richards 2008). This dummy variable equals 1 if a state engaged in torture frequently in the previous year (mean = 0.45, standard deviation = 0.50). States who torture their citizens regularly are less likely to sign and ratify the Rome Statute, as we might expect, although the effect of domestic legal traditions on ratification is robust to these additions; the p value is 0.009 for civil law and 0.025 for common law. In short, even if we control for other factors that may reduce states' willingness to join international criminal courts, we still find a robust relationship between domestic legal traditions and support for the ICC.

Finally, we compare our results to another important explanation for ICC ratification based on a credible commitment theory. Simmons and Danner (2010) argue that low credibility states (autocracies) are more likely to ratify the Rome Statute if they have experienced recent civil war in comparison to high credibility states (democracies) with histories of internal violence. On the other hand, democratic states with no history of civil war should be amenable to ratifying the Statute because they have internal judicial mechanisms for prosecuting crimes against humanity, and thus fear the ICC less than other states. In Table 4.5, we estimate the same model for ratification as presented in Table 4.4, Model 4 (all states).

Here, we control for the occurrence of civil war in the 1992–1997 time period as coded by the Uppsala/PRIO Armed Conflict Dataset, where the threshold for violence is twenty-five casualties. This coding

---

[30] This data is available at www.paulhensel.org/icow.html#mtops.

Table 4.5 *Controlling for the Simmons/Danner
credible commitment variables*

Variable	Ratification, all states
Civil law system	0.87**
	(0.38)
Common law system	0.97**
	(0.40)
Mixed legal system	0.56
	(0.46)
Rule of law	0.04
	(0.07)
Democracy	1.26**
	(0.25)
Military expenditures	−(0.00)**
	(0.00)
Civil war	−0.05
	(0.41)
Democracy* Civil War	−0.91*
	(0.48)
Constant	−2.53**
	(0.51)
Sample size	806
Chi–square	82.57**

Entries are coefficients followed by robust standard errors:
$*p < 0.10; ** p < 0.05$.

is taken from Simmons and Danner's (2010) Appendix A.[31] We interact this recent civil war measure with our dummy variable for democracy. The results are consistent with Simmons and Danner's theory, as democracies that have experienced recent civil wars are significantly less likely to ratify the Rome Statute in comparison to democracies with no civil war.[32] Our legal variables for civil law and common law are still positive and significant, showing that these are complementary explanations

---

[31] See the UCDP/PRIO Armed Conflict Dataset Codebook 3.10, Version 1–2006, (www.prio.no/sptrans/1795428530/Code_book.pdf).

[32] We also created a version of the model (not reported herein) that employs the same measures as Simmons and Danner (2010) based on the data in their appendix. This creates three categories for democracies without civil wars, democracies with civil wars, and non-democracies with civil wars. We find in this specification that only one of these variables is significant: democracies with no history of civil war are significantly more likely to ratify the ICC. Part of these differences can be attributed to different model specifications as well as different statistical modeling approaches; they employ a Cox proportional hazard model.

for ICC ratification.[33] These results demonstrate that political and legal explanations can be fruitful for explaining states' decisions to accept the jurisdiction of international courts, such as the International Criminal Court.

Conclusion

In this chapter, we presented and empirically evaluated our theoretical arguments about the motives facing the "originators" of new courts. The empirical results regarding the originators of the ICC support our general claim that states' domestic legal systems determine their bargaining positions at the negotiating table. Domestic legal traditions also influence states' decision-making processes about whether or not to join adjudicatory bodies. Originators of a new international court invest a great amount of effort into shaping the basic legal structure of the court. Once these states have locked in a particular legal design, they face very high costs for reneging in their commitment to the court in comparison with states that join the court at a later date. The fact that no originating states have left the ICC accords with this expectation. Civil and common law states purposively designed the ICC to best suit their interests. Thus, these states continue to support this international court. As we will see in the next chapter, similar patterns emerge in the context of the PCIJ/ICJ. The World Court's rules and procedures clearly reflect the civil law tradition, which helps explain why civil law states are much more likely than common, Islamic, and mixed law states to support the Court.

The ICC emerged as an interesting amalgamation of civil and common law principles. Its two *ad hoc* predecessors, the ICTY and ICTR, were largely based on common law principles. A US-composed draft of rules of procedure was quickly adapted with minor changes by the Yugoslav tribunal, and then duplicated by the Rwandan tribunal. The Rome Statute, on the other hand, emerged as a product of lengthy and meticulous negotiations. By 1998, the year of the Statute's adoption, negotiating states were able to learn from the experiences of the ICTY and ICTR. Rules of procedure and issues of jurisdiction regarding the ICC were of interest to many more states since the Court has jurisdiction over "the most serious crimes of concern to the international community as a whole" (Article 5 of the Rome Statute), and it is not limited to

---

[33] We should note, however, that the rule-of-law measure becomes insignificant when the civil war and interaction variables are added. This stems in part from the fairly sizable correlation between civil war experiences and rule of law (-0.38). Thus it is difficult to disentangle the effects of rule of law from other prominent explanations for ICC signature and ratification.

a specific conflict like the *ad hoc* tribunals. Despite the strong position of the United States, adapting a purely adversarial set of procedures was just not viable during the Rome negotiations. Both civil and common law states exerted a large influence on the creation of the Court's procedural rules.

Because the structure of the ICC successfully incorporates elements of both civil and common law, the Court is able to acquire support from a wider swathe of countries in comparison to the PCIJ/ICJ. There is an interesting selection process at work, whereby states are not equally predisposed to recognize the jurisdiction of international courts. The originators of an international court have incentives to lock in an institutional design that favors future judicial behavior, while later joiners to the court must decide if the adjudicator will be fair and balanced. The latter process, by which the joiners make decisions whether to join an existing international court, constitutes the main focus of the next two chapters.

5 Domestic legal traditions and state support for the World Court

For nearly ninety years, a World Court (PCIJ, 1920–1945; ICJ, 1946–present) has been accessible to all countries for the peaceful settlement of disputes. However, initial hopes that states would view the Court as a legitimate and effective conflict manager have not been fully realized. Only one third of countries in the world accept the compulsory jurisdiction of the Court, and an overwhelming majority of these states (84 percent) place reservations on their optional clause declarations, which can limit the Court's adjudication prerogatives. On the other hand, it is much more common for states to recognize the PCIJ/ICJ's jurisdiction through compromissory clauses in bilateral or multilateral treaties. For example, close to 80 percent of countries in the world are signatories to one or more treaties that recognize the Court's jurisdiction should a dispute arise in the context of the treaty (Powell and Mitchell 2007).[1]

In this chapter, we explore states' decisions to recognize the jurisdiction of a pre-existing international court to adjudicate interstate disputes. Why do some states accept the jurisdiction of an international court, like the ICJ, while other states do not? How do expectations about international bargaining influence unilateral state decisions to accept or not accept the jurisdiction of an international court?[2] In Chapter 3, we linked characteristics of domestic legal families (civil law, common law, and Islamic law) to our rational legal design theory of adjudication, which focuses on how adjudicators can help disputants resolve coordination problems by correlating strategies, constructing focal points, and signaling information. We also noted that states can signal information about their types through an international court by recognizing its jurisdiction.

---

[1] This figure is based on our own collection of data on compromissory clauses, described in more detail in the research design section of this chapter. The basic data on relevant treaties was obtained from the ICJ's website: www.icj-cij.org/documents/index.php?p1=4.

[2] In Chapter 7, we look at the bargaining side of the story more carefully by analyzing the effect of jurisdictional acceptance of the World Court on bargaining outcomes (e.g. reaching agreements, compliance) and bargaining failures (e.g. failed mediation, militarized conflict).

In this chapter, we argue that civil law states can correlate their bargaining strategies and generate clear focal points for coordination through the PCIJ/ICJ more easily than common law or Islamic law states due to the legal similarities between the rules and principles used by the World Court and those found in the civil tradition. This leads to our primary hypothesis that civil law states are more likely to accept the jurisdiction of the World Court than common law or Islamic law states.

We begin this chapter by providing historical background information about the formation of the PCIJ and the ICJ. Next, we provide a brief description of the substantive international law that the World Court applies. We then summarize our theoretical argument relating the institutional features of domestic legal traditions to states' unilateral choices to accept or not accept the jurisdiction of the World Court. Finally, we present a series of empirical analyses of states' acceptance of PCIJ/ICJ compulsory jurisdiction.[3] We find that civil law states are significantly more likely to accept compulsory jurisdiction than common law or Islamic law states, although civil law states' commitments to the PCIJ/ICJ are less durable than commitments made by common or Islamic law countries. Our theory highlights the importance of legal systems in world politics and sets the stage for exploring further the relationship between domestic legal institutions, commitments to international legal institutions, and interstate bargaining processes.

Historical background

The use of arbitration in world politics became more popular following the Jay Treaty of 1794 signed between the United States and the United Kingdom to resolve post-war disputes; a similar commission was established after the American Civil War to resolve the *Alabama* claims (Rosenne 1963, 13). The Hague Conferences of 1899 and 1907 further articulated legalized dispute settlement in the international arena, developing an elaborate code of procedures should bilateral negotiations fail. During World War I, several Scandinavian states, Switzerland, the Netherlands, and the United States pushed for the creation of a centralized judicial organ (Rosenne 1963, 17–20). Many NGOs and transnational groups were active in the promotion of international adjudication, including William Ladd in the Massachusetts Legislature (adopting a resolution of arbitration in 1838), the Quakers in the United States, the British Society for the Promotion of Permanent and Universal Peace, and activist groups in France and Switzerland

---

[3] We also analyze compromissory clause jurisdiction in Chapter 6.

(Allain 2000, 11–13).[4] In February 1920, a Commission of the League of Nations set out to create a new, supranational court. The project was begun despite reservations expressed by the great powers of the early twentieth century, which centered on the compulsory jurisdiction of international institutions with powers to make and enforce international law on the supranational level. After a series of thirty-five meetings, the Advisory Committee produced a draft plan for the PCIJ, with the jurists on the committee backing a plan for the Court's compulsory jurisdiction (Lloyd 1985, 30–31).[5]

The inclusion of compulsory jurisdiction in the PCIJ statute was favored for several reasons. First, the Commission believed that compulsory jurisdiction was a characteristic of a "true" court. The experience of World War I prompted the jurists to develop judicial procedures that could resolve disputes between states in a peaceful manner and, most specifically, with the aid of arbitration mechanisms that were already inserted into a sizable number of treaties. Second, the Commission believed that the Court should have compulsory jurisdiction so as to be engaged in adjudication and not in arbitration, since many states expressed reservations to the use of arbitration when their interests were not fully satisfied (Lloyd 1985, 34). Third, "parties to arbitration had to set out in the *compromis* their agreement to arbitrate and the precise nature of the dispute. In adjudication, however, the court was seen as having the powers of compulsory jurisdiction upon the application of any party to a dispute" (Lloyd 1985, 34). Therefore, a country could bring a dispute to the Court without having the adversary country present. Furthermore, the Court could establish predictability in conflict management by articulating a clear set of rules and procedures for adjudication.

Yet, the precise legal principles and rules to be employed by the PCIJ were strongly contested in negotiations surrounding the Court's establishment. For example, the inclusion of compulsory jurisdiction in the formative documents of the PCIJ led to a disagreement between the United Kingdom, France, Italy, and Japan, who opposed the idea, and the smaller powers, who demanded it (Lloyd 1985, 29). The United Kingdom, the leading common law state in the negotiations, was the first country to object to the adoption of compulsory jurisdiction, with Italy and Japan following soon after. Their objections were based on three arguments: First, the laws of naval welfare and the interpretation of belligerent maritime rights were irreconcilable across states. Second, the

---

[4] Allain (2000) also points out that compromissory clauses for arbitration were actively used by Latin American states early in the nineteenth century.
[5] For a detailed look at the committee's deliberations, see Vogiatzi (2002).

Anglo-American and European camps adopted different approaches to international law, and an international court would necessarily be forced to choose one approach over the other (Lloyd 1985, 36–37). Finally, "an international court with compulsory jurisdiction would provide the weak with a forum where they could take their grievances against the strong, and where the outcome would not be decided by the number of guns or economic power. In other words, the small stood to gain what Britain stood to lose" (Lloyd 1985, 40).[6]

Under the tutelage of the Brazilian delegate Raoul Fernandes, the League of Nations Commission reached a compromise to quiet objections to compulsory jurisdiction through inclusion of Article 36(2) in its Statute, which came to be known as the optional clause (Allain 2000, 40). Upon its reception, signatory countries accepted the Court's jurisdiction *ipso facto* and without special Convention, yet states accepting the PCIJ Statute in general were under no corresponding obligation to accept the optional clause. The PCIJ was a functioning international court between 1922 and 1940, hearing sixty cases (Hudson 1957, 569).[7]

The Court's justices pushed for relocation of the PCIJ to a neutral location in 1939 following the outbreak of World War II. While still intact, the Court remained on the sidelines throughout the war. In 1942, an Inter-American Juridical Committee advocated for the extension of the PCIJ after the war. The United Kingdom pushed for the creation of the Inter-Allied Committee in 1943; the committee developed a proposal for the successor to the PCIJ, which laid the ground work for the Dumbarton Oaks Proposals. At Dumbarton Oaks in 1944, the United Kingdom, the United States, and the Soviet Union agreed to the creation of an International Court of Justice, a proposal that was approved by the UN Conference on International Organization in 1945 (Hudson 1957; Rosenne 1957/1962).

Most legal scholars agree that the ICJ was created in the aftermath of World War II as a *successor* of the PCIJ (Gamble and Fischer 1976; Jennings and Watts 1992; Allain 2000; Janis 2003; Shaw 2003). The

---

[6] Interestingly, the British representative on the Advisory Committee, Lord Phillimore, supported compulsory jurisdiction. However, his position encountered staunch domestic opposition to the plan. Lord Curzon, the British Foreign Secretary, expressed this sentiment: "It would seem to me that Lord Phillimore or whoever represented us in framing this scheme must have been singularly oblivious to British interests" (Lloyd 1985, 35). The draft document was scrutinized carefully by British diplomats and lawyers and the British government's opposition to compulsory jurisdiction ultimately prevailed in the final design of the Court's optional clause.

[7] Rosenne (1963, 24) reports a slightly larger number than Hudson (1957); he identifies sixty-six cases brought before the PCIJ, with thirty-eight of those being contentious cases and twenty-eight being advisory.

statutes of both courts, the scope of their jurisdiction, organization, procedures, and their purposes are virtually identical. Both courts rely on equivalent sources of international law, both are to be comprised of fifteen members that shall be elected for nine years, and both are to provide states with an alternative to a forceful resolution of disputes. Declarations granting jurisdiction to the PCIJ in the optional clause or treaties/conventions continue to be in force with respect to the ICJ (Shaw 2003, 980). Article 37 of the ICJ Statute declares: "Whenever a treaty of convention in force provides for reference of a matter to a tribunal to have been instituted by the League of Nations, or to the Permanent Court of International Justice, the matter shall, as between the parties to the present Statute, be referred to the International Court of Justice." Moreover, no distinction is made between cases decided by the PCIJ and those by the ICJ (Shaw, 2003, 960); many PCIJ judgments have been highly influential for the development of international adjudication.

The most crucial difference between the Statute of the ICJ and that of its predecessor is that the ICJ was established as the principal judicial organ of the UN. The Statute of the ICJ constitutes an integral part of the Charter, and all members of the UN become *ipso facto* parties to the ICJ Statute (Gamble and Fischer 1976, 4). The PCIJ, although established under the auspices of the League of Nations, was entirely independent from the Covenant. Despite the official "independence" of the PCIJ from the League of Nations, these two international bodies were inescapably interconnected: "In spite of the formal autonomy of the two institutions, functionally the Court was a part of the machinery for the settlement of international disputes envisaged in the very conception of the League of Nations" (Gamble and Fisher 1976, 4).

The PCIJ and ICJ came into existence in the context of major systemic changes following the world wars. The crux of the problem in the negotiations for both courts, most notably the PCIJ, was a potential clash between opposing legal traditions. The originators of these new courts were enmeshed in a struggle to determine the courts' legal rules and principles. For example, negotiators of the ICJ agreed that the common law doctrine of *stare decisis* would not be applied in international law; rather the ICJ would be bound in its decision making by Article 59, which states: "The decision of the Court has no binding force except as between the parties and in respect of that particular case." As most legal scholars agree, the object of this article is simply to prevent legal principles accepted by the Court in a particular case from being binding on other states or in other disputes (Brownlie 2003). The lack of formal judicial precedent in the activity of the ICJ makes it very similar to civil legal systems where this doctrine is forbidden for the most part (Rosenne 1957/1962).

The PCIJ and ICJ, as courts of international law, also lean in the civil law direction of favoring the *bona fides* principle.[8] *Bona fides* constitutes one of the general principles of law and is considered to be one of the formal sources of international law (O'Connor 1991).[9] The ICJ has recognized the doctrine of good faith in several judgments, including the *Norwegian Fisheries* case (1951), the *North Sea Continental Shelf* cases (1969), the *Nuclear Test* cases (1973), and the *Arbitral Award made by the King of Spain on 23 December 1906* (1960).[10] Additionally, the principle of good faith is articulated in the Court's basic documents, including Article 38 of the ICJ Statute, as well as Article 2(2) of the UN Charter. The principle of good faith is sometimes viewed as an overarching principle, from which the *pacta sunt servanda* derives, and not surprisingly, the World Court also treats contractual compliance as an important part of international and customary law (O'Connor 1991).

With respect to procedural rules for evidence and admissibility, the PCIJ (and later the ICJ) adopted a set of general provisions, recognizing the Court's *compétence de la compétence*:

Only the most general provisions were included in the PCIJ Statute with respect to evidence and procedure. The stipulations that were made, which were adopted in the ICJ Statute, largely supported the freedom of action of the International Court – in both its incarnations – as to presentation and admission of evidence. In addition to articles 30 and 48, which empower the ICJ to frame rules for carrying out its functions and to "make all arrangements connected with the taking of evidence," article 49 provides that the ICJ can request the production of evidence from parties, and if the requested evidence is not produced, "formal note shall be taken of any refusal." Under article 50, the ICJ may at any time "entrust any individual, body, bureau, commission, or other organization that it may select, with the task of carrying out an enquiry or giving an expert opinion." Article 51 empowers the ICJ to put "any relevant questions" to the witnesses and experts during the hearing, and under article 52, the ICJ can refuse to admit any further oral or written evidence after the

---

[8] As noted in Chapter 2, the *bona fides* principle has three constitutive moral elements: honesty, fairness, and reason (Zimmermann and Whittaker 2000).

[9] Several international law scholars consider good faith a cornerstone of relations between nations in that it can ensure international order and guard against arbitrary behavior and even anarchy (Bull 1977; Virally 1983; Lukashuk 1989).

[10] In the *Norwegian Fisheries* case, the ICJ upheld Norway's right to establish maritime baselines, arguing that the United Kingdom could not contest them after a long period of inaction (Kolb 2006, 21). In the *North Sea Continental Shelf* cases, the ICJ recognized *estoppel*, an important doctrine derived from good faith (O'Connor 1991). In the *Nuclear Test* cases, the ICJ argued that "[o]ne of the basic principles governing the creation and performance of legal obligations, whatever their source, is the principle of good faith" (cited in Virally 1983, 130). In the *Arbitral Award* case, the ICJ argued that Nicaragua could not renege on the territorial award in the arbitration because it had agreed to carry out its terms in good faith (Kolb 2006, 22–23).

expiry of the time specified for the purpose, unless the other side consents. (Brown 2007, 87)

The more general point here is that the negotiations that gave birth to the PCIJ and ICJ produced two courts with rules and procedures that are very similar to those found in civil law systems.[11] Potential joiners to these standing international courts have considered whether or not the adjudicator would be fair, a decision that we assert is influenced by states' domestic legal institutions. In the next section, we discuss the broad relationship between international law and the World Court. This is followed by a summary of our rational legal design theory of adjudication and the primary hypotheses that we test in this chapter. To understand the expansion of state support for international courts, we must journey into the nexus of domestic and international law.

International law and the World Court

While performing its functions, the Court is to apply the rules of international law as included in Article 38 of its Statute (treaties, custom, general principles of law, etc.). Additionally, under Article 38(2), the ICJ may, at the request of the disputants, decide a case *ex aequo et bono*, i.e. relying on justice and equity. This method of reaching a decision has certain merits, such as absolute flexibility, but at the price of uncertainty regarding the basis of the decision (Merrills 2005, 162). Perhaps that is why this provision has never been put into practice. Article 36(2), known as the optional clause, is of great importance in broadening the ICJ's jurisdiction:[12]

The states parties to the present Statute may at any time declare that they recognize as compulsory ipso facto and without special agreement, in relation to any other state accepting the same obligation, the jurisdiction of the Court in all legal disputes concerning:

(a) The interpretation of a treaty;
(b) Any question of international law;
(c) The existence of any fact which, if established, would constitute a breach of an international obligation;
(d) The nature or extent of the reparation to be made for the breach of an international obligation.

[11] This is an interesting outcome given that the United States and the United Kingdom were strong advocates for the creation of an international court during World War II (Gross 1987, 19). The failure of the United States to join the League of Nations, as well as domestic opposition to a strong court in the United Kingdom, contributed to the establishment of a world court with civil law design features.

[12] This is available at www.icj-cij.org/documents/index.php?p1=4&p2=2&p3=0.

Importantly, Article 36(2) of the Statute also declares that any matter brought before the Court should be a legal, not a political, dispute. The PCIJ adopted this approach in the *Mavromatis Palestine Concessions (Jurisdiction)* case,[13] where it declared that a dispute must constitute "a disagreement over a point of law or fact, a conflict of legal views or of interests between two persons."[14] Later, the ICJ emphasized that "a legal dispute is one capable of being settled by the application of the principles and rules of international law and that it cannot concern itself with the political motivation of a state in seeking judicial settlement of a dispute" (Shaw 2003, 971). The principle of adjudicating only legal disputes is very important and yet very difficult to satisfy on the international arena, as states constitute political entities often involved in political quarrels. Even cases considered to be "legal" frequently have a political dimension (Merrills 2005, 167). For example, when the United States announced that it ceased to take any part in the case brought to the ICJ by Nicaragua, one of the underlying reasons put forth by the United States was the question of the legality of the dispute. The United States argued that "the Court should have held the case to be inadmissible on the ground that it raised a political and therefore a non-justiciable issue" (Merrills 2005, 166).

The PCIJ and ICJ have had a great impact on international law, oftentimes providing a bit more than its interpretation. As a court of law that is enmeshed in an international legal system full of vague definitions and loop holes, the World Court has addressed numerous important legal issues in countless substantive areas of international law. Some include boundaries disputes, rights of passage, maritime delimitation, transborder armed actions, legality of the threat or use of nuclear weapons, performing nuclear tests, continental shelf delimitation, fisheries, and taking hostages. The issue of gaps in international law can make the working of the Court challenging, as sometimes there may not be a straightforward and immediate rule applicable to each international dispute. The problem of gaps in international law arose in the Advisory Opinion concerning *The Legality of the Threat or Use of Nuclear Weapons.*[15] Here, the ICJ was not able to give its opinion on a very important issue in international law. In the words of the ICJ, it could not "conclude definitively whether the threat or use of nuclear weapons would be lawful or unlawful in an extreme circumstance of self-defense, in which the very survival of a state would be at stake."[16] The nature of rules and principles, the vagueness

---

[13] 1924, PCIJ, Series A, No. 2, p. 11.
[14] Also quoted in Shaw (2003, 969).
[15] 1966 ICJ Rep. 1966, 226.
[16] 1966 ICJ Rep. 226, 263 and 266, also quoted in Shaw (2003, 983).

of sources of law, and presence of gaps in the system constitute unique attributes of international law – the system in which the World Court operates. They stand in sharp contrast to many domestic legal systems where a well-structured and hierarchically organized system of courts operates.

Interstate bargaining and the World Court

In this section, we summarize the theoretical argument articulated in Chapter 3. We consider a potential adjudicator's role to be important in helping states resolve coordination problems, such as the drawing of a territorial or maritime boundary. States would like to convince others that they are strong and resolved, but because conflict is costly, they also have incentives to signal their intentions to resolve interstate disputes peacefully. These pacific intentions are difficult to convey in world politics, because they are often viewed as mere cheap talk. The interesting question is why states would coordinate their dispute resolution processes with the assistance of an adjudicator.

The first answer is provided by the expressive theory of adjudication, which demonstrates that unbiased adjudicators may be effective at helping parties strike cooperative agreements by correlating strategies, creating focal points, and signaling information (Garrett and Weingast 1993; Ginsburg and McAdams 2004; McAdams 2005, 1049). Adjudicators help parties to converge on particular solutions to coordination problems by establishing focal points in the bargaining process. Adjudicators also reduce uncertainty in bargaining by bringing new information to light about the disputed issues in question. We can consider this an *active* effect of adjudication (Mitchell and Hensel 2007), in that the court helps the parties reach an acceptable settlement by being directly involved in the dispute resolution process.

The second answer about why states might resolve coordination problems with the assistance of international courts stems from the indirect or *passive* effect that they might create in the dispute resolution process. In this sense, the threat of being sued in court can be sufficient to alter the strategies that disputants select in bilateral bargaining situations. The signal of jurisdictional recognition makes credible a state's intention to take a dispute before a court should other avenues of dispute resolution fail. However, as we noted in Chapter 3, not all courts are equally effective for all disputants. The jurisdictional cheap talk signal is more effective when a state's domestic legal characteristics are similar to the rules and procedures employed by the court. Cheap talk promotes cooperation more readily in bargaining settings if the parties have common interests. In the case where a court utilizes familiar legal principles, a disputant would be willing to allow the court to intervene because it is perceived to be fair and unbiased. Furthermore, the court's active efforts (should they arise) will be much more effective because the court will correlate strategies, create focal points, and provide information more efficiently to disputants with similar legal principles. In short, the active and passive effects of the adjudicator enhance the likelihood of bargaining success.

Consider how this argument works in the context of the World Court. In this context, the cheap talk signal is a decision by a state to make an optional clause declaration, which recognizes the compulsory jurisdiction of the PCIJ or ICJ. Alternatively, states could also recognize the jurisdiction of the World Court in a more limited sense, by placing compromissory clauses in bilateral or multilateral treaties. In both of these scenarios, states would like to convince other states that they prefer to settle interstate disputes peacefully, and recognition of the World Court's jurisdiction sends information about a state's willingness to view the adjudicator as a legitimate third party conflict manager. Furthermore, the similarities between civil law states and the practices of the PCIJ/ICJ produce great benefits for civil law states' use of jurisdictional cheap talk.

As noted in Chapter 2, a majority of states in the world have civil domestic legal systems (see Figure 2.1). The high number of civil law states increases the likelihood that any two states in a dyadic interstate negotiation will both represent the civil law tradition. If two states were drawn randomly from the international system in a given year, the probability of selecting a pair of civil law states would at a minimum be 0.23 (for 48%) and at a maximum be 0.61 (for 78%). In short, any dyadic interaction for a civil law state has the highest chance of being with another civil law state. Because civil law states dominate in the international arena, and because cheap talk works best when sent to similar states, civil law countries stand to benefit most from acceptance of the PCIJ/ICJ's jurisdiction. There are more states like themselves in the international system, which suggests that acceptance of the Court's adjudicative powers is an effective conflict management strategy for civil law states. In addition to the PCIJ/ICJ creating focal points more easily with civil law states that share its basic principles, civil law states are better equipped than common or Islamic law states to use optional clause declarations as cheap talk. The Court's active and passive effects are stronger for civil law countries than common or Islamic law states.

Finally, the ability of a court to signal private information works more efficiently in civil law dyads. Shared legal principles that civil law states project onto the interstate bargaining process, such as *bona fides* and the lack of judicial precedent, play a significant role in reducing each side's private information. All states present at the bargaining table are aware of the shared rules that govern contractual relations, which substantially reduces uncertainties regarding future compliance. At the same time, an agreement can be reached much easier between negotiators that bring similar legal training and experience to the table. These assertions about legal institutional similarity accord with previous research on regime, economic, or cultural similarity: The likelihood of cooperation increases as similarity increases. Yet the PCIJ/ICJ as an adjudicator plays an important role in interstate bargaining between civil law states. The PCIJ/ICJ is more likely to be perceived by civil law states as an unbiased and fair adjudicator, increasing the likelihood that the disputants will believe the signals sent by the institution. The high probability for civil law states to interact with one another increases the number of times that the Court can signal private information effectively. To sum up, the expressive power of adjudication in the form of correlated strategies, focal points, and information signaling are all enhanced in situations where the disputing states represent the civil legal tradition. Therefore we expect that:[17]

> *Hypothesis 5.1: States with civil law systems are more likely to accept the compulsory jurisdiction of the World Court than states with common law or Islamic law systems.*

In addition to providing leverage for understanding why certain states are more likely to recognize the Court's jurisdiction than others, domestic legal systems and their prominent characteristics can also give us insight into the success of international legal commitments. Freedom of contracting and lack of religious principles will increase international commitments made by common law and civil law states relative to Islamic law states. These states are simply free to sign more contracts. On the other hand, the lack of good faith and compliance principles in common law systems suggests that common law states will be much more cautious and specific about their international obligations. We also believe that states design their international commitments in a way that resembles design of contracts in their domestic legal system. Common law contracts are elaborate and very detailed, including all principles and issues that will govern the contractual relationship. Thus we anticipate

---

[17] We do not fully consider the relationship between common and Islamic law institutions and the PCIJ/ICJ. Common law and Islamic law states face greater costs when negotiating with the assistance of an international court that employs less familiar legal rules and principles. They also experience greater uncertainty with respect to the Court's potential rulings. Furthermore, because the ICJ does not base its decisions on religious laws (especially Islamic law), Islamic law states are least likely to view the Court as a legitimate conflict manager.

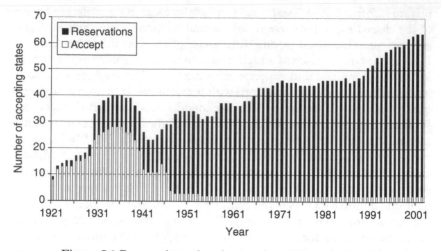

Figure 5.1 Reservations placed on optional clause declarations

that common law states will be hesitant to accept the PCIJ/ICJ's compulsory jurisdiction, but if they do accept the optional clause, they will place a large number of reservations on their commitments. These restrictions should enhance the durability of common law states' commitments to the Court because they will limit the Court's jurisdiction, especially over highly salient matters (this concerns Figure 5.1: reservations placed on optional clause declarations).

For example, Canada, a common law state, recognized the compulsory jurisdiction of the PCIJ in 1930, placing seven reservations on its initial commitment relating to certain states (*ratione personae*), certain times of disputes (*ratione temporis*), and divergent areas of international law (*ratione materiae*) (Alexandrov 1995). Several of these reservations were targeted to deal with very important issues to Canada, such as their sovereignty rights over resources of the sea off their coasts (e.g. Northwest Atlantic Fisheries). Canada added three other reservations across time, bringing the total to ten, although such reservations arguably strengthened Canada's long-standing commitment to the Court.

Contracts in civil law are much shorter than common law contracts. We believe that this factor coupled with the prime position of the *bona fides* principle in civil law systems should produce optional clause declarations with a small number of reservations. Civil law states are aware of the fact that the fulfillment of their contractual obligation to the PCIJ/ICJ will be governed by the principle of good faith, which should substantially decrease the number of reservations on their declarations. As we discussed in Chapters 2 and 3, contracts in civil law are not overly detailed due to the fact that most of the overarching legal principles that govern contractual relationships are clearly spelled out in codes. Moderate compliance principles in civil law states should also produce long-standing commitments to the Court, although such commitments may be shorter than those for Islamic law states. It is simply much easier to break an international commitment that is not as clearly specified. Islamic law states, while very reluctant to make any optional clause declarations, will remain firmly committed to the PCIJ/ICJ once they recognize its jurisdiction due to the preeminence of the *pacta sunt servanda* norm in Islamic law. Islamic law states will design their commitments to the PCIJ/ICJ carefully, making them more likely to stay steadfastly committed to the Court. It is much easier to keep a commitment that has been carefully and meticulously crafted.

> *Hypothesis 5.2: Islamic law states will have more durable commitments to the World Court than civil or common law states.*

In the next chapter, we explore more fully the rational design features of states' commitments to the World Court. Our analysis at this stage focuses on states' decisions to recognize the jurisdiction of the PCIJ/ICJ through compulsory jurisdiction and the durability of states' commitments to these international courts.

Research design

The temporal domain of this study is 1921–2001, which includes the eras of both the PCIJ (1921–1945) and the ICJ (1946–2001). As noted earlier, we believe that these two judicial organs can be treated empirically as an equivalent and functionally unchanged highest court of international law, or as a "World Court." The basic unit of analysis in our empirical model is the state-year. A state can accept compulsory jurisdiction without any reservation; after some time, however, the same state may add a restrictive reservation to its declaration, or else withdraw its declaration. Using state-year as our unit of analysis allows us to capture the behavior of states over time.[18]

One issue with employing a state-year design is the potential to equate transitions to compulsory jurisdiction acceptance with continued

---

[18] Reservations are "restrictions relating to the content of the commitments entered into a particular declaration" (Szafarz 1993, 46). There are numerous types of reservations that states may place on their optional clause declarations, relating to other states (*ratione personae*), certain times of disputes (*ratione temporis*), or specific areas of international law (*ratione materiae*) (Szafarz 1993). We discuss these categories in much greater detail in Chapter 6.

acceptance year to year. In other words, if we simply coded in each year whether a state accepts the compulsory jurisdiction of the World Court or not, we would be treating the emergence and survival of commitments as equivalent. Such an approach would also assume implicitly that the probability of transition is equivalent to the probability of survival. We employ the Markov transition logit model, because this allows us to distinguish between states that transition from not accepting to accepting compulsory jurisdiction in a given year from those that continue to recognize the jurisdiction of the PCIJ/ICJ each year.[19] The model can be represented as follows:

$$P(y_{i,t} = 1 \mid y_{i,t-1} = 0) = \text{Logit}(x_{i,t}\beta)$$
$$P(y_{i,t} = 1 \mid y_{i,t-1} = 1) = \text{Logit}(x_{i,t}\alpha)$$

Our theoretical hypotheses are expressed as relationships where the independent variable (e.g. civil legal system) increases or decreases the likelihood that a state will accept the compulsory jurisdiction of the PCIJ/ICJ. The transition model, when the lagged dependent variable equals zero, is best suited to testing hypothesis 5.1 because this demonstrates an active decision by a state to deposit an optional clause declaration with the League of Nations or the UN. However, we also examine the influence of our independent variables on the survival of PCIJ/ICJ commitments to evaluate our second hypothesis (5.2) about the durability of such commitments.

Accepting compulsory jurisdiction

The primary dependent variable in this chapter is acceptance of compulsory jurisdiction under the PCIJ and/or ICJ. We code the dependent variable into two categories: (1) a state accepts the compulsory jurisdiction with or without reservations, or (0) a state does not recognize the jurisdiction of the World Court. The data are collected from the annual volumes of the *Yearbook of the International Court of Justice*,[20] noting any declarations by states with respect to the optional clause and any reservations placed on these declarations. Box 5.1 provides a list of countries grouped by legal system tradition and the years of PCIJ/ICJ compulsory

---

[19] This model can be estimated one of two ways. First, we can condition the logit model on the value of the lagged dependent variable, running separate models for transition (lagged DV = 0) and continued acceptance (lagged DV = 1). We could also create an interaction term between the lagged dependent variable and each independent variable in the model. We employ the former strategy in this chapter, although as we show in Chapter 6, we get identical results when we use interaction terms.

[20] See www.icj-cij.org.

Box 5.1 Domestic legal traditions and years of PCIJ/ICJ compulsory jurisdiction acceptance

Common law countries

Antigua & Barbuda, Australia (1940–), Bahamas, Bangladesh, Barbados (1980–), Belize, Bhutan, Canada (1930–), Cyprus (1988–), Dominica (2006–), Federated States of Micronesia, Fiji, Ghana, Grenada, Guyana, India (1940–), Ireland (1930–1946), Jamaica, Kiribati, Lesotho (2000–), Liberia (1952–), Malawi (1966–), Malaysia, Marshall Islands, Mauritius (1968–), Nauru (1988–), Nepal, New Zealand (1930–), Palau, Papua New Guinea, Philippines (1947–), Samoa, Sierra Leone, Singapore, Solomon Islands, St. Lucia, St. Kitts-Nevis, St. Vincent and Grenadines, Tanzania, Tonga, Trinidad and Tobago, Tuvalu, Uganda (1963–), United Kingdom (1930–), United States of America (1946–1985), Zimbabwe, Zambia, Zanzibar

Civil law countries

Albania (1930–1940), Andorra, Angola, Argentina, Armenia, Austria (1922–1942, 1971–), Azerbaijan, Belgium (1926–1941, 1948–), Belarus, Benin, Bolivia (1936–1953), Bosnia-Herzegovina, Brazil (1921–1953), Bulgaria (1921–1946, 1992–), Burkina Faso, Burundi, Cambodia (1957–), Cape Verde, Central African Republic, Chad, Chile, Congo, Colombia (1937–), Costa Rica (1973–), Croatia, Cuba, Czech Republic, Democratic Republic of the Congo (1989–), Denmark (1921–), Djibouti (2005–), Dominican Republic (1924–), East Timor, Ecuador, El Salvador (1930–1988), Equatorial Guinea, Estonia (1923–1946, 1991–), Ethiopia (1926–1936), Finland (1922–1946, 1958–), France (1931–1941, 1947–1974), Gabon, Georgia (1995–), Germany (1928–1938), Greece (1929–1944, 1994–), Guatemala (1947–1952), Guinea (1998–), Guinea-Bissau (1989–), Haiti (1921–), Honduras (1948–), Hungary (1929–1939, 1992–), Iceland, Indonesia, Italy (1931–1936), Ivory Coast (2001–), Kazakhstan, Kyrgyz Republic, Laos, Latvia (1930–1946), Liechtenstein (1950–), Lithuania (1922–1940), Luxembourg (1930–), Macedonia, Madagascar (1992–), Mali, Mexico (1947–), Moldova, Monaco, Mongolia, Mozambique, Netherlands (1921–), Nicaragua (1939–), Norway (1921–), North Korea, Panama (1929–), Paraguay (1933–1938, 1996–), Peru (1932–1946, 2003–),

Poland (1990–), Portugal (1921–1946, 1955–), Republic of Vietnam, Romania (1931–1941), Russia, San Marino, Sao Tome and Principe, Slovakia (2004–), Slovenia, South Korea, Spain (1928–1938, 1990–), Surinam (1987–), Swaziland (1969–), Sweden (1921–), Switzerland (1921–1946, 1948–), Taiwan (1949–1971), Tajikistan, Togo (1979–), Turkey (1947–1972), Turkmenistan, Ukraine, Uruguay (1921–), Uzbekistan, Venezuela, Vietnam, Yugoslavia (1930–1935, 1999–)

Islamic law countries

Afghanistan, Algeria, Bahrain, Comoros, Egypt (1957–), Gambia (1966–), Iraq, Iran (1932–1951), Jordan, Kuwait, Lebanon, Libya, Maldives, Morocco, Nigeria (1965–), Oman, Pakistan (1948–), Qatar, Saudi Arabia, Sudan (1958–), Syria, Tunisia, United Arab Emirates, Yemen, Yemen Arab Republic, Yemen People's Republic

Mixed law countries

Botswana (1970–), Brunei, Cameroon (1994–), China (1922–1927, 1946–1948), Eritrea, Israel (1950–1985), Japan (1958–), Kenya (1965–), Malta (1966–), Myanmar, Namibia, Niger, Rwanda, Senegal (1985–), Seychelles, Somalia (1963–), South Africa (1930–1967), Sri Lanka, Thailand (1930–1960), Vanuatu,

jurisdiction acceptance. From 1921 to 2001, states accepted compulsory jurisdiction in 34.2% of state-years, with a majority placing some reservations on their declarations (27.9% of state-years).

Legal traditions

In order to capture the impact of divergent legal systems on the propensity of states to accept the compulsory jurisdiction of the PCIJ/ICJ, we employ the four mutually exclusive dichotomous categories described in Chapter 2: civil law, common law, Islamic law, and mixed law. The first three categories capture our key legal traditions, while the mixed category captures the legal system of countries where two or more traditions apply interactively or cumulatively. As noted earlier, information about domestic legal traditions has been gathered using the *CIA Fact Book* (Central Intelligency Agency 2007), which describes major characteristics of legal traditions of each state in the international system, and several other subsidiary legal sources. Box 2.1 provides a classification of countries in the world by domestic legal tradition.

Control variables

Power constitutes one of the most frequently mentioned factors that influence whether states bring their disputes to the World Court (Lloyd 1985). Powerful states prefer to bargain bilaterally because their material advantages translate into bargaining leverage. "In theory, one may expect a particular reluctance to accept compulsory jurisdiction by powerful nations, or at least nations which see themselves as likely to be in a superior bargaining position in the kinds of disputes that they think might arise" (Bilder 1998, 249). Less powerful nations, on the other hand, see impartial adjudication more as a protection than a risk; it allows these states to feel "legally equal to the world's powers" (Scott and Carr 1987, 57). We therefore expect more powerful states to be less likely to accept the PCIJ/ICJ's compulsory jurisdiction. This is a similar expectation to what we argued in Chapter 4, namely that powerful states should be less likely to sign and ratify the Rome Statute. Because we have a longer period of time for analysis, we are able to employ a different measure of state power than military expenditures. We employ the national capabilities index (or CINC score) as developed by Singer *et al.* (1972), which captures a state's proportion of total system capabilities in six areas: iron/steel production, energy production, urban population, total population, military expenditures, and military personnel. We obtained these values from the Correlates of War Project's homepage.[21] This variable has a mean of 0.009, with a range from (near) 0 to 0.38.

Some legal scholars compare attitudes towards the World Court of relatively new states with the mind-set of well-established nations (Gamble and Fischer 1976). Typical of the conventional wisdom in this area is that new states view international law as an alien system that Western nations have imposed on others (Brierly 1963, 43) and are "the product of European imperialism and colonialism" (Rosenne 1957/1962, 173).[22] Newer states came to view the PCIJ/ICJ as conservative and strongly determined to preserve the status quo (Gamble and Fischer 1976), attitudes that were fueled by several unpopular ICJ judgments, such as the 1966 *South West Africa* decision.[23] Newer states should be more reluctant to make optional clause declarations. Our measure for state age captures the length of time a country has been recognized as a state (Central Intelligency Agency 2007). For countries that trace their origins to times BC, we chose 1200 AD as the starting point of statehood. We

---

[21] See www.correlatesofwar.org/COW2%20Data/Capabilities/NMC_3.02.csv.

[22] For an in-depth examination of new states and their attitudes towards the ICJ, see Shihata (1965).

[23] 1966 ICJ Rep. 6.

calculate the natural logarithm of state age to minimize the variance of the measure.[24]

The normative explanation for the democratic peace suggests that when two democratic states disagree over an issue, they should be more likely to resolve the dispute peacefully because they realize that their adversary is operating under a norm of bounded competition, which supports the use of compromise (Dixon 1994). These conciliatory democratic norms should increase the likelihood of democracies adopting peaceful methods of conflict resolution. Democratic states' respect for judicial processes and regard for constitutional constraints carries over into international relations, and democracies are apt to engage third parties in the resolution of disputes in binding ways such as adjudication or arbitration due to their trust in legal procedures (Teson 1992; Raymond 1994; Slaughter 1995; Mitchell 2002).

Our theoretical argument asserts that optional clause declarations as cheap talk work better between parties with similar preferences. While we focus on the similarity of legal institutions, we can also evaluate our argument by looking at the similarity of political institutions. Democratic states should be more likely to accept the compulsory jurisdiction of the PCIJ/ICJ than non-democratic states both because of greater preference similarity and the transparency of democratic regimes, which reduces privately held information that can impede cooperation. This accords with our empirical findings on the ICC in Chapter 4, which show democratic states are significantly more likely to sign and ratify the Rome Statute than non-democratic states.

In these analyses, we are also able to assess the durability of states' commitments to international courts. Research on the democratic peace suggests that commitments made by democratic countries are more credible (Lipson 2003), hence democratic states should be more likely to stay committed to the PCIJ/ICJ once they sign on to the Court. To measure each state's democracy level in a given year, we use the Polity IV dataset (Jaggers and Gurr 1995), which combines information from four institutional characteristics into a single democracy score ranging from 0 (least democratic) to 10 (most democratic). This includes the competitiveness of political participation, the level of constraints on the chief executive, and the openness and competitiveness of chief executive

---

[24] We also estimated models using an alternative measure of state age, the number of system membership years as recorded by the Correlates of War Project. Our results are similar to what we report herein. We do not control for age in the ICC analyses because the vast majority of states that could join the Court were present at the Rome negotiations. In contrast, only a small portion of states were at the bargaining table when the PCIJ was created, and thus did not have a say in its legal design.

Table 5.1 *Descriptive statistics for Chapter 5*

Variable	N	Mean	Std. dev.	Min.	Max.
Accept ICJ jurisdiction	9,420	0.340	0.474	0	1
Civil law	9,420	0.570	0.495	0	1
Common law	9,420	0.201	0.401	0	1
Islamic law	9,420	0.139	0.346	0	1
Mixed law	9,420	0.089	0.285	0	1
Democracy	8,157	3.823	4.177	0	10
Capabilities	9,228	0.009	0.028	3.59e−07	0.38
State age	9,294	3.931	1.491	0	7.44
British	8,918	0.284	0.451	0	1
French	8,918	0.492	0.499	0	1
Socialist	8,918	0.145	0.352	0	1
Scandinavian	8,918	0.043	0.202	0	1
German	8,918	0.037	0.190	0	1
Year	9,420	1971	22.633	1920	2001

recruitment.[25] We turn now to multivariate analyses to empirically evaluate our theoretical hypotheses. Descriptive statistics for all variables are summarized in Table 5.1.

Empirical analysis

In Figure 2.1, we presented the frequency of domestic legal traditions over time as a percentage of all states in the world. As we noted in Chapter 2, civil law is the most prevalent legal tradition in the world. In Figure 5.2, we plot the frequency of legal system types as a percentage of all states that have optional clause declarations in force for a given year. In Figure 5.3, we compare the percentage of states that are civil law in each year with the percentage of civil law states accepting PCIJ/ICJ compulsory jurisdiction.

Given the prevalence of civil law states overall in the international system, it is not surprising that they dominate the group of states accepting PCIJ/ICJ compulsory jurisdiction. Civil law states comprise 57% of all state-years in the dataset from 1921 to 2001, yet accepted compulsory jurisdiction in 61.2% of state-years ($\chi^2 - 35.2$, $p < .001$). However, this support does vary over time, as can be seen in Figure 5.3. Civil law

[25] As noted in Chapter 4, we utilize a different measure of democracy that collapses this index into a dummy variable. This was necessary due to the multicollinearity that arose in those analyses when the rule-of-law measure was included. We are unable to control for the rule of law in our PCIJ/ICJ analyses because most rule-of-law indicators are recorded only from the early 1980s to the present.

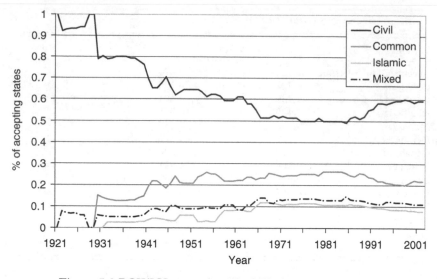

Figure 5.2 PCIJ/ICJ compulsory jurisdiction acceptance by legal system types

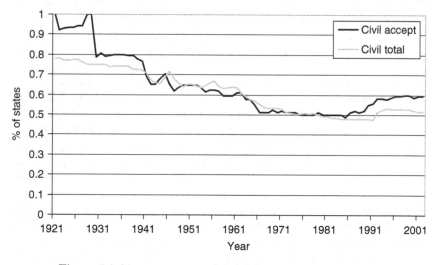

Figure 5.3 Acceptance rates for civil law states

states exhibited a high level of support for the PCIJ, they were "cooler" towards the ICJ, but they have shown increasing levels of support for the ICJ since the end of the Cold War. Furthermore, civil law states dominate the set of countries accepting the Court's jurisdiction without any

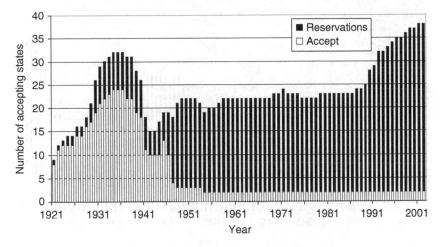

Figure 5.4 Optional clause declarations, civil law states

reservations (91%). As we can see in Figure 5.4, not only were civil law countries extremely supportive of the PCIJ, but a majority of those states recognized the Court's jurisdiction without reservations.

Common law states make up 20.1% of the state-year sample and have accepted compulsory jurisdiction in 20.9% of state years ($\chi^2 = 1.65$, $p < 0.20$). Most common law countries place reservations on their commitments to the World Court. In fact, as we see in Figure 5.5, that since the advent of the ICJ, all common law states with optional clause declarations have one or more reservations on their pledge to the Court. Common law state support for the World Court varies considerably over time. In Figure 5.6, notice that no common law countries recognized the PCIJ in the first seven years of its existence, and those few common law states that made optional clause declarations in the 1930s were very likely to limit the Court's jurisdiction through reservations (Figure 5.5). Common law country support was much stronger for the ICJ during the Cold War, a finding that is not surprising given the important role that the United States and the United Kingdom played in the establishment of the Court at Dumbarton Oaks. Between 1945 and 1989, common law states comprised 20.4% of all state-years and accepted compulsory jurisdiction of the ICJ in 24% of those cases ($\chi^2 = 20.6$, $p < 0.001$). On the other hand, the United States' withdrawal from the Court in 1986 corresponds with a more general decline in common law support for the ICJ.

Consistent with Hypothesis 5.1, Islamic countries make up 14% of the state-year sample and accept PCIJ/ICJ compulsory jurisdiction in

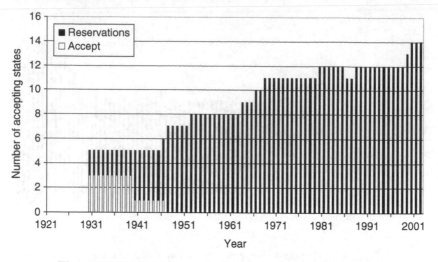

Figure 5.5 Optional clause declarations, common law states

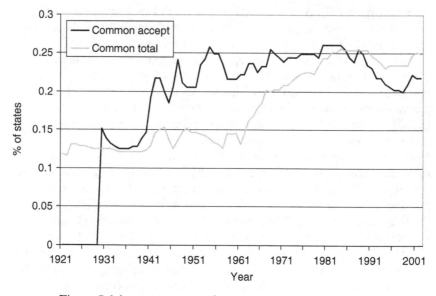

Figure 5.6 Acceptance rates for common law states

only 7.5% of state-years ($\chi^2 = 168.5$, $p < 0.001$). As we see in Figure 5.7, Islamic law countries showed greater support for the ICJ than the PCIJ, although there is a significant gap between the percentage of Islamic law states with optional clause declarations in force and the overall percentage

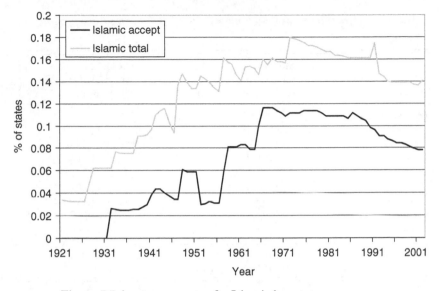

Figure 5.7 Acceptance rates for Islamic law states

of Islamic law states in the international system in all years. Interestingly, support for the World Court among Islamic law countries declined after the end of the Cold War. The percentage of Islamic law states with reservations on their optional clause declarations are not plotted because virtually all accepting states have one or more reservations in place.

Turning to multivariate analyses, Table 5.2 presents estimates from the Markov transition logit models. Model 1 presents the estimates for transition from non-acceptance to acceptance, while Model 2 provides estimates for durability, or whether states that accepted the jurisdiction of the PCIJ/ICJ last year continue to do so this year. Common law states are utilized as the omitted legal type category. Table 5.3 presents the predicted probabilities for each model to ascertain the substantive effect of each variable holding all others at their mean or mode.

The coefficient for the civil law dummy variable is positive and statistically significant in the transition model (Table 5.2, Model 1), providing support for hypothesis 5.1 that civil law countries are more likely than common or Islamic law states to accept the compulsory jurisdiction of the World Court. In Table 5.3, we see that the transition probability for civil law systems (0.017) is nearly three times as large as the probability of acceptance for common law states (0.006), and more than two and a half times as large as the probability of acceptance for Islamic law states (0.007). States with mixed legal systems have the highest probability

Table 5.2 *Markov transition logit model: PCIJ/ICJ compulsory jurisdiction acceptance*

Variable	Model 1: transition to compulsory Jurisdiction acceptance	Model 2: survival of existing Commitment
Theoretical variables		
Civil law	0.98 (0.36)**	−1.90 (1.16)*
Islamic law	0.15 (0.61)	−0.87 (1.49)
Mixed law	1.22 (0.46)**	−1.97 (1.10)*
Control variables		
Democracy	0.17 (0.03)**	0.09 (0.04)**
Capabilities	4.47 (3.42)	−13.6 (4.52)**
State age	−0.07 (0.09)	−0.20 (0.18)
Constant	−5.30 (0.47)**	6.86 (1.24)**
Sample size	5,076	2,767
Chi-square	51.35**	17.48**

Entries are coefficients followed by robust standard errors: * $p < 0.10$; ** $p < 0.05$.
Note: Common law is the omitted referent category.

Table 5.3 *Substantive effects: PCIJ/ICJ compulsory jurisdiction acceptance*

Variable	Model 1: transition prob. (change)	Model 2: survival prob. (change)
Legal system		
Civil law	0.017	0.989
Common law	0.006 (− 0.011)	0.998 (+ 0.009)
Islamic law	0.007 (− 0.010)	0.998 (+ 0.009)
Mixed law	0.021 (+ 0.004)	0.988 (− 0.001)
Democracy		
0 (min.)	0.010	0.981
10 (max.)	0.055 (+ 0.045)	0.992 (+ 0.011)
Capabilities		
0 (min.)	0.016	0.990
0.38 (max.)	0.083 (+ 0.067)	0.346 (− 0.644)
State age		
0 (min.)	0.022	0.995
7.44 (max.)	0.013 (− 0.009)	0.980 (− 0.015)

of acceptance overall (0.021). The eleven mixed law states that have accepted PCIJ/ICJ jurisdiction at some point in time are all influenced by the civil legal tradition, thus their acceptance fits with the theoretical relationship articulated for civil law states.[26] The low values of the transition predicted probabilities reflect the reality that most countries do not make new optional clause declarations in a given year. However, the variance in domestic legal system types does give us purchase for explaining why some states are willing to make optional clause declarations more readily than others.

The coefficient for the Islamic legal system dummy is positive, although not significantly different from zero. Thus while we cannot distinguish significantly between common law and Islamic law states in the transition analyses (Table 5.2, Model 1), we can conclude that countries with an Islamic legal tradition are less likely to accept compulsory jurisdiction than civil law states. These results clearly demonstrate the importance of taking into consideration domestic legal systems for understanding the expressive power of adjudication. Civil law states benefit most from acceptance of the Court's jurisdiction because they are more likely to view the PCIJ/ICJ as an unbiased adjudicator, which facilitates the adjudicator's ability to correlate strategies and create focal points. Taking potential disputes to the World Court is also more credible if the disputants are civil law states that recognize the Court's jurisdiction. This more passive effect of the PCIJ/ICJ is strongest for civil law countries. Islamic states prefer not to subject themselves to an alien legal system because Islamic law puts limits on the types of international commitments that Islamic states can make and because Islamic states are more likely to view the World Court as a biased adjudicator.

However, Hypothesis 5.2 predicted that Islamic law and common law states would have more durable commitments to the PCIJ/ICJ than civil law states. Islamic law states have very strong *pacta sunt servanda* norms, while common law states draft very precise contracts in international relations, enhancing the durability of their commitments. The durability results are presented in Table 5.2, Model 2. The coefficient for the Islamic variable has the wrong sign, although it is not statistically distinguishable from zero. However, this finding reflects a lack of variance; in only one state year in the entire dataset (Iran, 1952) did an Islamic country renege on its commitment to the PCIJ/ICJ. In all other cases, once an Islamic law country was committed to the ICJ, it did not withdraw its optional

[26] These states are Botswana, Cameroon, China, Israel, Japan, Kenya, Malta, Senegal, Somalia, South Africa, and Thailand. On the other hand, a handful of mixed law states with civil legal influences have stayed away from the World Court too (Eritrea, Niger, Rwanda, Seychelles, Sri Lanka, Vanuatu).

clause declaration. This is confirmed in Table 5.2 by the high predicted probability of continued compulsory jurisdiction acceptance for Islamic law states (p = 0.998). While Islamic states are wary of accepting international courts and rarely do accept them, any recognition of the PCIJ/ICJ by Islamic states remains durable over time due to strong norms of contractual compliance.

The negative and significant sign for the civil law dummy variable in the survival model (Table 5.2, Model 2) shows that civil law states are open to the World Court, but they are more likely to renege on their commitments over time. The substantive effects for the legal type variables, however, illustrate that all states are extremely likely to remain committed to the PCIJ/ICJ over time. The predicted probability of continued PCIJ/ICJ acceptance ranges from 0.989 (civil law states) to 0.998 (Islamic and common law states).

Two of the three control variables exert significant influences on commitments to the PCIJ/ICJ: capabilities and democracy. The coefficient for capabilities is positive but insignificant in the transition model (Model 1), while negative and statistically significant in the survival model (Model 2). We conjectured that powerful states would be less inclined to recognize the jurisdiction of the PCIJ/ICJ due to their bargaining advantages in bilateral negotiations. Our results suggest that both weak and powerful states may be willing to accept compulsory jurisdiction, although powerful states are much less likely to remain committed to the institution over time. Furthermore, the substantive effect of capabilities in the survival model is extremely large. The probability that a country as powerful as the United States will continue to recognize the ICJ's jurisdiction in a given year is only 0.346, while the weakest states in our sample (e.g. Lichtenstein) almost always remain committed (99 percent chance of survival). The lack of major power commitment to international legal institutions is perhaps best illustrated by the withdrawal of the United States' optional clause declaration in 1986. While the creation of new world orders after victory in major wars such as World War I and World War II may include the creation of international courts for adjudication, the major power victors may become less willing to support these institutions when their national interests are directly challenged (Posner 2004).

On the other hand, our results demonstrate that democratic states are much more willing to accept compulsory jurisdiction of the PCIJ/ICJ and they are also significantly more likely to maintain those commitments over time. Perhaps in this regard, the United States' behavior with respect to the Court is an outlier when compared to the rest of the democratic community. Fully democratic states are five times more likely

Table 5.4 *Markov transition logit model: PCIJ/ICJ compulsory jurisdiction acceptance for joiners separately*

Variable	Model 1: transition (joiners)	Model 2: survival (joiners)
Theoretical variables		
Civil law	0.91 (0.38)**	−1.69 (1.08)
Islamic law	0.15 (0.61)	−0.92 (1.43)
Mixed law	1.21 (0.48)**	−2.01 (1.13)*
Control variables		
Democracy	0.17 (0.03)**	0.02 (0.05)
Capabilities	5.93 (8.14)	−19.49 (6.41)**
State age	−0.10 (0.10)	−0.14 (0.20)
Constant	−5.21 (0.51)**	6.81 (1.24)**
Sample size	4,777	2,303
Chi-square	45.70**	24.46**

Entries are coefficients followed by robust standard errors: * $p < 0.10$; ** $p < 0.05$.
Note: Common law is the omitted referent category for legal tradition.

to recognize the World Court's jurisdiction than fully autocratic states. Furthermore, the commitments made by democratic states to these institutions are durable; there is only an 8 in 1,000 chance that a democratic state will withdraw its optional clause declaration. This provides additional support to our theoretical argument that optional clause declarations work more effectively as cheap talk between similar states.

Table 5.4 presents the same Markov Transition analyses as in Table 5.2, but only for later joiners to the PCIJ or ICJ. The originators are coded as the states that had representatives on the Committee of Jurists, including Belgium, Brazil, France, Italy, Japan, the Netherlands, Norway, Spain, the United Kingdom, and the United States (Lloyd 1985, 30). Thus, Table 5.4 estimates the model for non-originating states only.

We also attempted to estimate models for the set of originating states, but we ended up with too few cases for estimation when control variables were included. The legal system variables were seriously truncated in the set of originator cases as well, because no Islamic law or mixed law states were present at the bargaining table. Thus very few variables achieved significance in the few hundred cases where we had information for all relevant variables.

Table 5.4, Model 1 presents the transition results for the joiners, while Model 2 shows the survival results for the potential joiners. The results in Model 1 are virtually identical to the transition results for all states, with civil law and mixed law states being significantly more likely to join the World Court than common law or Islamic law states. Democratic states are also more supportive of the Court in the set of potential joining states. The survival estimates in Model 2 are somewhat different from what was reported in Table 5.2, as the civil law and democracy variables are no longer significant. This is most likely driven by the exclusion of several civil law countries from the originator set, as well as the fact that most of these states are democracies as well. However, we can see that the theoretical expectations are supported in the set of joining states, a relationship we articulated in Chapter 3. As we noted, the potential joiners were unable to negotiate the basic rules of the Court, thus they utilized information about their domestic legal systems as clues about the fairness of the Court and the efficacy of sending cheap talk signals through the Court. The significance of the democracy variable is also consistent with our theory, as democratic states share more similar preferences and can thus send cheap talk signals to each other through the adjudicator more effectively. Democratic support for international adjudication is also consistent with a more general democratic preference for legalistic dispute settlement, especially in situations where leaders may face electoral and domestic audience costs for making concessions on important issues (Huth and Allee 2002).

In order to check the robustness of our results further, we estimated our models in Table 5.2 with year as an independent variable. The coefficient for the year variable is negative and statistically significant, indicating a declining propensity for states to recognize compulsory jurisdiction over time. However, the coefficient for the civil law variable is still positive and statistically significant ($p = 0.02$). This shows that our results are not driven by the fact that in the early years of the PCIJ there were far more civil law countries than common law or Islamic law states. Clustering by year produces similar results, although the p-value for civil law becomes a bit larger ($p = 0.078$). In an analysis of data in more recent years (1984–2002), Powell (2006a) finds that the effect of the civil law tradition on states' propensity to transition to ICJ acceptance is positive and significant, consistent with our findings for the entire sample.

Once courts have been in existence for a long time, they may develop a reputation that is distinct from their original legal design. To capture the effect of states' learning based on an international court's performance, we also estimated the models in Table 5.2 including two measures in the second stage of the model to control for states' experience with the World Court. Coding all judgments rendered by the PCIJ or ICJ, we generated two count measures for total wins and total losses in these courts over time. Interestingly, neither variable has a statistically significant effect on whether states continue to accept compulsory jurisdiction of the PCIJ/ICJ in a given year. Furthermore, the results reported in Table 5.2 for domestic legal traditions hold when these past experience measures are included. This suggests that legal similarity between domestic law and international courts serves as a stronger cue for joiners than experience with the court as it renders a series of judgments. It also suggests that the US decision to leave the ICJ in light of the *Nicaragua* case in 1986 might be exceptional when examining all states' experience with the World Court.

Similar to our robustness checks in Chapter 4, we also include the measure of membership in multilateral treaties of pacific settlement in Models 1 and 2, as coded by Paul Hensel in the MTOPS project.[27] We expect a higher number of treaty memberships to correspond with a greater willingness to support the World Court, especially if some states are more amenable to peaceful forms of dispute resolution in general. In the transition model, the IO membership measure is not significant, while the civil law variable is still positive and statistically significant (p = 0.009). The mixed law variable (p = 0.009) and the democracy variable (p = 0.000) are both still positive and highly significant. When considering the durability of states' commitments to the World Court, the MTOPS variable is positive and significant (p = 0.053). States that belong to more regional and global treaties with dispute settlement clauses in their charters are indeed more likely to remain committed to the World Court once they recognize its compulsory jurisdiction. However, the results for the other variables are unchanged; civil law states are still more likely to withdraw from the PCIJ/ICJ than common law or Islamic law states (p = 0.020), democratic states have more durable commitments (p = 0.011), while powerful states leave the Court at higher rates than weaker ones (p = 0.001). In short, the effect of domestic legal traditions holds even when controlling for membership in other types of pacific dispute-resolution organizations.

We also check the robustness of our results by controlling for colonial legacy using the legal origin coding scheme developed by La Porta *et al.* (1999). This variable has five legal origin categories: English, Socialist, French, German, and Scandinavian. As expected, the English colonial legacy correlates highly with the common law tradition in our state-year dataset (r = 0.72). Countries with French legal origins also tend to have civil law systems, although the correspondence is weaker (r = 0.33). A similar civil law pattern obtains for countries with a Socialist (r = 0.27) or Scandinavian (r = 0.19) legal origin. A German legal origin is not highly correlated with any of the major legal traditions.

---

[27] See www.paulhensel.org/icow.html#mtops.

Table 5.5 *PCIJ/ICJ compulsory jurisdiction acceptance and colonial legal origin*

Variable	Model 1: transition	Model 2: survival	Model 3: transition	Model 4: survival
Theoretical variables				
Civil law	1.67 (0.36)**	−2.05 (1.31)		
Islamic law	0.62 (0.81)	−1.01 (1.34)		
Mixed law	1.36 (0.51)**	−1.70 (1.21)		
Colonial legal origin				
British	0.08 (0.72)	−0.14 (0.87)	−1.04 (0.49)**	1.00 (0.84)
French	−0.70 (0.48)	0.37 (0.65)	−0.76 (0.47)	0.49 (0.63)
Socialist	−0.69 (0.56)	−0.77 (0.75)	−0.58 (0.54)	−0.73 (0.80)
Scandinavian	1.56 (0.74)**	1.21 (1.14)	1.61 (0.72)**	1.15 (1.12)
Control variables				
Democracy	0.14 (0.03)**	0.07 (0.05)	0.15 (0.03)**	0.08 (0.05)*
Capabilities	5.43 (3.13)*	−11.3 (4.79)**	3.26 (3.07)	−7.91 (4.21)*
State age	−0.07 (0.10)	−0.29 (0.19)	−0.02 (0.10)	−0.30 (0.19)
Constant	−5.15 (0.92)**	7.31 (1.68)**	−3.83 (0.67)**	5.21 (1.22)**
Sample size	4,703	2,768	4,703	2,768
Chi-square	75.93**	23.97**	66.88**	22.16**

Entries are coefficients followed by robust standard errors: * $p < 0.10$; ** $p < 0.05$.
Note: Common law is the omitted referent category for legal tradition. German legal origin is the omitted reference category for colonial legal origin.

Table 5.5 presents results adding the legal origin variables to our estimated Markov transition logit models. In Models 1 and 2, we add the legal origin variable to our original specification. The results for transition to PCIJ/ICJ acceptance are not altered, with civil and mixed law states still having a significantly higher likelihood of transition to acceptance than common or Islamic law states. The control variable results are similar also, although the coefficient for capabilities is positive and (now) marginally significant ($p = 0.08$). The inclusion of the legal origin measures in the survival equation, however, eliminates the statistical significance of all legal variables. This is most likely a function of increased multicollinearity in the smaller sample due to the non-random selection effects by legal type for transition into the World Court.

In Models 3 and 4 in Table 5.5, we remove our legal tradition variables and retain the La Porta *et al.* (1999) legal origin measures. States with a British legal origin are significantly less likely to accept compulsory jurisdiction in comparison to states with German legal origins (the omitted category). This result is consistent with our results for common law in

Table 5.2. We also see that Scandinavian countries have a significantly higher likelihood for transition to acceptance, which is consistent with our results for civil law. On the other hand, states with a French legal origin are not significantly more accepting of the PCIJ/ICJ in comparison to those with a German legal origin. These results reveal some interesting distinctions across states within legal families, something that we hope to parse apart more carefully in future research.[28]

Discussion

Our theoretical hypotheses find robust empirical support. However, we focus exclusively on acceptance of compulsory jurisdiction, which might be problematic if common and Islamic law states recognize the Court's jurisdiction frequently through other means, such as the placement of compromissory clauses in interstate treaties. This form of jurisdiction is granted much more frequently, with 80 percent of all states belonging to one or more compromissory clause treaties (Powell and Mitchell 2007). One might argue theoretically that common law countries prefer recognition of the World Court's jurisdiction through compromissory clauses because such commitments are more precise and limited only to the treaty at hand. The lack of good faith in bargaining creates specific and limited obligations, which can be done more easily through a bilateral or multilateral treaty. Compulsory jurisdiction is a more risky proposition, because it can be applied to any legal matter in international law. Thus while the placement of reservations might help to limit the Court's prerogative, common law states may nonetheless prefer to limit the Court's potential involvement to the more specific subject matter of interstate treaties. If our theory is apt, on the other hand, then all forms of PCIJ/ICJ jurisdictional acceptance should exhibit similar empirical patterns. Civil law states have greater incentives to employ jurisdictional acceptance of the World Court as cheap talk, and this should hold whether we are examining compulsory or compromissory jurisdiction.

To assess these arguments, we have taken an initial cut at identifying the members of all bilateral and multilateral treaties with compromissory clauses, available on the ICJ's website.[29] Bilateral treaty members are listed on the website, while multilateral treaties are listed by simply the

---

[28] We have begun to explore the issues of colonial legacies more explicitly in the area of human rights, finding that common law countries have better human rights records than civil law or Islamic law countries, but that these distinctions become minimal in states with colonial legacies, who exhibit worsened human rights performance overall (Ring *et al.* 2009). See also Powell and Staton (2009) for an analysis of how judicial independence influences states' willingness to sign and comply with human rights treaties.

[29] See www.icj-cij.org/jurisdiction/index.php?p1=S+p2=1+p3=4.

Table 5.6 *Monadic count of treaty memberships with compromissory clauses*

Variable	Coefficient (S.E.)
Common law	−6.15 (2.38)*
Mixed law	−7.88 (3.43)*
Islamic law	−4.52 (3.02)
Accept ICJ Compulsory Jurisdiction (in 2002)	11.44 (2.08)*
Constant	27.43 (1.55)*

N = 192 (Number of States in 2002)
$F_{(4,187)} = 11.09$ (p < 0.00)
$R^2 = 0.19$
Entries are coefficients followed by robust errors: * p < 0.05.

name of the treaty and signature year. Using information from the UN Treaty Database and other sources, we obtained copies of each multilateral treaty to determine the member states and years of acceptance. We created a count measure of the total number of bilateral and multilateral treaty memberships for each of the 192 Correlates of War system members as of 2002. The average state belongs to twenty-eight treaties (twenty-six multilateral, two bilateral) with compromissory clauses, with a standard deviation of approximately fifteen treaty memberships.

In Table 5.6, we present the results of a regression analysis, where the dependent variable is the total number of treaty memberships with compromissory clauses. In addition to our legal system type variables (omitting civil law), we also include a dummy variable coded 1 if a state also accepted the compulsory jurisdiction of the PCIJ/ICJ and 0 otherwise. The results provide further support to our theoretical argument, showing that civil law states have the highest average number of treaty memberships. Common law states have 6 fewer (p = 0.01), mixed law states 8 fewer (p = 0.023), and Islamic law states 4.5 fewer treaty memberships with compromissory clauses (although not significant, p = 0.136) than civil law states. Thus civil law states use both forms of jurisdiction as cheap talk. The positive and significant sign for the compulsory jurisdiction variable demonstrates the positive correlation between the two; states recognizing compulsory jurisdiction belong to eleven more treaties with compromissory clauses.[30]

---

[30] In the next chapter, we expand these analyses by counting the number of bilateral, multilateral, and total compromissory clause treaty memberships for each state-year in our

The question remains, however, whether simply accepting the World Court's jurisdiction in any form has any significant influence on bargaining over contentious issues in international relations. Pessimists would still point to the large number of reservations states place on their optional clause declarations, and would argue that even though the number of cases before the Court has increased, the increase in the number of states has far outpaced this growth (Posner and Figueiredo 2004). We address this question more directly in Chapter 7 by examining the influence of dyadic PCIJ/ICJ acceptance on bargaining outcomes and failures. Previous research has shown that once cases involving territorial, maritime, or cross-border river issues come before the PCIJ or ICJ, compliance with judgments is almost guaranteed. Contending parties have complied with twenty-eight of twenty-nine PCIJ and ICJ decisions over these coordination issues, an impressive record indeed (Mitchell and Hensel 2007).[31]

As noted above, similarity of legal institutions should promote cooperation between states in general. However, the logic of our theory suggests that the use of optional clause declarations as cheap talk will work best for civil law states. Peaceful bargaining should succeed most often when two states have civil legal systems *and* when they both accept the jurisdiction of the PCIJ/ICJ. In these situations, the threat of being sued in Court is most credible, and thus, out-of-court negotiations will be more efficient. We test these conjectures more explicitly in Chapter 7, discriminating between the general effect of legal system similarity and the specific effect of the PCIJ/ICJ signal, and we consider their interactive effects as well.[32] Our results in that chapter show that the interactive effect of the PCIJ/ICJ jurisdictional signal improves bargaining only in civil law dyads. This indicates that the legal design put into place at the negotiating table between the originating states has important consequences for state support for the court as well as the efficacy of the court as a conflict manager.

---

dataset. We estimate more sophisticated statistical models for these count data (negative binomial models). The separation of the data into bilateral and multilateral forms of cooperation produces more surprising and nuanced results.

[31] Ginsburg and McAdams (2004, 1229) argue that judicial resolution is more likely for territorial disputes because the underlying dispute is a coordination problem. In an analysis of ICJ cases, they find that 86% of border dispute judgments have been complied with, in comparison to 40% compliance in cases involving the use of force and 43% compliance in cases involving diplomatic relations (Ginsburg and McAdams 2004, 1315). See also Huth and Allee's (2002) work on legalized dispute settlement in territorial claims.

[32] It would also be interesting to consider the interactive effects of other sources of state similarity, such as regime type and shared culture. Democratic states are more accepting of international legal institutions and make more durable commitments to these institutions than non-democratic states. The growth in democratic states worldwide suggests that a larger percentage of states may accept the legitimacy of the ICJ in the future.

Conclusion

In this chapter, we argue that domestic legal systems have important effects on foreign policy behavior and interstate bargaining, and that civil law countries are more likely to recognize the jurisdiction of the ICJ than common law or Islamic law countries. On the other hand, common and Islamic law states make more durable commitments to the Court. These results speak more broadly to our theoretical ideas about the motives of states joining pre-existing courts, or the potential *joiners*. Our argument and empirical analyses for the World Court suggest that states look to the similarity between the Court's legal principles and rules and their own domestic legal tradition when sending cheap talk signals about their willingness to resolve conflicts peacefully. It is easier for potential joiners to coordinate through an adjudicator that they perceive to be unbiased and fair because the adjudicator is advantaged for mitigating information asymmetries and providing independent and trusted information to disputants. Potential joiners are also likely to seek out international courts created in their own legal image because this increases the chances that the adjudicator and joiners will converge on the same focal points in bargaining. The joiners are more confident in the types of rulings that the court will render should they require the assistance of the court to resolve interstate disputes.

Our argument speaks more broadly to the liberal research tradition in international relations. Liberals argue that domestic political variables play an important role in states' behavior on the international arena, and our analyses of domestic legal institutions and regime type support this view. A domestic legal system, which constitutes an embodiment of societal preferences, interests, and ideas, can determine a state's behavior towards other states and international institutions (Moravcsik 1997). We find that the characteristics of internal legal systems account for a great deal of variance in the acceptance rates and durability of interstate commitments. Our argument also bolsters democratic peace research, showing that democratic states are more accepting and committed to international legal institutions than autocratic states.

Understanding the characteristics of states' legal systems may give us leverage for analyzing a wide variety of international courts and peace-promoting institutions. Powell (2006b) finds that common law states tend to lend higher levels of support to the ECJ than civil law states because the ECJ embraces the *stare decisis* principle. As shown in Chapter 4, civil and common law states have similar signature and ratification rates for the ICC, which reflects the legal compromise struck by civil and common law negotiators in Rome. We anticipate similar patterns for other international courts, such as the ITLOS and the proposed IICJ. Potential joiners to these courts will look to the legal design principles established by the originators when deciding whether or not to open themselves up to adjudication by the court. Extending our argument to other international courts will further our understanding of the intricate relationship between domestic legal structures and foreign policy choices.

6 The rational design of state commitments to international courts

States join international institutions and sign treaties with other states frequently in world politics. The depth of cooperation and design of these commitments varies considerably. Some treaties are extremely detailed and span hundreds of pages, such as the United Nations Convention on the Law of the Sea (UNCLOS), while others spell out the terms of the treaty in a few hundred words, such as the original North Atlantic Treaty Organization (NATO) agreement. International relations scholars have pointed to a variety of factors that may explain the rich variation in the design and depth of cooperation in states' international commitments, including relative capabilities, number of signatories, and regime types of the negotiating parties.

In this chapter, we focus on a factor that has received less attention in the rational design literature: domestic legal systems. As we explained in Chapter 2, there is considerable variation in the form and design of contracts in civil law, common law, and Islamic law systems. Contracts signed in these legal traditions differ in terms of their attention to detail, their length, and their inclusion of general principles. We assert that these contractual differences in the domestic realm carry over onto the international arena, where states make commitments with international institutions and with other states. International negotiators bring their legal backgrounds to the negotiating table, which influences both their willingness to sign treaties and the design of the resulting agreements. Negotiators are forward looking in the sense that they consider how international commitments will affect future interstate bargaining situations. States can protect their self-interests by refusing to join international institutions, refusing to sign treaties, or by embedding reservations in treaties that they sign and ratify.

While our theoretical framework can be applied broadly to states' commitments to international institutions and other states, we focus our attention on the relationship between domestic legal systems and states' commitments to international courts. We examine the design of states' commitments to the PCIJ and the ICJ. States have considerable leverage in their ability to place reservations on declarations to the PCIJ/ICJ, making these courts interesting empirical testing grounds for institutional design hypotheses. We argue that characteristics of domestic legal systems help to account for the manner by which states recognize the PCIJ/ICJ (e.g. compulsory vs. compromissory clause jurisdiction), the length of states' optional clause declarations (i.e. number of words), as well as the types of reservations that states place on compulsory jurisdiction declarations (e.g. *ratione temporis*, *ratione personae*).

Empirical analyses of states' commitments to the PCIJ/ICJ show that civil law states are more likely to recognize the jurisdiction of the PCIJ/ICJ through both optional clause declarations and compromissory clause treaty memberships than common law or Islamic law states. Common law states place more restrictions on their declarations than civil law or Islamic law states, with the majority of those restrictions relating to specific areas of international law (*ratione materiae*). This is reaffirmed in analyses of the total number of words found in states' optional clause declarations: common law and Islamic law states have a significantly higher number of words in their declarations, reflecting the tendency for these countries to embed more reservations in their commitments to the World Court. However, when looking at recognition of the Court's jurisdiction through compromissory clauses in interstate treaties, there are notable differences with respect to bilateral and multilateral forms of cooperation. Civil law states embed compromissory clauses more often in multilateral treaties, while common and Islamic law states prefer bilateral compromissory clause treaties. Even more fascinating is that Islamic law states belong to the highest average number of bilateral compromissory clause treaties.

Our chapter is organized as follows. First, we describe the various ways that states can recognize the jurisdiction of the PCIJ/ICJ. Second, we present our theoretical argument relating the characteristics of domestic legal systems to the design of states' commitments to the PCIJ/ICJ. Third, we describe our research design to evaluate our hypotheses and we present the results from several empirical tests. Finally, we talk about the broader implications of our findings for research on international courts and the rational design of interstate cooperation more broadly.

The design of state commitments to the World Court

The process of cooperation between states and international institutions is somewhat different from cooperation between states because institutions have a finite set of rules and procedures in place before negotiations with a particular state commence. In other words, the basic legal core of the relationship between a state and an institution is not usually negotiable. Consider, for example, the situation states face when they are considering whether or not to accept the jurisdiction of the ICJ. The basic rules and procedures of the ICJ are spelled out in its Statute and are not subject to negotiations or bargaining: "[W]hile the Statute as interpreted in practice permits reservations to its jurisdiction, it does not permit reservations as to the functioning and the organization of the Court."[1] Moreover, these core rules cannot differ in relation to each particular state. For example, the formal prohibition of precedent (Article 59 of the ICJ Statute) relates to the ICJ's method of deciding all cases, regardless of the domestic legal systems of the litigating parties.

The World Court's jurisdiction may derive from multiple sources, as explained by Szafarz (1993, x).

Special emphasis should be placed on the fact that the jurisdiction (competence) of an international court has its source in the consent of the states which are parties to a given dispute. The consent may be expressed *ad hoc*, once a dispute has arisen. It may also be expressed *post hoc* by a party to the dispute when the case has been brought before the court by the other party. Finally, consent may be expressed *ante hoc*, in advance, with reference to all legal disputes to be submitted in the future or to certain categories of such disputes. The latter form of jurisdiction is usually ... termed compulsory or obligatory jurisdiction.

With respect to the ICJ, *ante hoc* consent is expressed through recognition of the optional clause (Article 36(2) of the ICJ Statute), indicating that a nation is willing to acknowledge the adjudication powers of the ICJ in all legal disputes regarding the interpretation of a treaty, any question of international law, and the interpretation of other international obligations (Bederman 2001, 243). The Court's jurisdiction may also be established in compromissory clauses contained in multilateral or bilateral treaties. As noted by Szafarz (1993), a party may also express its consent when the case has already been brought before the Court by the other disputant (*post hoc*) or once a dispute has arisen (*ad hoc*).[2] Among these forms of jurisdictional recognition, compromissory clauses are the most common, with 80% of countries in the world belonging to one or more treaties with compromissory clauses. Compulsory jurisdiction

---

[1] Separate opinion of Judge Lauterpacht, *Case Concerning Certain Norwegian Loans* (*France* v. *Norway*), Judgment of July 6, 1957, 1957 ICJ Rep. 9, 45–46.

[2] States may also recognize ICJ jurisdiction by special agreement, or *forum prorogatum*: "Exercise of jurisdiction by virtue of the principle of *forum prorogatum* takes place whenever, after the initiation of proceedings by joint or unilateral application, jurisdiction is exercised with regard either to the entire dispute or to some aspects of it as the result of an agreement, express or implied, which is given by either or both parties and without which the Court would not be in the position to exercise jurisdiction" (Alexandrov 1995, 3).

is less common, with one third of states making optional clause declarations. However, eighty-nine different countries have recognized the compulsory jurisdiction of the PCIJ/ICJ since 1920, representing 46% of all states in the world today.

While states cannot renegotiate the procedures or rules of the World Court, they do have the ability to make decisions about the Court's competence and jurisdiction in situations where interstate disputes may arise. States can accept the jurisdiction of the PCIJ/ICJ in a limited way by placing reservations on their optional clause declarations. Reservations are "restrictions relating to the content of the commitments entered into a particular declaration" (Szafarz 1993, 46).[3] Paving the way for future reservations, in 1921 the Netherlands restricted the PCIJ's jurisdiction "only to future disputes, and excluded disputes with respect to which the parties had agreed upon a different means of settlement" (Szafarz 1993, 47). Formally, the admissibility of reservations was established in relation to the PCIJ by the resolution of the Assembly of the League of Nations, which stated that reservations may relate "either generally to certain aspects of any kind of dispute, or specifically to certain classes of lists of disputes." The right of states to limit the competence of the Court via reservations was further upheld by the Statute of the ICJ (Article 36, Section 3). The doctrine of international law admits the existence of all types of reservations that restrict the jurisdiction of the Court. The general logic behind this approach is that since a state is able to refuse the jurisdiction of the PCIJ/ICJ altogether, it should also have the option to accept the jurisdiction in a limited way.

For compulsory jurisdiction, this inherent competence is embodied in the institution of a reservation.[4] There are numerous types of reservations that states may place on their optional clause declarations (see Table 6.1), relating to other states (*ratione personae*), certain times of disputes (*ratione temporis*), or specific areas of international law (*ratione materiae*) (Szafarz 1993).

---

[3] For an informative discussion about various legal definitions of reservations and systemic level trends in their use in treaties over time, see Gamble (1980).

[4] The widespread practice of placing many reservations on a declaration is often criticized: "[T]he reason for making reservations in declarations include: viewing judicial procedure as improper in certain disputes, lack of full confidence in the Court, excessive caution, political sensibility of certain issues" (Szafarz 1993, 50). Bolton (2001, 170) points to the lack of reservations as a major impediment to American support for the ICC: "Stripped of the reservation power, the United States would risk expansive and mischievous definitional interpretations by a politically motivated court. Indeed, the 'no reservations' clause appears obviously directed against the United States and its protective Senate, and is a treaty provision we should *never* agree to."

Table 6.1 *Reservations on PCIJ/ICJ optional clause declarations*

Reservation type	Percentage of state-years among states accepting compulsory jurisdiction		
	Civil law	Common law	Islamic law
General reservations	N = 2,068	N = 645	N = 241
Relation to any other state accepting the same obligation*	82	45	73
Reciprocity*	73	82	54
Declarations are in conformity with Article 36(2)	59	84	92
Refer to the four categories of disputes in Article 36(2)	21	46	57
Ratione materiae			
Recourse to other method of peaceful settlement*	36	82	76
Territorial dispute	4	4.5	0
Rights and status of adjacent sea areas, islands, sea resources	< 1	13	0
Adjacent airspace	3	10	0
Domestic jurisdiction as determined by international law*	11	58	52
Matters essentially within the domestic jurisdiction	0	9	0
Matters within the domestic jurisdiction as determined by the state	3	19	38
Disputes relating to multilateral treaties	< 1	9	23
Relating to a treaty or treaties	4	4	0
Suspension of proceedings regarding a dispute under consideration by the League of Nations or the UN	3	50	0
Subject to the right to submit the dispute to the council of the League of Nations	< 1	0	0
Excluding disputes that arose during hostilities	< 1	38	0
Excluding disputes relating to hostilities, armed conflict, individual and collective self-defense, resistance to aggression and occupation, fulfillment of obligations imposed by IGOs	3	10	19
National security reservation	< 1	7	0
Other reservations *ratione materiae*	< 1	7	19
Ratione temporis			
Object of exclusion	34	81	72
Exclusion date	29	68	72

Table 6.1 (*cont.*)

| Reservation type | Percentage of state-years among states accepting compulsory jurisdiction | | |
	Civil law	Common law	Islamic law
Ratione personae			
Excluding British Commonwealth countries	2	56	0
Requiring recognition, diplomatic relations	< 1	7	0
Excluding non-sovereign states or territories	0	4	0
Only states party to the statute or members of the UN	3	8	0
Others			
Reserve the right to add, amend, withdraw declarations★	11	20	0
The declaration of the other party should be deposited no less than twelve months prior to the filing of an application or the other party should not have accepted the compulsory jurisdiction exclusively for the purposes of the dispute	4	20	0
Declaration made for specific types of dispute	0	0	0

Note: We placed an asterisk (★) near each reservation considered by most international law scholars as "unnecessary."

In the famous *Mavrommatis* case,[5] the Court established that declarations made by states under the optional clause have retroactive force: "[I]n cases of doubt, jurisdiction based on an international agreement embraces all disputes referred to it after its establishment" (p. 6 of the judgment). States that want to exclude pre-existing disputes place *ratione temporis* reservations on their optional clause declarations, which limit the PCIJ/ICJ's jurisdiction to disputes arising after a certain date.[6] For example, numerous states place reservations excluding World War II (declaration of Poland, 1931) or World War II (Australia, 1940; United Kingdom, 1940; South Africa, 1940) from the Court's jurisdiction. The main justification for reservations *ratione temporis* is that they constitute

---

[5] *Mavrommatis Palestine Concessions* (*Greece* v. *United Kingdom*), Judgment of August 30, 1924 (Jurisdiction), 1924 PCIJ Series A, No.2.
[6] As Alexandrov (1995, 41) notes, "the exclusion date itself can be determined in declarations of acceptance in different ways: signature, ratification, entry into force or depositing of a declaration, date of previous declaration, a fixed date, date or period relating to certain events, etc."

a precautionary measure against unforeseen cases originating from the past (Alexandrov 1995, 15).

The largest group of reservations relate to *ratione materiae*, which exclude certain types of disputes from the jurisdiction of the PCIJ/ICJ, including territorial disputes, disputes over sea resources, armed conflicts, and individual self-defense. If a state places a reservation *ratione materiae* on its declaration, all disputes dealing with the particular reservation's subject area do not fall under the adjudication powers of the PCIJ/ICJ. For example, the United Kingdom's optional clause declaration of 1957 contained a provision that excluded the ICJ's jurisdiction from any question "which in the opinion of the Government of the UK affects the national security of the UK or any of its dependent territories" (Alexandrov 1995, 91). Reservations *ratione personae* limit the jurisdiction of the PCIJ/ICJ by excluding disputes with certain states. The most common reservation of this type is the reservation placed by members of the British Commonwealth, which excludes disputes with any other member of the British Commonwealth. Another quite popular reservation *ratione personae* excludes disputes with states with which the declaring state has no diplomatic relations.

All of these restrictions on states' commitments to the PCIJ/ICJ can vary across time as states modify declarations by adding new restrictions and removing old ones. France, for example, joined the ICJ in 1945, making an optional clause declaration. Two years later, it placed a reciprocity reservation on its declaration. In 1959, France added a reservation *ratione materiae*, which excluded the ICJ's jurisdiction in disputes arising out of any war or international hostilities and disputes arising out of crises affecting French national security. In 1966, France added a general provision to its declaration which states: "The Government of the French Republic also reserves the right to supplement, amend, or withdraw at any time the reservations made above, or any other reservations which it may make hereafter, by giving notice to the Secretary-General of the United Nations" (Declaration of France).

Restrictions can also vary across space because the declarations of each state can be unique as far as the number and types of reservations placed on optional clause declarations. The number of reservations placed by states on optional clause declarations varies from zero to nineteen, with an average of five reservations per state. Some states choose not to place any type of reservation on their declarations (Gabon, Georgia, Iceland, Laos, and Turkey), some states place a moderate amount of restrictions (Canada's ten reservations), while other states restrict the jurisdiction of the PCIJ/ICJ in a wide variety of situations (India's nineteen reservations).

The diversity and use of reservations for optional clause declarations is well established in international law. However, states may also recognize the jurisdiction of the PCIJ/ICJ through compromissory clauses in bilateral or multilateral treaties. As discussed earlier, this is a common occurrence in world politics, with over three quarters of countries belonging to one or more compromissory clause treaties. Unlike optional clause declarations, which are negotiated between a state and a standing IO, compromissory clauses are negotiated between states in bilateral or multilateral negotiations. In these cases, the terms of the treaty negotiations may involve a wide variety of issues; dispute resolution mechanisms via the PCIJ/ICJ may constitute a small part of the overall negotiations. Design differences in compromissory clause commitments stem primarily from the nature of the treaty in which the clause is embedded, which may vary with respect to mandate (political, economic, security), membership scope (regional, global), and membership size (bilateral, multilateral). Our analyses focus on a comparison of bilateral and multilateral treaties, which constitute distinct forms of cooperation due primarily to the number of actors involved. We turn now to a description of how domestic legal systems influence the design of international commitments to the PCIJ/ICJ.

Domestic legal systems and the design of contractual relations

It is clear that the scope of the PCIJ/ICJ's jurisdiction varies tremendously across time and space. To understand this rich variation, we build upon the theoretical argument articulated in Chapter 3, where we uncovered important linkages between domestic legal systems, interstate bargaining, and commitments to the World Court. We argued that states can send cheap talk signals about their willingness to bargain peacefully with other states through international courts. International courts are able to facilitate these signals by correlating strategies, creating focal points, and signaling information. States with similar preferences are better able to send jurisdictional cheap talk signals to each other, which enhances their bargaining efficiency in the shadow of the Court. The PCIJ and ICJ are designed as civil law courts, which makes it easier for the PCIJ or ICJ as an adjudicator to create focal points, signal information, and correlate strategies if the claimants are civil law states. Furthermore, because civil law systems are so prevalent in the international system, they can more easily coordinate their behavior through the PCIJ/ICJ because their dyadic bargaining interactions are very likely to involve other civil law states. Thus civil law states are more likely to recognize the jurisdiction of the PCIJ/ICJ than states with other domestic legal systems. The empirical analyses in Chapter 5 provided robust support for this hypothesis (5.1), showing that civil law states are significantly more likely to recognize the compulsory jurisdiction of the PCIJ/ICJ than common and Islamic law states.

In this chapter, we expand upon our previously developed theoretical framework to understand the relationship between the characteristics of domestic legal systems and the *design* of states' commitments to the PCIJ/ICJ. We focus on three design features of states' commitments to the PCIJ/ICJ: (1) thoroughness of contracts, (2) necessary vs. unnecessary reservations, and (3) the substantive form of selected reservations (*ratione materiae, temporis,* and *personae*). Our argument rests on a key assumption that the law of contracts varies significantly across civil law, common law, and Islamic law traditions, and that these differences influence states' choices about the form of their commitments to international courts.

Domestic legal systems and the thoroughness of contracts

In Chapter 2, we compared the three major legal traditions in the world along several dimensions (Table 2.1), noting that differences across legal traditions stem from divergent structures, legal philosophies, and varied histories. Civil, common, and Islamic legal systems are quite different from each other with respect to contract law. Divergent substantive and procedural rules apply to contracts drafted under each of these legal traditions. As a result, contracts concluded under civil law are different from common law or Islamic law contracts. These differences pertain to length and the thoroughness of a contract, conditions of fulfillment, and consequences of breach of a contract. In this section, we summarize differences across legal systems with respect to contract law. We also discuss how the prominent features of domestic contract law influence the design of states' commitments to international courts.

Contracts concluded in a civil law system are relatively straightforward, due primarily to the structure of the civil legal tradition. The main feature of a civil legal system is a system of law codified in various codes, which are "systematic, authoritative, and guiding statute[s] of broad coverage" (Schlesinger *et al.* 1998, 271). Civil law is, to a large extent, classified, well-structured, and "contains a great number of general rules and principles" (Pejovic 2001, 819). With regards to contractual relationships, all of the main principles that are to apply to contracts are contained in codes. Usually, these general principles appear in the front sections of the codes, implying their application to all contractual relations enumerated in a code. For example, the *bona fides* and the *pacta sunt servanda* principles are included in civil codes. The first of these principles, *bona fides* or "good faith," requires that contracting parties refrain from deceit. The principle originated in Roman law and has significantly affected the civil law tradition. Although modern civil legal systems vary to some extent, the general concept of *bona fides* constitutes one of the most important abstract rules in this system (Powell 2006a).

The *pacta sunt servanda* principle is also firmly established in the civil legal tradition and it is included in general provisions of civil codes. When individuals sign contracts, such pacts are supposed to be binding and observed by the parties. According to civil law, when the subject of the contract has been destroyed, or the obliged party is prevented from keeping his promises due to illness, a contractual party may be partially released from a contract until the contract can be fulfilled. These situations are examples of *force majeure* (greater force), or unforeseen events beyond the control of a contracting party that prevents him/her from fulfilling contractual obligations. Because these and other general principles are included in the front stipulations of civil codes, there is no need to include them in the terms of a specific contract. The *force majeure* clause "operates independently of party agreement, which means that it will protect an obligee even if the contract does not contain a *force majeure* clause" (Pejovic 2001, 824). The same rule applies to both *bona fides* and *pacta sunt servanda* principles.

Negotiators from civil law countries bring to the table their experience with civil contract law, and thus they will be more amenable to signing and designing an international commitment that reflects the principles governing domestic contracts in civil law systems. The brevity of civil law contracts should carry over into commitments to international courts. Civil law states' optional clause declarations signed with the PCIJ/ICJ should be straightforward, with relatively few reservations. Civil law states should also be amenable to signing treaties with compromissory clauses, viewing these choices as complements rather than substitutes (Powell and Mitchell 2007). However, civil law states may be more willing to embed compromissory clauses in multilateral treaties than common law or Islamic law states because their acceptance of general legal principles allows for multilateral negotiations to be more successful. The basic idea is that when fewer contractual terms need to be negotiated, it is easier to strike an accord.

The strong commitment to *bona fides* and *pacta sunt servanda* principles in civil law systems enhances the probability of success in multilateral negotiations. Simply put, civil law states constitute relatively desirable contractual partners. Furthermore, multilateral treaties must take all of the parties' competing interests into account, and the more civil law states there are at the bargaining table, the more likely it is that a relatively simple agreement will satisfy the parties' needs. Civil law states have been dominant in the international system (Figure 2.1). This dominance suggests that negotiations for large multilateral treaties are more likely to include multiple states with civil law systems and that such states should be amenable to recognizing the PCIJ/ICJ's jurisdiction for resolving disputes.

In a similar vein, the international commitments of common law states should reflect characteristics of common law contracts. Contracts in this legal tradition are much more detailed and meticulous than civil law contracts. Because there is much less codified law that incorporates overarching general principles, the parties are responsible for including certain stipulations (clauses) in their contract. For example, in common law, *force majeure* is not precisely defined. The parties must enumerate in a contract any events of *force majeure* that will preclude them for being liable on the grounds of nonperformance: "This is why the *force majeure* clauses in common law are often very long and comprehensive trying to cover as many *force majeure* events as possible" (Pejovic 2001, 824). When contractual disputes arise in common law systems, judges look to the written terms of the contract, which is why negotiating parties try to foresee as many future contractual compliance situations as possible when drafting a contract. This is different than civil law contracts, where only the specifics of the particular contract are negotiated; the rest is left to the legal system (Moss 2007b, 234)

English common law does not recognize a general duty to negotiate or to perform contracts in good faith. In the United Kingdom, for example, the doctrine of good faith is often perceived by lawyers as threatening and unworkable in the British common law system. Despite the fact that some efforts have been made to incorporate *bona fides* into the common law tradition, the position of *bona fides* in this legal family is still much weaker than under civil law (Zimmermann and Whittaker 2000). *Pacta sunt servanda* and *force majeure* principles are also regulated slightly differently from the civil legal tradition. Common law systems recognize that events occurring after the signing of a contract, or a *force majeure*, might render a contractual relationship impossible or impracticable to fulfill, because the subject of the contract has been destroyed, or the obliged party is prevented from keeping his promises due to illness. Such circumstances in the common law tradition usually release all parties from their contractual obligations (Rayner 1991; Whincup 1992).

These characteristics of common law contracts lead us to expect that common law states will place a higher number of reservations on their optional clause declarations. These restrictions ensure that all of the states' rights and obligations are clearly specified, which resembles the "all-inclusive" approach of domestic common law contracts. Common law states should also find the use of compromissory clauses attractive because they limit the Court's jurisdiction to the subject matter negotiated in a specific treaty. We also expect common law states to embed compromissory clauses more often in bilateral treaties than in multilateral treaties because it should be easier to strike a bilateral agreement than to reach a settlement in a multilateral negotiation if negotiators are very precise about contractual commitments. It is less costly to negotiate with only one contractual partner if the terms of the contract are diligently drafted. Also, the common law approach to the *bona fides* principle should prompt common law states to sign bilateral agreements. Just as civil law's strong adherence to good faith warrants the high likelihood of multilateral agreements, common law states' relatively weak support for this principle makes them more likely to sign bilateral agreements in interstate cooperation situations.

Islamic law regulates contractual relationships in a way that is strikingly different from that of common and civil law. The Koran plays a crucial role in establishing the types of contracts admissible to the faithful, their rights, and obligations. Islamic law lacks a general theory of contracts comparable to its Western counterparts. However, the Koran does act in some ways as a code, in which general principles are included. Parties to a contract are also free, with some limitations, to place stipulations in a contract. These clauses cannot negate the legal purpose of a contract, or violate specific laws in the Koran or the Sunna (Arabi 1998). The design of contracts under Islamic law is closely connected to its treatment of the *bona fides* and *pacta sunt servanda* principles. Good faith is very firmly established in the Islamic legal tradition. Both the Koran and the Sunna permit cooperative interstate agreements as long as they are conducted according to the principles of good faith and honesty. Islamic law identifies fraud and dishonesty as a "serious moral wrong" (Rayner 1991, 206).

The principle of *pacta sunt servanda* has also been granted a prime position in the Islamic legal tradition. All contracts and treaties are subject to the *pacta sunt servanda* rule "whether such action takes the form of an administrative, judicial or even legislative act" (Rayner 1991, 87). The Koran (Sura V:1) states: *"Aufū bi al-'Uqūd"* or "Fulfill your obligations." Muslims believe that "this is an order from God to fulfill a promise, whether it be a contract proper ('*aqd*') or an agreement or obligation created by any means other than verbal" (El-Hassan 1985, 54). This rule is binding in relation to other Muslims and non-believers.[7] As noted in Chapter 2, Islamic law expects the faithful to keep their commitments. This rule, *ipso facto*, encourages careful and detailed contractual design, as both parties want to ensure that their obligations and rights are clearly stated.

We anticipate international commitments of Islamic law states to reflect the general design of contracts in Islamic law. Thus, we expect that Islamic states will be very careful in signing international contracts with international institutions. If a state knows that it has to keep its international commitments, it will want to make sure that its obligations are very clearly specified and thorough. This strong commitment to contractual compliance (strong *bona fides* and *pacta sunt servanda* principles), as well as cultural differences between Islam and the West, should make Islamic law states hesitant to recognize the jurisdiction of the World Court through compulsory jurisdiction or compromissory clauses.[8] However, when Islamic law states recognize the Court, their commitments should be durable and specific. The number of restrictions placed on their optional clause declarations should be rather substantial, although not as large as for common law states.

Islamic law states are also more likely to recognize the PCIJ/ICJ's jurisdiction in bilateral rather than multilateral compromissory clause treaties. Islamic law puts substantial limitations on states' contracting freedom, which implies that bilateral bargains will be easier to strike. Religious principles in Islamic law limit states' contracting freedom, which should result in a smaller number of interstate agreements. However, strong norms of *pacta sunt servanda* produce expectations that contracts negotiated under Islamic law will be upheld, even as circumstances change.

We can summarize our theoretical expectations with the following hypotheses:

> *Hypothesis 6.1: Civil law states will place fewer reservations on optional clause declarations than common law or Islamic law states.*

> *Hypothesis 6.2: Civil law states will have shorter optional clause declarations than common law or Islamic law states.*

---

[7] Despite such a strong position of the *pacta sunt servanda* rule under Islamic law, a contract may become temporarily invalidated if its fulfillment is impossible (*rebus sic stantibus*).
[8] The analyses in Chapter 4 made this clear, as only six Islamic law countries have ever recognized the compulsory jurisdiction of the PCIJ/ICJ. However, only one of these six states (Iran) reneged on their commitment to the Court.

Hypothesis 6.3: Civil law states are more likely to sign multilateral treaties with compromissory clauses than common law or Islamic law states.

Hypothesis 6.4: Common law and Islamic law states are more likely to sign bilateral treaties with compromissory clauses than civil law states.

Necessary vs. unnecessary reservations

In addition to the expectations regarding the number of optional clause reservations, our theory also allows us to formulate predictions dealing with specific types of reservations. Several of the reservations utilized in states' optional clause declarations are general in nature and merely repeat general principles inherent to international law or provisions of the PCIJ/ICJ statute (Alexandrov 1995, 21). For example, Article 36(2) of the ICJ Statute states that declarations of acceptance of the compulsory jurisdiction of the ICJ shall be "in relation to any other state accepting the same obligation." This article clearly establishes the principle of reciprocity. Thus the ICJ is bound by reciprocity "whether or not it is mentioned in the declaration of the state involved and there is no need to specifically make the reservation of reciprocity in a unilateral declaration" (Alexandrov 1995, 27; see also Briggs 1958, 267). Nevertheless, numerous states place the unnecessary reservation of reciprocity on their optional clause declaration.

Several states limit the jurisdiction of the PCIJ/ICJ in matters exclusively within the domestic jurisdiction as determined by international law, although such a clause is unnecessary. This reservation was first made by a common law country, the United Kingdom in 1929. As time went on, similar reservations appeared in twenty-one other PCIJ declarations, and in twenty-six ICJ declarations (Alexandrov 1995, 67). Similarly unnecessary is the reservation that excludes disputes in regard to which the parties agreed to have recourse to another method of peaceful settlement from the PCIJ/ICJ's jurisdiction. This quite popular reservation is not needed since "the Court, however, may take into account an agreement to resort to other method of peaceful settlement even without such a reservation" (Alexandrov 1995, 104). Finally, quite a few states place on their optional clause declaration a reservation which reserves the right to add, amend, or withdraw reservations or declarations. Yet even states that do not include such reservations can freely add, amend, or withdraw a reservation or a declaration. While many of these general reservations are redundant from an international law perspective, almost all states (95 percent) recognizing compulsory jurisdiction place one or more general reservations on their optional clause declarations.

Because domestically drafted contracts in common law states often contain general principles of law, we anticipate that these countries will also be more likely to place the above described "unnecessary" restrictions on their declarations. Common law states will feel more secure by including them in their commitments to the Court. Civil law states and Islamic law states should refrain from restrictions that repeat basic principles of international law or rules expressed in the Statute of the PCIJ or ICJ.

> *Hypothesis 6.5: Common law states are more likely to place unnecessary reservations on their optional clause declarations than civil law or Islamic law states.*

Reservation types: ratione materiae, ratione temporis, and ratione personae

Our theory also allows us to construct hypotheses regarding specific types of reservations relating to time, space, and other states. The use of reservations *ratione materiae* and *ratione personae* reflects the willingness of a state to accept the jurisdiction of the PCIJ/ICJ as far as its substantive scope. Common law countries are more likely than civil or Islamic law states to employ *ratione personae* reservations, especially those that exclude fellow British Commonwealth countries from the Court's jurisdiction. The general pattern we expect to observe is a higher likelihood of *ratione materiae*, *ratione temporis*, and *ratione personae* reservations for common law and Islamic law states in comparison to civil law states, with common law systems having the highest chances for reservations in all categories due to the nature of contract law in common law systems.

> *Hypothesis 6.6: Common law countries are more likely to place ratione personae and ratione materiae reservations on their optional clause declarations than civil law or Islamic law states.*

However, all states should be inclined to place *ratione temporis* reservations on their optional clause declarations regardless of the breadth of their substantive commitment to the PCIJ/ICJ. Even states that are less willing to limit the jurisdiction of the Court across space should value legal predictability that stems from placing a reservation *ratione temporis*. An optional clause declaration, which does not include any reservations *ratione temporis*, makes a state very vulnerable to potential suits regarding past and often unforeseen grievances.

Research design

Our theoretical argument suggests that civil law states should be more accepting of the World Court's jurisdiction than common law or Islamic law states, and less likely to place reservations on their optional clause declarations. Common law states are expected to place a large number of reservations on their declarations, especially those that restrict the Court's jurisdiction over specific disputes or issues. We also expect common and Islamic law states to embed compromissory clauses more often in bilateral treaties, due to the difficulties they face in striking multilateral agreements. To evaluate these hypotheses empirically, we analyze data from the PCIJ (1921–1945) and the ICJ (1946–2001) eras.

As noted in Chapter 5, information on compulsory jurisdiction is compiled from the annual volumes of the *Yearbook of the International Court of Justice*.[9] These volumes record optional clause declarations deposited with the UN' Secretary General, including the text of the declarations, from which information about reservations can be coded. Our coding of reservations is based upon Alexandrov's (1995) typology, which identifies restrictions related to certain states (*ratione personae*), certain times of disputes (*ratione temporis*), divergent areas of international law (*ratione materiae*), general reservations (such as reciprocity), and others. Table 6.1 provides a comprehensive list of all reservations in each category. States have utilized twenty-eight separate reservations, although the empirical range for individual states ranges from zero to nineteen, with an average of five reservations per state.

A list of bilateral and multilateral treaties with compromissory clauses was collected from the ICJ's website.[10] The list of bilateral treaties includes each member state and the start year of the treaty. Multilateral treaties are listed only by the treaty name and the treaty start date, thus we did additional research to determine the members of each treaty and the signature and ratification dates for each member. The data includes 159 bilateral treaties and 93 multilateral treaties. We created a monadic state-year dataset that allowed us to count the number of compromissory clause treaties that each state belongs to in a given year. The empirical range for this variable is zero to ninety-seven, with an average of seven per year. In Figure 6.1, we show how the aggregate number of compromissory clause treaty memberships in the international system has changed over time. The vast majority of temporal growth stems from the increasing number of multilateral treaties with compromissory clauses, with over 4,000 state level memberships in multilateral treaties in 2001. Bilateral treaty memberships grew in the inter-war period, but reached a steady number in the low 300s by the mid-1960s.[11]

---

[9] See www.icj-cij.org.
[10] *Ibid.*
[11] Given that other forms of cooperation, such as military alliances, have become more prevalent in bilateral treaty format following the Cold War (Powers and Goertz 2009), it will be interesting to see if compromissory clause treaties follow a similar pattern.

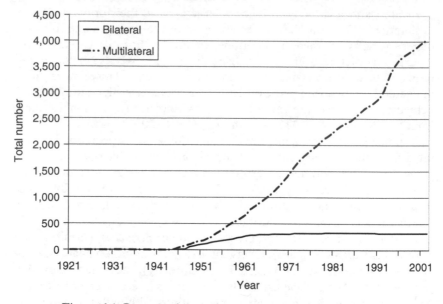

Figure 6.1 Compromissory clause treaty memberships

Our coding of domestic legal traditions is based on the four mutually exclusive dichotomous variables described in previous chapters: civil law, common law, Islamic law, and mixed law. We also include the same control variables that we utilized in Chapter 5: state capabilities, state age, and democracy. First, we include a measure of state power because powerful states are less likely to recognize the PCIJ/ICJ's jurisdiction (Scott and Carr 1987; Bilder 1998), which may also increase their willingness to place more restrictions on their reservations if they recognize the Court's jurisdiction. Given their advantage in bilateral bargaining, more powerful nations have incentives to limit the situations in which the PCIJ/ICJ has jurisdiction. As noted previously, we measure capabilities using the Correlates of War's CINC score.

The second measure is state age. Newer states should be more reluctant to make optional clause declarations, although older states may declare more reservations or join more compromissory clause treaties, simply because their commitments to the PCIJ/ICJ are longer. As described in Chapter 5, the measure for state age captures the length of time a country has been recognized as a state, starting in 1200 AD (Central Intelligence Agency 2007). We calculate the natural logarithm of a state's age to minimize its variance.

The third control variable is regime type. The democratic peace literature suggests that democracies are more likely to adopt peaceful methods of conflict resolution (Dixon 1994), and are more amenable to legalistic procedures, such as adjudication or arbitration (Raymond 1994). While democracies may be supportive of the PCIJ/ICJ in general (Powell and Mitchell 2007), they may be cautious about their international commitments because they face higher audience costs for reneging on agreements (Fearon 1994). Thus our expectation is that democracies will be more likely than autocracies to place restrictions on the Court's prerogative in the form of reservations on optional clause declarations. To measure each state's democracy level, we use the Polity IV 0–10 democracy score (Jaggers and Gurr 1995). We turn now to multivariate analyses to empirically evaluate our theoretical hypotheses.

Empirical analyses

In order to test our legal design hypotheses, we employ a wide variety of tests. We begin by examining the number of words in states' optional clause declarations (compulsory jurisdiction), including the number of words on initial commitments to the World Court and the total number of words in optional clause declarations as of 2001. We then compare our results for compulsory jurisdiction to analyses of compromissory jurisdiction, breaking down treaties into bilateral and multilateral forms of cooperation. Next, we analyze the design of states' optional clause declarations in more detail, focusing on five different categories of reservations. In all three testing grounds, we find support for our general contention that the characteristics of domestic legal traditions carry over into world politics, influencing not only whether states work with international courts but also the conditions under which states are comfortable ceding jurisdictional control to international courts.

Word counts for optional clause declarations

We begin our analyses with a simple regression analysis of the number of words contained in states' optional clause declarations. We make a distinction between the initial word count, which is the number of words in the first year of a state's optional clause declaration (561 maximum), and the total (or current) word count, which includes all subsequent declarations made by a state (1,025 maximum). The mean number of words in the initial count is 155, while the mean number of words for the total

Table 6.2 *Regression analyses of optional clause declaration word counts*

Variable	Model 1: initial declarations	Model 2: initial[a] declarations	Model 3: current[b] declarations	Model 4: current declarations
Common law	49.75 (32.94)	62.92 (38.68)	163.49 (63.88)**	279.81 (72.75)***
Islamic law	18.48 (49.34)	25.64 (48.65)	94.23 (90.84)	188.57 (98.98)*
Mixed law	56.08 (38.12)	29.38 (35.85)	50.97 (70.24)	37.18 (75.41)
Democracy	—	3.11 (3.11)	—	15.67 (8.50)*
Capabilities	—	−73.92 (279.75)	—	−981.41 (1123)
State age	—	−4.86 (6.92)	—	−6.35 (25.50)
Constant	129.19 (16.6)**	120.53 (36.99)**	200.93 (30.86)**	120.95 (115.16)
Sample size	80	62	77	67
F	1.22	0.98	2.32	3.48***
R^2	0.05	0.10	0.09	0.26

Entries are coefficients followed by robust standard errors: * $p < 0.10$; ** $p < 0.05$; *** $p < 0.01$.
[a] The control variables are recorded in the same year as a state's initial entry into the PCIJ/ICJ.
[b] These are current only up through 2001, the last year in which the Correlates of War capabilities data is available.

(current) count is 245. The regression models are reported in Table 6.2. Models 1 and 3 estimate the effects of domestic legal systems only, while Models 2 and 4 add the control variables for democracy, capabilities, and state age.

As we can see in Models 1 and 2, there is no significant difference between the initial word counts for civil law, Islamic law, mixed law, and common law states. None of the control variables has a statistically significant effect on initial declaration word counts. However, once we take into consideration the variance that is added over time as states insert more reservations into their declarations (Models 3 and 4), we find that common law states have a significantly higher number of words than states with other domestic legal traditions, which provides support for hypothesis 6.2. Common law states have 280 more words in their optional clause declarations than civil law states. In the model with control variables, Islamic law states also exhibit a higher average number of words in their declarations (189), although this is weakly significant ($p = 0.06$). Democratic countries have a higher number of words than autocratic countries (Model 4), which is consistent with audience cost arguments (Fearon 1994). The explanatory power for Model 4 is fairly decent, with the six variables explaining 26 percent of the variance in word counts.

Table 6.3 *Negative binomial analyses of monadic compromissory clause treaty memberships*

Variable	Model 1 Bilateral treaties Coefficient (S.E.)	Model 2 Multilateral treaties Coefficient (S.E.)	Model 3 All treaties Coefficient (S.E.)
Civil law	0.250 (0. 080)**	1.066 (0.120)**	0.903 (0.100)**
Common law	0.625 (0.106)**	0.798 (0.124)**	0.724 (0.103)**
Islamic law	2.040 (0.101)**	−1.297 (0.183)**	−0.308 (0.113)**
Democracy	0.190 (0.006)**	0.072 (0.004)**	0.083 (0.003)**
Capabilities	8.889 (0.664)**	−3.213 (0.543)**	−0.179 (0.492)
State age	0.406 (0.016)**	0.180 (0.014)**	0.213 (0.012)**
Constant	−3.055 (0.111)**	0.440 (0.119)**	0.467 (0.105)**
α	2.563 (0.086)** N = 8,359 χ^2 = 2,910.62 (p < 0.0001) Pseudo-R^2 = 0.096	4.568 (0.104)** N = 8,359 χ^2 = 1,485.38 (p < 0.0001) Pseudo-R^2 = 0.024	2.931 (0.057)** N = 8,359 χ^2 = 2,426.71 (p < 0.0001) Pseudo-R^2 = 0.025

Entries are coefficients followed by robust standard errors: * $p < 0.05$; ** $p < 0.01$.

Compromissory clauses

Table 6.3 presents negative binomial analyses of state-year commitments to treaties with compromissory clauses, divided into bilateral, multilateral, and all treaties.

We utilize an event-count model due to the truncated nature of the dependent variable and the fact that Ordinary least squares (OLS) can produce biased and inefficient estimates when estimated on event-count data. We selected the negative binomial event-count model to control for non-independence among our event counts (Long 1997), which makes sense theoretically, given that legal traditions influence PCIJ/ICJ jurisdictional acceptance in multiple forms. The similarity of results in Model 2 (multilateral) and Model 3 (all treaties) reflects the dominance of multilateral memberships in the dataset. There are 5,518 state-year commitments to multilateral treaties vs. 3,059 state-year commitments to bilateral treaties. Civil law states belong to a higher number of multilateral treaties than common, Islamic, or mixed law states. As Table 6.4 shows, civil law states belong on average to eleven multilateral treaties with compromissory clauses, compared to nine for common law states, four for mixed law states, and one for Islamic law states. A similar pattern emerges in Model 3 when examining all treaties (12.5 for civil law, 10.5 for common law, 5 for mixed law, and 3.7 for Islamic law).

Table 6.4 *Substantive effects: monadic compromissory clause treaties*

Variable	Number of bilateral treaty memberships, expected count (S.E.)	Number of multilateral treaty memberships, expected count (S.E.)	Number of all treaty memberships, expected count (S.E.)
Legal system			
Civil law	0.67 (0.02)	11.66 (0.21)	12.49 (0.21)
Common law	0.99 (0.07)	8.93 (0.30)	10.46 (0.32)
Islamic law	4.03 (0.24)	1.11 (0.16)	3.73 (0.21)
Mixed law	0.52 (0.04)	4.02 (0.47)	5.07 (0.49)
Democracy			
0 (min.)	0.33 (0.01)	8.91 (0.23)	9.15 (0.22)
10 (max.)	2.21 (0.08)	18.24 (0.53)	20.89 (0.50)
Capabilities			
0 (min.)	0.62 (0.02)	12.03 (0.21)	12.50 (0.21)
0.36 (max.)	19.79 (4.87)	3.60 (0.75)	11.89 (2.31)
State age			
0 (min.)	0.14 (0.01)	5.75 (0.38)	5.37 (0.32)
7.31 (max.)	2.63 (0.14)	21.32 (0.95)	25.60 (0.99)

Note: Values are calculated using Clarify, Version 2.0 (King *et al.* 2000).

These results are consistent with our expectations that contract law in domestic legal systems influences the design of international commitments. As expected, civil law states are more likely to be part of multilateral treaties with compromissory clauses (hypothesis 6.3), since the number of contracting parties does not deter these states from contracting successfully. Because civil law contracts are not overly detailed, the costs for negotiations on the international arena are not as high for these states as they are for Islamic or common law states. While we expected common law states to be less open to the Court, we did anticipate a preference for compromissory clause jurisdiction over compulsory jurisdiction, and this seems to be borne out in our analysis. Common law states are also more likely to embed compromissory clauses in bilateral treaties than in multilateral treaties, providing support for hypothesis 6.4. It is easier to sign a bilateral contract than a contract with multiple contracting parties if negotiators are very careful about each particular obligation. The same is true for Islamic law states, as they prefer to embed compromissory clauses in bilateral treaties.

Islamic law states, whose systems integrate law and religion, are not very amenable to resolving disputes with the assistance of the PCIJ/ICJ. However, Islamic law states have the highest number of bilateral treaty memberships (4) with compromissory clauses, much higher than for any other legal system (civil law, 0.67; common law, 0.99; mixed law, 0.52). Thus while the results in Chapter 5 show that Islamic law states are significantly *less* likely to recognize the compulsory jurisdiction of the PCIJ/ICJ, our analyses in this chapter suggest that Islamic law states are more open to compromissory clauses in restricted bilateral treaties.

These results are somewhat puzzling, especially since Islamic law states are least likely to accept the compulsory jurisdiction of the PCIJ/ICJ. It is plausible that these states see the compulsory jurisdiction of the Court as constituting a permanent and firm submission to a Western judicial institution. Acceptance of the PCIJ/ICJ jurisdiction via a compromissory clause embedded in a relatively limited international contract (a bilateral treaty) seems to these states less threatening and easier to change if desired. Also, withdrawal of the optional clause declaration is much more visible on the international arena, and thus it affects a state's reputation to a much larger degree. Changing a compromissory clause in a bilateral treaty constitutes a relatively "low key" action that does not damage a state's reputation in the eyes of other "law-abiding" states. This behavior is somewhat consistent with the attitude of Islamic law in general towards keeping one's promises in the domestic realm and the survival of international commitments. Withdrawal of the optional clause declaration constitutes a much more severe breach of Islamic law. We can interpret this act as constituting a breach of contract not only with the PCIJ/ICJ but also with other states accepting compulsory jurisdiction. Breaking a promise given to multiple contracting partners is much graver in Islamic law than breaking a promise given to only one party. These results constitute a fascinating venue for future research.

The legal design of optional clause declarations

In this section, we analyze the design of states' commitments to the PCIJ/ICJ by focusing on the specific forms of reservations that states place on optional clause declarations. The full list of reservations employed by states is listed in Table 6.1. We report the percentage of reservation state-years for each domestic legal system type. These percentages include only those years in which states' optional clause declarations are in force. We find support for our theoretical conjecture that common law states will place the highest number of reservations on their commitments to the Court (hypothesis 6.1). In the majority of reservation categories (twenty of twenty-eight), common law states have a higher percentage of years with the reservations in force compared to civil law and Islamic law states. There are also some types of reservations that are fairly unique to common law systems, such as the declaration excluding British Commonwealth countries from the Court's jurisdiction (56%) and the exclusion of disputes that arose during hostilities (38%).

With respect to differences across reservation types, we see a fairly large use of general reservations by all states. As noted above, this reflects in many cases a restatement of principles already embodied in the League/ UN Charter or international law more broadly. As expected in hypothesis 6.5, common law states feel more compelled to place these "unnecessary" restrictions on their optional clause declarations. As Table 6.1 shows, these states are most likely to place a general reservation of reciprocity (82%) and a reservation *ratione materiae*, excluding matters exclusively within the domestic jurisdiction as determined by international law, from the World Court's jurisdiction (58%). A similar pattern emerges with regard to the remaining two "unnecessary" restrictions: a reservation containing the right of a state to add, amend, or withdraw declarations (20%) and a reservation *ratione materiae* excluding disputes in which the parties have recourse to another method of settlement (82%).

Consistent with hypothesis 6.6, the exclusion of the Court's jurisdiction in areas relating to particular issues or disputes (*materiae*) is much more widely used by common and Islamic law states than civil law states. The lack of good faith and *pacta sunt servanda* principles in common law systems produces more detailed international commitments and a broader set of reservation categories. Islamic law states exclude disputes where there is recourse to other methods of peaceful settlement or the issue falls within domestic jurisdiction. Both common and Islamic law states frequently exclude disputes that arose prior to their optional clause declaration (*temporis*) from the ICJ's purview. The use of *personae* reservations is fairly limited and employed mostly by common law states.

Table 6.5 presents logit analyses of each reservation category, where the dependent variable equals one if a state declares one or more reservations of each type in a given year and zero otherwise. The excluded reference category for legal systems is civil law.

The positive and significant coefficients for all other legal types across the reservation categories supports our claim that civil law states will place the fewest restrictions on their optional clause declarations (hypothesis 6.1). The substantive effects for these models are presented in Table 6.6. We see a large increase in the probability of *materiae* reservations for common (p = 0.699), Islamic (p = 0.726), and mixed law (p = 0.689) systems relative to the baseline category for civil law (p = 0.262). A similar ordering obtains for *temporis* reservations, with civil law states having a moderate probability for these restrictions (p = 0.404)

Table 6.5 *Logit analyses of PCIJ/ICJ optional clause reservation types*

Variable	Model 1: general	Model 2: *materiae*	Model 3: *temporis*	Model 4: *personae*	Model 5: other
Common law	2.43 (0.72)**	1.88 (0.14)**	2.38 (0.13)**	3.45 (0.15)**	1.48 (0.13)**
Islamic law	—	2.01 (0.24)**	2.60 (0.22)**	—	—
Mixed law	−0.06 (0.48)	1.83 (0.17)**	1.22 (0.16)**	2.25 (0.17)**	1.67 (0.14)**
Democracy	0.09 (0.03)**	0.06 (0.01)**	0.11 (0.01)**	0.09 (0.02)**	−0.01 (0.01)
Capabilities	1,616.56 (180.42)**	74.73 (31.85)*	65.55 (31.09)*	−9.00 (1.28)**	−10.84 (1.83)**
State age	−0.33 (0.15)*	−0.13 (0.04)**	0.21 (0.05)**	−0.03 (0.05)	−0.11 (0.05)*
Constant	2.59 (0.63)**	−0.57 (0.21)**	−2.53 (0.21)**	−3.14 (0.33)**	−1.32 (0.24)**
Sample size	2,785	3,001	3,001	2,785	2,785
Chi-square	186.42**	487.19**	571.01**	650.24**	283.87**
Pseudo-R^2	0.25	0.22	0.24	0.33	0.10

Entries are coefficients followed by robust standard errors: * $p < 0.05$; ** $p < 0.01$.
Smaller sample sizes in Models 1, 4, and 5 result from Islamic law cases being excluded from the model due to lack of variance.

Table 6.6 *Substantive effects: PCIJ/ICJ optional clause reservations*

Variable	General reservations, prob. (change)	*Materiae* reservations, prob. (change)	*Temporis* reservations, prob. (change)	*Personae* reservations, prob. (change)
Legal system				
Civil law	1.00	0.262	0.404	0.055
Common law	1.00 (none)	0.699 (+0.437)	0.879 (+0.475)	0.645 (+0.590)
Islamic law	—	0.726 (+0.464)	0.901 (+0.497)	—
Mixed law	1.00 (none)	0.689 (+0.427)	0.696 (+0.292)	0.354 (+0.349)
Democracy				
0 (min.)	1.00	0.203	0.268	0.034
10 (max.)	1.00 (none)	0.317 (+0.114)	0.524 (+0.256)	0.079 (+0.045)
Capabilities				
0 (min.)	0.835	0.154	0.273	0.059
0.36 (max.)	1.00 (+ .165)	1.00 (+0.846)	1.00 (+0.727)	0.002 (−0.057)
State age				
0 (min.)	1.00	0.608	0.210	0.062
7.31 (max.)	1.00 (none)	0.122 (−0.486)	0.552 (+0.342)	0.050 (−0.012)

and common (p = 0.879) and Islamic (p = 0.901) law states being much more likely to employ one or more restrictions related to time.

As expected, all states regardless of their domestic legal system type are likely to include reservations *ratione temporis* in their declarations. The probabilities for these reservations are very high (0.404 for civil law states, 0.879 for common law states, 0.901 for Islamic law states, and 0.696 for mixed law states). Each state perceives these reservations as a guarantee that old disputes from the past will not be brought before the Court. The multivariate analysis also confirms what we observed in Table 6.1, namely that common law states use *personae* reservations much more frequently than states with other domestic legal systems.

The control variables reveal some interesting differences across reservation categories. As states' democracy scores increase, they become increasingly likely to employ all types of reservations. As previous research shows, democracies sign only those international commitments that they are likely to keep in the future (Gaubatz 1996; Leeds 1999; Simmons 2000). Because democratic states know that they are very likely to keep their promises, they design their commitments in a very cautious way, making sure that all of their obligations and possible future circumstances are accounted for. This is interesting because it suggests that democracies are open to international adjudication, but that they place more restrictions on the situations where the courts have jurisdiction.

The effect of state power varies across reservation types. More powerful states are significantly more likely to employ general, *materiae*, and *temporis* reservations, and significantly less likely to employ *personae* and other reservations. The substantive effects for capabilities are quite large as well, with great powers being almost certain to place general, *materiae*, and *temporis* reservations on their optional clause declarations. We also see varying effects for state age across reservation categories. Older states are less likely to employ general, *materiae*, and other reservations, while significantly more likely to restrict disputes occurring prior to the declaration (*temporis*). The probability of the submission of cases originating from the past is much smaller for new states.

We check the robustness of these findings in various ways. To control for potential selection effects, we present the results of a Heckman selection model in Table 6.7, which includes all state-years in the international system from 1921 to 2001.

The first stage of the model captures a state's acceptance of compulsory jurisdiction, while the second stage captures the reservation categories analyzed in Table 6.5. The baseline model for compulsory jurisdictional acceptance is taken from Chapter 5, Table 5.2. In those earlier analyses, we employed a Markov logit model, which is duplicated here by multiplying each independent variable by the value of the lagged dependent variable in stage one (0 = a state did not accept jurisdiction in the previous year, 1 = a state did accept jurisdiction in the previous year). In order to identify the Heckman model, the variable for regime type is employed in Stage 1 only, while the variable for state age is employed in Stage 2

Table 6.7 Heckman probit analyses of PCIJ/ICJ optional clause reservation types

Variable	Model 1: general	Model 2: materiae	Model 3: temporis	Model 4: personae	Model 5: other
Stage 2: design					
Common law	1.10 (0.30)**	0.97 (0.07)**	1.23 (0.07)**	1.71 (0.07)**	0.84 (0.07)**
Islamic law	—	—	2.26 (0.17)**	—	—
Mixed law	−0.22 (0.20)	1.02 (0.10)**	0.40 (0.09)**	0.83 (0.10)**	1.13 (0.09)**
Capabilities	906.32 (218.3)**	22.10 (2.05)**	20.05 (1.99)**	−2.58 (0.98)**	−6.82 (1.55)**
State age	−0.22 (0.05)**	−0.03 (0.02)	0.16 (0.02)**	−0.05 (0.02)*	−0.04 (0.02)
Constant	1.86 (0.24)**	−0.21 (0.11)**	−1.17 (0.11)**	−1.17 (0.11)**	−0.96 (0.10)**
Stage 1: acceptance					
Common law	−0.28 (0.12)*	−0.27 (0.12)*	−0.27 (0.12)*	−0.27 (0.12)*	−0.27 (0.12)*
Islamic law	−0.41 (0.18)*	−0.42 (0.18)*	−0.42 (0.18)*	−0.42 (0.18)*	−0.42 (0.18)*
Mixed law	−0.004 (0.17)	−0.00 (0.17)	0.00 (0.17)	−0.00 (0.17)	0.00 (0.17)
Democracy	0.06 (0.01)**	0.06 (0.01)**	0.06 (0.01)**	0.06 (0.01)**	0.06 (0.01)**
Lagged acceptance	4.20 (0.12)**	4.20 (0.12)**	4.19 (0.12)**	4.20 (0.12)**	4.21 (0.12)**
Islamic law* lag (acc.)	0.91 (0.40)*	0.90 (0.40)*	0.92 (0.40)*	0.91 (0.40)*	0.87 (0.40)*
Common law* lag (acc.)	0.62 (0.24)*	0.60 (0.25)*	0.60 (0.24)*	0.57 (0.25)*	0.60 (0.25)*
Mixed law* lag (Acc.)	0.24 (0.32)	0.23 (0.32)	0.23 (0.32)	0.25 (0.32)	0.24 (0.32)
Democracy* lag (acc.)	−0.01 (0.02)	−0.01 (0.02)	−0.00 (0.02)	−0.00 (0.02)	−0.00 (0.02)
Constant	−2.27 (0.07)**	−2.27 (0.07)**	−2.27 (0.07)**	−2.26 (0.07)**	−2.27 (0.07)**
Sample size	8,499 (2994)	8,498 (2993)	8,499 (2294)	8,499 (2994)	8,499 (2,994)
Chi-square	70.97**	446.85**	572.67**	673.52**	271.18**
Rho	−0.39 (0.11)**	−0.09 (0.06)	−0.10 (0.06)	−0.22 (0.09)**	−0.12 (0.07)

Entries are coefficients followed by robust standard errors: * p < 0.05; ** p < 0.01.

Table 6.8 *Logit analyses of PCIJ/ICJ optional clause reservation types, controlling for UK colony*

Variable	Model 1: general	Model 2: *materiae*	Model 3: *temporis*	Model 4: *personae*	Model 5: other
UK colony	2.84 (0.76)**	1.97 (0.17)**	0.91 (0.16)**	2.71 (0.20)**	1.21 (0.16)**
Common law	2.02 (0.73)**	0.52 (0.15)**	1.46 (0.15)**	1.84 (0.16)**	0.63 (0.15)**
Islamic law	—	—	3.38 (0.38)**	—	—
Mixed law	−0.61 (0.45)	1.12 (0.20)**	0.34 (0.18)*	0.59 (0.20)**	1.33 (0.17)**
Democracy	0.06 (0.03)*	0.05 (0.01)**	0.10 (0.01)**	0.05 (0.02)**	−0.02 (0.01)
Capabilities	1,848.99 (298.4)**	71.72 (8.40)**	62.77 (8.08)**	−1.50 (1.72)	−7.18 (2.70)**
State age	−0.13 (0.13)	0.04 (0.04)	0.26 (0.04)**	0.39 (0.06)**	0.03 (0.05)
Constant	1.57 (0.61)**	−1.32 (0.20)**	−2.70 (0.21)**	−4.93 (0.31)**	−1.99 (0.23)**
Sample size	2,996	2,815	2,995	2,815	2,815
Chi-square	262.12**	860.56**	1,030.02**	1,036.74**	318.45**
Pseudo-R^2	0.29	0.22	0.25	0.36	0.11

Entries are coefficients followed by robust standard errors: * $p < 0.05$; ** $p < 0.01$.

only. The results are very similar to those reported in Table 6.5, with common and Islamic law states having higher numbers of reservations in all categories than civil law states. Thus, even when we control for the non-random selection of states into the World Court, the rational design hypotheses that we identified find robust empirical support.

We also consider colonial legacies in our models. If we add a variable for British colony to each model in Table 6.5, which we present in Table 6.8, we find that common law, Islamic law, and mixed law states are significantly more likely to have reservations in all categories than civil law states.

The dummy variable for the UK colony is positive and significant for each reservation category, which is consistent with our argument for common law systems. We also estimated the models in Table 6.5 using the alternative scheme for domestic legal systems which focuses on colonial legacy, as discussed in Chapter 5 (La Porta *et al.* 1999).[12] Our logit models in Table 6.9 suggest that states with an English legal origin are significantly more likely to employ reservations in their optional clause declarations, consistent with our findings for common law states.

On the other hand, states with French or German legal origins have significantly fewer reservations than the other legal systems, which is also consistent with our findings that civil law states have the fewest number of reservations. Even when we employ an alternative coding for legal

[12] La Porta *et al.* (1999) identify the following legal system categories: English, Socialist, French, German, and Scandinavian.

Table 6.9 Logit analyses of PCIJ/ICJ optional clause reservation types with La Porta et al.'s legal origin classifications[a]

Variable	Model 1: general	Model 2: materiae	Model 3: temporis	Model 4: personae	Model 5: other
English legal origin	3.44 (0.32)**	1.36 (0.19)**	1.83 (0.21)**	0.30 (0.19)	1.83 (0.30)**
French legal origin	0.01 (0.50)	−0.39 (0.18)*	0.46 (0.21)*	−3.49 (0.25)**	0.79 (0.30)**
German legal origin	—	−1.84 (0.27)**	−3.03 (0.41)**	—	—
Scandinavian legal origin	—	—	−0.56 (0.24)*	—	−0.06 (0.36)
Democracy	0.08 (0.03)**	0.15 (0.01)**	0.14 (0.01)**	0.19 (0.02)**	0.03 (0.01)**
Capabilities	1317.34 (285.3)**	76.87 (8.04)**	103.81 (8.78)**	−10.76 (1.75)**	−8.92 (2.44)**
State age	−0.05 (0.14)	−0.14 (0.04)**	0.13 (0.04)**	0.37 (0.05)**	−0.02 (0.04)
Constant	1.27 (0.55)**	−0.09 (0.22)	−2.38 (0.24)**	−2.64 (0.26)**	−2.51 (0.32)**
Sample size	2,480	2,687	2,994	2,480	2,786
Chi-square	239.15**	869.00**	1,019.58**	980.33**	188.00**
Pseudo–R^2	0.28	0.24	0.25	0.36	0.07

Entries are coefficients followed by robust standard errors: * p < 0.05; ** p < 0.01.
[1] The five categories include "(1) English Common Law; (2) French Commercial Code; (3) German Commercial Code; (4) Scandinavian Commercial Code; and (5) Socialist/Communist laws" (La Porta et al. 1999: 238). In our analyses, the Socialist/Communist legal system is treated as the omitted category.

families, we arrive at very similar conclusions regarding the rational design of states' commitments to the World Court.

Conclusion

In this chapter, we argue that domestic legal systems have important effects on the way that states design their commitments to international courts. We show that states belonging to different legal traditions design their commitments to the PCIJ/ICJ in quite different ways. Our results support theoretical conjectures that differences in the design of contracts in the domestic realm carry over onto the international arena. More broadly, our theory and empirical analyses suggest that scholars should consider the two-level relationship between domestic and international law more carefully when seeking to understand the design of states' international commitments.

Our findings contribute to the expanding literature on the rational design of international institutions. Not only do institutions vary in their design features (scope, mandate, size, etc.), but state-level commitments to institutions vary as well. In some instances, such as optional clause declarations recognizing the compulsory jurisdiction of the World Court, states are able to negotiate the form of their commitments to institutions. This kind of variance in institutional support most certainly influences the institution's effectiveness. In the case of international courts, this may imply that courts are more effective conflict managers for member states who place fewer restrictions on the court's jurisdictional mandate. This also suggests that international courts that do not allow for restrictions/ reservations on state commitments, like the ICC or the ECJ, may fare better in their attempts to resolve member states' conflicts.

In the next chapter, we explore these effectiveness questions more carefully by analyzing the effect of the World Court on interstate conflict management. We return to Bilder's (1998) conjecture that countries will be able to resolve conflicts out of court more effectively if they can credibly sue each other in court. We look at the effect of joint acceptance of compulsory jurisdiction of the World Court on the peaceful and militarized management of contentious issues. Are states able to reach peaceful agreements to resolve coordination issues, such as border disputes, more effectively if they can take each other to court? Do states eschew the use of militarized force to pursue their issue-related goals in these instances? More broadly, are relations between countries more peaceful if states open themselves up to international adjudication?

While states have standing in the World Court, individuals can be brought to justice in the ICC. To examine the influence of this Court on states' behavior, we look within the state and consider the influence of ICC membership on human rights practices. Do countries have better human rights records when their leaders and citizens can be brought to justice? Is the ICC more effective at promoting sound human rights practices than human rights treaties because of the Court's unique, hybrid design (e.g. independent prosecutor)? By focusing on the influence of international courts on states' foreign policy and states' internal behavior towards their citizenry, we can obtain a more complete understanding of the role and importance of international courts in the interstate system.

7 The consequences of support for international courts

In this book, we have shown that a rich relationship exists between domestic law and international courts. Originators of new international courts seek to design the courts in their own legal image, while joiners of pre-existing courts seek out adjudicating institutions that operate with familiar legal rules and principles. Domestic legal traditions influence states' willingness to support international courts and shape the design of states' commitments to courts as well. However, what difference do states' commitments to international courts make? Are international courts effective forums for conflict management? Do they alter states' domestic behavior, such as human rights practices?

Our theory suggests that international courts are not equally effective adjudicators for all states. Because the originators of new courts design them in their own legal image, this creates greater efficacy for member states with domestic legal traditions similar to the court's originating states. The World Court, for example, was designed according to civil law principles. As we demonstrated in the previous two chapters, this design feature resulted in greater support for the Court by states with civil legal traditions. This natural alliance of civil law states to the World Court should also enhance the Court's efficacy when managing conflicts between civil law states. In those instances, the adjudicator is better able to create focal points, provide information, and correlate the disputants' strategies. Bargaining in the shadow of an effective adjudicator in turn creates more efficient out-of-court bargaining, allowing the parties to reach agreements more easily and avoid costly strategies for dispute resolution, such as militarized force.

Our perspective sits between the traditional theoretical poles in the international relations field that view international institutions as either epiphenomenal (Mearsheimer 1994/1995) or as effective tools for interstate cooperation (Keohane 1984). Rather, our theory builds upon a growing literature which suggests that international institutions have *contingent* effects on interstate cooperation (Boehmer *et al.* 2004; Hafner-Burton *et al.* 2008; Hansen *et al.* 2008). International courts can

194

be effective conflict managers for some but not all member states. Our empirical findings build upon the rational design literature, showing that institutional design influences both the likelihood of state support for institutions and the chances that institutions will in turn be efficacious on the international scene.

In this chapter, we empirically explore the consequences of state support for the two international courts examined in this book: the ICC and the World Court (the PCIJ/ICJ). Our analyses show that both courts have significant, albeit contingent, effects on states' human rights practices and the propensity for successful conflict management. We begin by analyzing the effect of ICC signature and ratification on states' human rights practices. This is followed by an analysis of the out-of-court effects of the World Court on interstate bargaining, focusing on bargaining successes (e.g. reaching agreements, compliance) and bargaining failures (e.g. militarized conflict). We conclude the chapter by discussing the broader theoretical implications of our empirical findings.

Consequences of state support for the International Criminal Court

The issue of compliance with international human rights regimes has received a lot of scholarly attention.[1] Despite the fact that there is some hope that international treaties and institutions can put a stop to human rights violations (Chayes and Chayes 1993; Lutz and Sikkink 2000), there are serious doubts about the efficacy of human rights institutions. For example, states that ratified the Convention Against Torture and Other Cruel, Inhuman or Degrading Treatment or Punishment routinely violate their obligations stemming from this treaty (Powell and Staton 2009). Compliance is often linked to the parties' regime types, with democratic countries having better records of compliance with human rights treaties than autocracies (Neumayer 2005). States also have better records of compliance when they are more integrated into a system of international non-governmental organizations (INGOs) (Sikkink 1993; Hafner-Burton and Tsutsui 2005; Neumayer 2005).

While some scholars have examined the practices of specific international courts in the human rights arena, such as the ECHR, the vast majority of attention has been focused on human rights treaties. The findings in the literature regarding the effect of human rights treaties on states' human rights practices are mixed. Keith (1999) shows that being a party to the International Covenant on Political and Civil Rights

[1] For a detailed review of this literature, see Neumayer (2005).

is unlikely to produce an observable direct impact on states' behavior. Similar results are reported by Hathaway (2002, 1989), who shows that "not only is treaty ratification not associated with better human rights practices than otherwise expected, but it is often associated with worse practices."[2] Hafner-Burton and Tsutsui (2005) report similar results as well, showing that signature of major international human rights treaties actually worsens member states' human rights scores. However, human rights treaties can be effective at improving states' human rights practices if they have a mechanism to ensure compliance. Hafner-Burton (2005), for example, finds that human rights treaties are more successful if they are linked explicitly to Preferential Trade Agreements (PTAs).

Mechanisms for compliance have also been linked to institutions that enhance domestic enforcement of human rights treaties. According to von Stein (2004), democracies are more likely to be compliant with human rights treaties because they have stronger mechanisms for enforcement of the agreements. Ratification of human rights treaties does not significantly affect the subsequent behavior of autocracies in large part because of their weak domestic legal enforcement. Domestic enforcement may also create a selection effect, whereby fully democratic states may not join human rights treaties because they are able to effectively prosecute war crimes (Simmons 2009). Along these lines, Powell and Staton (2009) show that states with effective judiciaries are significantly less likely to ratify the Convention Against Torture because they have domestic means for punishing crimes against humanity.

In short, much of the existing work on human rights treaties paints a fairly grim picture about their effectiveness for improving states' human rights practices. However, we believe that the ICC is different. Unlike other human rights treaties, the ICC has a great deal of autonomous authority for prosecuting crimes against humanity. The Rome Statute created an independent prosecutor, with the ability to bring war criminals to justice (e.g. prosecution against the Democratic Republic of the Congo in 2004). Investigations can also be instigated by states party to the Rome Statute (e.g. Uganda in 2003) and by the UN Security Council (e.g. Sudan in 2005). Cases come before the prosecutor in the form of situations rather than as specific cases, which gives the ICC additional leverage for prosecuting crimes against humanity. The prosecutor's independence from the UN, combined with its support from the UN Security Council, puts the ICC in a unique position for investigating and prosecuting crimes against humanity.

---

[2] See Goodman and Jinks (2003) for a critique of Hathaway (2002).

A good example of the Court's authority stems from the recent charges brought against several individuals in Sudan.[3] In October 2004, the International Commission of Inquiry on Darfur was established by UN Secretary-General Kofi Annan. The Commission's report to the UN in January 2005 identified a series of crimes against humanity and war crimes that had been committed in Darfur, recommending that the situation be referred to the ICC. In March 2005, the Security Council referred the situation in Darfur to the prosecutor of the ICC. Three months later, the prosecutor initiated an investigation of the activities in the Darfur region of Sudan, resulting in the issuance of two arrest warrants in May 2007 against Ahmad Muhammad Harun, the Minister of State for Humanitarian Affairs of Sudan, and alleged Janjaweed leader, Ali Muhammad Ali Abd-Al-Rahman. More recently in March 2009, the ICC issued an arrest warrant for the President of Sudan, Omar Hassan Ahmad Al Bashir. Bringing charges against an acting head of state was a bold move by the ICC, as most previous arrest warrants issued by the ICC in the Congo and Uganda had been directed at rebel leaders.

However, while the ICC's prosecution powers are much more widespread than those normally covered by human rights treaties, the Court faces jurisdictional limits. The ICC has jurisdiction over "the most serious crimes of concern to the international community as a whole" (Article 5.1 of the Rome Statute), which include genocide, crimes against humanity, war crimes, and the crime of aggression. Article 5.2 stipulates, however, that the Court's jurisdiction over the crime of aggression depends on the adoption of a definition of this crime, which has not yet happened. Thus, at present, the jurisdiction of the ICC is limited to the first three categories of crimes listed in Article 5.1. This relatively narrow jurisdiction has encouraged widespread acceptance of the Rome Statute, despite the fact that "the range of international crimes over which the ICC can exercise jurisdiction may be expanded with the consent of the States parties" (Cassese 2005, 456).

Thus, while the ICC has a great deal more leverage to prosecute criminal acts, its relatively limited scope of jurisdiction may have increased the attractiveness of the Court to potential joiners. It remains a question, though, whether these limitations led to expressive commitments through the Court without any real intention for compliance. If joining the ICC is mere window dressing, then signature alone should not significantly improve human rights' behavior. The more significant act

---

[3] Information on this case was taken from the ICC's website at www.icc-cpi.int/Menus/ICC/Situations+and+Cases/Situations/Situation+ICC+0205.

of ratification should push member states to prosecute their own war criminals more vigorously, and should result in better overall human rights practices.

Research design

Descriptive statistics for the data utilized in this chapter are presented in Table 7.1. We estimate the effect of the ICC on human rights in the same time period that we analyzed in Chapter 4, 1998–2004. Models 1 through 8 in Table 7.2 are designed to capture the effect of ICC signature/ratification on states' human rights practices.

Our data on human rights scores come from the CIRI Human Rights Database (Cingranelli and Richards 2008), which contains information about government respect for a wide range of human rights. We utilize several different measures of human rights practices, including: (1) "Frequent torture" (Models 1 and 2), (2) "Extra-judicial killings" (Models 3 and 4), (3) "Political imprisonment" (Models 5 and 6), and (4) "Disappearance" (Models 7 and 8). These variables are coded based on US State Department country reports, as well as Amnesty International annual human rights reports. We selected variables in the CIRI Database that best capture crimes against humanity covered by the Rome Statute. We think this strategy makes more sense than examining overall human rights indices, such as the Political Terror Scale, because it allows us to better capture the fact that the jurisdiction of the ICC is limited to prosecuting only certain types of human rights abuses.

Our first human rights measure, "Frequent torture," is coded one if a state experienced fifty or more instances of torture in a given year, and zero otherwise. "Torture refers to the purposeful inflicting of extreme pain, whether mental or physical, by government officials or by private individuals at the instigation of the government" (Cingranelli and Richards 2008, 18). This definition of torture includes the use of physical and other force by police and prison guards that is cruel, inhuman, or degrading; deaths in custody due to negligence by government officials; simple beatings; rape; water-boarding; and electrocution. Our measure for frequent torture is a recoding of the CIRI database's indicator of torture into values of one when the original variable takes on a value of zero; in our state year dataset, there are 531 instances of frequent torture.[4]

---

[4] Most CIRI variables are coded in declining levels of human rights abuses as one increases along a given scale. The torture variable, for example, is coded as follows: 0 = frequent torture (fifty or more instances), 1 = occasional torture (one to forty-nine instances), and 2 = no torture.

Table 7.1 *Descriptive statistics for Chapter 7*

Variable	N	Mean	Std. dev.	Min.	Max.
A: ICC data					
Frequent torture	1,187	0.447	0.497	0	1
Extra-judicial killings	1,187	0.490	0.500	0	1
Political imprisonment	1,187	0.471	0.499	0	1
Disappearance	1,186	0.215	0.411	0	1
Ratification	1,353	0.265	0.442	0	1
Signature	1,353	0.650	0.477	0	1
Democracy	1,042	0.569	0.495	0	1
Military expenditures	1,123	5,659.372	31,109.89	0	480,451
Population	1,278	33,448.16	123,999.5	18.1	1,294,846
Threat	1,183	0.241	0.428	0	1
B: Politically relevant dyad year data					
MID onset	70,516	0.024	0.152	0	1
Both civil law	70,516	0.313	0.464	0	1
Both common law	70,516	0.068	0.251	0	1
Both Islamic law	70,516	0.032	0.176	0	1
Both PCIJ/ICJ	70,516	0.135	0.341	0	1
Civil law interaction	70,516	0.047	0.213	0	1
Common law interaction	70,516	0.013	0.111	0	1
Islamic law interaction	70,516	0.001	0.026	0	1
Democratic dyad	70,516	0.155	0.362	0	1
Relative capabilities	70,516	0.584	0.411	0	1
Distance	70,516	3,418.063	2,792.72	5	11,989
Peace years	70,516	25.235	27.804	0	185
C: ICOW claim dyad year data					
Issue MID onset	6,097	0.034	0.181	0	1
Both civil law	6,097	0.419	0.493	0	1
Both common law	6,097	0.098	0.297	0	1
Both PCIJ/ICJ	6,097	0.250	0.433	0	1
Civil law interaction	6,097	0.097	0.295	0	1
Common law interaction	6,097	0.041	0.198	0	1
Democratic dyad	6,097	0.354	0.478	0	1
Challenger's capabilities	6,097	0.474	0.369	0.0002	0.999
Issue salience	6,097	6.479	2.367	0	12
Recent conflict	6,097	0.163	0.511	0	5.4
D: ICOW settlement attempt data					
Reach agreement	1,136	0.547	0.498	0	1
Comply with agreement	621	0.826	0.379	0	1
Agreement ends issue claim	621	0.237	0.425	0	1
Both civil law	1,136	0.463	0.499	0	1
Both common law	1,136	0.079	0.270	0	1
Both PCIJ/ICJ	1,136	0.179	0.384	0	1
Civil law interaction	1,136	0.088	0.284	0	1
Common law interaction	1,136	0.037	0.188	0	1
Democratic dyad	1,136	0.404	0.491	0	1
Challenger's capabilities	1,133	0.452	0.334	0.0002	0.999
Issue salience	1,136	7.11	2.349	0	12
Recent conflict	1,136	0.367	0.482	0	1
Functional/procedural	1,136	0.403	0.491	0	1

Table 7.2 *Effects of signature/ratification of the ICC Statute on state human rights practices, 1998–2004*

Variable	Model 1: frequent torture, signature	Model 2: frequent torture, ratification	Model 3: extra-judicial killings, signature	Model 4: extra-judicial killings, ratification
Ratification	—	-0.60 (0.21)**	—	-0.21 (0.22)
Signature	-0.58 (0.24)**	—	-0.16 (0.24)	—
Lagged torture	2.41 (0.20)**	2.41 (0.20)**	—	—
Lagged killings	—	—	2.76 (0.21)**	2.76 (0.21)**
Democracy	-0.44 (0.20)**	-0.42 (0.21)**	-0.58 (0.22)**	-0.56 (0.22)**
Military expenditures	-0.00 (0.00)**	-0.00 (0.00)**	-0.00 (0.00)	-0.00 (0.00)
Population	0.00 (0.00)**	0.00 (0.00)**	0.00 (0.00)**	0.00 (0.00)**
Threat	0.71 (0.25)**	0.68 (0.25)**	0.52 (0.22)**	0.56 (0.22)**
Constant	-1.02 (0.25)**	-1.28 (0.19)**	-1.32 (0.27)**	-1.38 (0.21)**
Sample size	787	787	787	787
Chi-square	231.17**	235.67**	264.54**	264.23**

Variable	Model 5: political imprisonment, signature	Model 6: political imprisonment, ratification	Model 7: disappearance, signature	Model 8: disappearance, ratification
Ratification	—	-0.70 (0.25)**	—	-1.41 (0.32)**
Signature	-0.22 (0.22)	—	-0.10 (0.28)	—
Lagged pol. imprisonment	2.65 (0.21)**	2.54 (0.21)**	—	—
Lagged disappearance	—	—	3.00 (0.24)**	2.86 (0.25)**
Democracy	-1.72 (0.23)**	-1.64 (0.23)**	-0.82 (0.26)**	-0.56 (0.26)**
Military expenditures	-0.00 (0.00)**	-0.00 (0.00)**	-0.00 (0.00)	-0.00 (0.00)
Population	0.00 (0.00)**	0.00 (0.00)**	0.00 (0.00)**	0.00 (0.00)**
Threat	0.61 (0.23)**	0.61 (0.23)**	1.47 (0.26)**	1.56 (0.27)**
Constant	-0.67 (0.25)	-0.61 (0.23)**	-2.40 (0.27)**	-2.26 (0.22)**
Sample size	787	787	786	786
Chi-square	255.07**	263.40**	205.33**	196.06**

Entries are coefficients followed by robust standard errors: * $p < 0.10$; ** $p < 0.05$.

Our second measure, "Extra-judicial killings," captures "killings by government officials without due process of law" (Cingranelli and Richards 2008, 7). This includes murders by private groups ordered by the government, illegal and excessive uses of force by the police, and deaths from torture or military hazing. We recode this measure into a dummy variable that equals one if a state is characterized by occasional or frequent extra-judicial killings. Our dataset records 582 such incidents in the 1998–2004 period.

The third measure, "Political imprisonment," records the incarceration of people by government officials for political reasons. This variable is coded one if in any given year in a state there were a few or many people imprisoned because of their political, religious, or other beliefs, and zero otherwise. There are 559 incidents of political imprisonment in our dataset. The final human rights variable, "Disappearance," refers to cases in which "people have disappeared, agents of the state are likely responsible, political motivation may be likely, and the victims (the disappeared) have not been found" (Cingranelli and Richards 2008, 13). The "Disappearance" variable is coded one if in any given year disappearances have occurred frequently or occasionally, and zero otherwise. There are 255 state-years characterized by political disappearances. For each of these measures, we anticipate that ratification of the ICC statute will improve states' treatment of their citizens, meaning a reduction in the likelihood of each of these violations of basic human rights. Whether or not signature will improve states' behavior depends on whether or not states use treaty commitments for primarily expressive purposes. Given that all four of our dependent variables are dichotomous, we estimate logit models with robust standard errors.

Independent variables

Our key independent variable captures whether or not a state has signed or ratified the Rome Statute. We also include several control variables that are fairly standard in the literature linking state membership in human rights treaties and human rights scores. A state's costs of using violent means to repress its citizens and its perceptions of threats to its sovereignty should influence human rights practices (Poe and Tate 1994). In order to measure the costs of repression to a state, we employ the SIPRI (Stockholm International Peace Research Institute) data on military expenditures (millions of US dollars at constant 2005 prices and exchange rates).[5] As described in Chapter 4, this data covers a wider time

---

[5] Data available at www.sipri.org/databases/milex.

span than the CINC index used to measure the material capabilities of each state in Chapters 5 and 6 (Singer *et al.* 1972). Higher levels of military expenditures indicate lower costs of repression, which would make it easier for a state to torture its citizens.

In order to capture a state's perceived level of threat, we construct a variable called "Threat," derived from the Uppsala/PRIO Armed Conflict Dataset (International Peace Research Institute 2009). This variable is binary, taking a value of one if the state faced any form of conflict identified by the Armed Conflict Dataset, and zero otherwise. States should be more likely to torture their citizens if they face higher levels of domestic threat (Poe and Tate 1994). We also include controls for democracy and population size. Several scholars have theorized that regime type has a substantial impact on states' propensity to sign and comply with international treaties, including treaties on human rights (Poe and Tate 1994; von Stein 2004; Landman 2005). To measure each state's democracy level in a given year, we use the Polity IV dataset (Jaggers and Gurr 1995), which combines information from four institutional characteristics into a single democracy score ranging from zero (least democratic) to ten (most democratic). We use the same measure as employed in Chapter 4, a dummy variable that equals one if a state's democracy score is six or higher on the Polity IV index. Finally, population has been identified as a positive predictor of state torture behavior (Henderson 1993; Poe and Tate 1994; Davenport 1995; Keith 1999; Poe *et al.* 1999), thus we also include this measure in our models. This measure is taken from the World Bank.[6]

Empirical results

The logit models are presented in Table 7.2 and the substantive effects for all variables are presented in Table 7.3; the predicted probabilities are generated with Clarify (King *et al.* 2000), setting each variable at its mean or mode, while varying the variable of interest.

We begin by examining the effect of ICC signature on states' human rights behavior. Signature has a statistically significant effect for only one of our four human rights indicators, "Frequent torture," with torture being 53 percent less likely in states that have signed the Rome Statute (reducing the probability of torture from 0.29 to 0.19). On the other hand, treaty signature alone has no discernable impact on extra-judicial killings, political imprisonment, or disappearance. This supports arguments made in the human rights literature about signature (alone) of human rights treaties acting as "window dressing."

[6] See http://databank.worldbank.org/ddp/home.do.

Table 7.3 *Substantive effects: ICC signature and ratification*

A: *ICC signature (Models 1, 3, 5, 7)*

Variable	Torture	Extra-judicial killings	Political imprisonment	Disappearance
Signature (0 to 1)	0.29, 0.19	0.23, 0.20	0.13, 0.10	0.04, 0.04
Democracy (0 to 1)	0.26, 0.19	0.31, 0.20	0.39, 0.10	0.08, 0.04
Military expenditures (0 to 480,451)	0.26, 0.00	0.22, 0.06	0.11, 0.01	0.04, 0.08
Population (18.1 to 1,294,846)	0.08, 1.00	0.10, 0.98	0.07, 0.99	0.04, 0.37
Threat (0 to 1)	0.19, 0.32	0.20, 0.31	0.10, 0.17	0.04, 0.14

B: *ICC ratification (Models 2, 4, 6, 8)*

Variable	Torture	Extra-judicial killings	Political imprisonment	Disappearance
Ratification (0 to 1)	0.25, 0.15	0.22, 0.19	0.14, 0.07	0.06, 0.01
Democracy (0 to 1)	0.33, 0.25	0.34, 0.22	0.45, 0.14	0.10, 0.06
Military expenditures (0 to 480,451)	0.33, 0.00	0.25, 0.06	0.14, 0.01	0.06, 0.07
Population (18.1 to 1,294,846)	0.11, 1.00	0.12, 0.99	0.09, 0.99	0.06, 0.42
Threat (0 to 1)	0.25, 0.39	0.22, 0.33	0.14, 0.23	0.06, 0.23

On the other hand, ratification of the Rome Statute is quite significant. States that ratify the ICC treaty are significantly less likely to experience frequent torture (Model 2), political imprisonment (Model 6), and disappearances (Model 8). The substantive effects are fairly impressive as well, with ratification reducing the rate of torture by 67%, the rate of political imprisonment by 100%, and the likelihood of disappearance by 500%. The effect of ICC ratification is larger substantively in Model 2 ("Frequent torture") than the effects of democracy (32%) and domestic threat (56%). The substantive effects of the ICC on disappearances are also larger than the maximum effects for democracy (67%), military expenditures (17%), and threat (283%). Unlike other human rights treaties, the ICC is consequential for human rights behavior. States that join this international court seek to avoid ICC prosecution by enforcing crimes against humanity domestically. This in turn creates improved practices by the state towards its citizenry.[7]

[7] Simmons and Danner (2010) show another positive effect of ICC ratification: a reduced likelihood of civil war recurrence and an improved chance for peaceful settlements to end existing civil wars.

The control variables show effects that are fairly similar to those found in other human rights studies, with democratic states having better human rights practices, and states with large populations and significant domestic threats having worse records. Among these control variables, population size has the largest substantive effect on repression. As we saw in Table 7.3, states with the largest populations are virtually certain to engage in human rights violations, while small states have a low probability of repression. Our measure for state capabilities, "military expenditures," typically has the incorrect sign and is insignificant in several models (3, 4, 7, and 8). While we expected stronger states to experience lower costs of repression, these results show that states with larger militaries are less likely to violate their citizen's human rights.

In addition to the model specification presented in Table 7.2, we also tried including our measures for domestic legal traditions, as well as interaction terms of ICC signature or ratification with each type of legal system. The interaction specification fits with our theoretical model in the sense that the Court should have its strongest effects on members with similar legal rules and principles. In the case of the ICC, this would imply that ratification by civil law and common law states would be more consequential for human rights behavior due to the hybrid nature of the Court's legal design. However, none of the interaction terms is significant due to the sizable correlation between the interaction variables and the component terms. For example, the bivariate correlations range between 0.5 and 0.8 for civil or common law states with ICC ratification. This is not too surprising given how well domestic legal traditions predict ICC signature and ratification decisions (Chapter 4). If we include the effects of domestic legal traditions alone, most of these variables have insignificant effects on the various indicators for human rights violations. Civil law states do show higher levels of torture than common law, Islamic law, or mixed law states, but we see no other significant relationships between legal families and extra-judicial killing, political imprisonment, and disappearance. Even when controlling for domestic legal traditions, the effects of ICC ratification that we observe in Table 7.2 hold (Models 2, 6, and 8).

One might contend that there is a selection effect at work here. States with better human rights practices may simply join the Court more often than states with bad human rights behavior, which is why ICC ratification appears to reduce torture, political imprisonment, and disappearances. We find some evidence for an endogenous relationship. As noted in Chapter 4, when we add the variable for "Frequent torture" to our ICC signature/ratification models (Table 4.3), we find that states who engage in frequent torture are significantly less likely to sign or ratify the Rome Statute. On the other hand, as Simmons and Danner (2010) note, there are a group of states that might fall into this category of "frequent torturers" that find the ICC attractive, namely autocratic states who have recently experienced civil war. These states can use ratification of the Rome Statute as a mechanism for credibly committing to democracy and peace. Yet, there are certainly countries that engage in bad human rights practices that eschew the ICC altogether. The ICC may fail to attract members most in need of its criminal proceedings, painting a potentially grim view that international human rights law matters least where it is needed most (Hafner-Burton and Tsutsui 2005). On the other hand, the ICC does at least have the intended effect of improving the human rights behaviors of member states, which is a better record than what the literature suggests for human rights treaties in general.[8] This is at best, though, an indirect way to evaluate the effect of the ICC more broadly. We should reserve judgment on the court's efficacy until we have more information about how successfully it prosecutes war criminals in the Congo, Uganda, Sudan, and other places.

In the next section, we evaluate the effect of the World Court on inter-state conflict management. The Court's long history gives us ample evidence to evaluate its influence on interstate bargaining.

Consequences of state support for the World Court

In domestic disputes, courts often play a role in pushing parties towards conflict resolution, even if the disputants never go to court. The threat of either side taking the case to court can be sufficient to induce some type of settlement. Some scholars have suggested that a similar phenomenon operates at the international level. Bilder (1998), for example, asserts that the presence of the ICJ could increase the likelihood of successful conflict resolution between states because it provides a legal course of action for the disputants (Gamble and Fischer 1976). This effect should be strongest for those disputants who accept the World Court's compulsory jurisdiction clause. Bilder's argument suggests that the influence of the ICJ on conflict management could be substantial: even if disputants never submit their claims to the ICJ, the Court could have an *indirect* effect on conflict management simply by providing a "last resort" outlet for dispute resolution.

Other international law scholars paint a more pessimistic view of the ICJ's influence in international conflict management. As noted in Chapter 5, only one third of states in the world accept the compulsory

---

[8] We hope to look at this endogenous relationship more carefully in future analyses, perhaps by examining Heckman models of ICC signature/ratification in stage one and human rights practices in stage two.

jurisdiction of the World Court (Alexandrov 1995). Even among countries accepting the optional clause, there are a plethora of reservations that states have included in their declarations, which limit the scope of the Court's jurisdiction. Some view the optional clause as an internal weakness of the Court because it provides justification for the violation of the legal notion of binding settlements (Elkind 1984, xiv; Singh 1989, 24–25). Furthermore, because such reservations are reciprocal, states may find themselves even further restricted in their ability to sue other states.[9] The combination of substantive reservations and reciprocity severely restricts the effect of the ICJ on conflict management: "Multiplied in effect by their reciprocity, these escape devices are capable of limiting the acceptance of compulsory jurisdiction of the Court to a pitiful and absolute minimum of actual commitment" (Oduntan 1999, 70). Other scholars argue that the historical under-use of the World Court stems from a preference for the political process in the UN Security Council (Gross 1987, 46) and power disparities between disputants, which gives little incentives for powerful states to submit themselves to adjudication by the Court (Scott and Csajko 1988). In short, pessimists see the role of the World Court in conflict management as quite limited and largely ineffective due to both the internal organization of the Court and various external factors, such as relative capabilities.

This debate presents an interesting puzzle for exploration. Pessimistic claims about the World Court generally arise from studies looking at cases where the ICJ was directly involved, situations where one state sued another before the Court. While this approach tells us something useful about the types of conflicts that come before the PCIJ/ICJ, and the factors that influence the chances of cases being heard, we learn little about the indirect effect of the World Court. If the mere threat of going to the Court influences bargaining over contentious issues, we would miss this effect by looking only at cases of adjudication.

One finds a similar debate in the liberal peace literature linking state membership in IOs and militarized conflict. Some initial dyadic studies found a significant negative relationship between shared dyadic IO memberships and the onset of militarized disputes (Russett *et al.*

---

[9] The most ironic application of reciprocity stems from one of the original US reservations to the optional clause declaration in 1946. Called the Connally Reservation, it stated that the United States would accept the jurisdiction of the Court except in situations where it viewed the issue as falling under its domestic jurisdiction. What happened was that every time the United States sued another state through the ICJ, it simply invoked the Connally Reservation. So what was intended as a shield against litigation ultimately placed limits on the ability of the United States to resolve conflicts with the assistance of the ICJ (Bederman 2001, 244–245).

1998), although that relationship became weaker as more post-Cold War data years were added to empirical analyses (Russett and Oneal 2001). More recent analyses have suggested that only certain types of IOs may be effective at preventing conflict, such as those with security mandates that are highly institutionalized (Boehmer *et al.* 2004). These studies capture the indirect effect of IOs on conflict management, with IOs playing a passive role as conflict manager (Mitchell and Hensel 2007). When IOs take a more direct or active role as a conflict manager, as international courts often do, their success rates depend on factors such as conflict management strategies and design features of the IOs. Binding, legalistic attempts by IOs to resolve conflicts have a much greater success rate than non-binding forms of mediation or good offices (Mitchell and Hensel 2007). Furthermore, IOs that are more institutionalized and have more democratic members also experience greater success rates in managing interstate conflicts (Hansen *et al.* 2008). These more recent studies point to a richer, more contingent relationship between IOs and conflict management, paralleling the debate about the efficacy of international courts in the international law literature.

Our theory in Chapter 3 helps to address the puzzling results in the literature regarding the effectiveness of the World Court or conflict management by IOs more broadly, showing that there is an important interaction between states' domestic legal systems and cheap talk signals through international courts. The World Court was designed according to civil law principles, which makes it easier for civil law states to send cheap talk signals through the Court about their willingness to bargain peacefully in interstate relations. Civil law states perceive the PCIJ/ICJ to be a fair and impartial adjudicator, which enhances the adjudicator's ability to correlate strategies, construct focal points, and signal information. Our analyses in Chapter 5 confirmed the hypothesis that civil law states are more likely to recognize the jurisdiction of the World Court than common law or Islamic law states.

Yet, what difference does this make for interstate bargaining? We speculated that the PCIJ/ICJ should work most effectively as a conflict manager between civil law states that accept the jurisdiction of the Court because in these cases both sides can credibly sue each in court, and the similarity of legal principles in interstate negotiations makes it easier to strike a bargain. The plethora of general principles in civil law systems also facilitates the process of interstate bargaining by reducing the number of terms that must be negotiated in a treaty. In short, the debate about the effectiveness of the PCIJ/ICJ as an institution is a bit misplaced because it does not consider the conditional effects of domestic legal traditions. The World Court may have important indirect effects on interstate bargaining, but these effects vary across states depending on their domestic legal traditions, with civil law states benefiting the most from conflict management through the Court. In the next section, we describe the data we have compiled in order to test the effect of PCIJ/ICJ jurisdictional acceptance on interstate bargaining; our analyses focus on both successes and failures in the bargaining process.

Research design

We employ a variety of empirical tests to evaluate the effect of jurisdictional acceptance of the PCIJ/ICJ on interstate bargaining. First, we utilize militarized dispute onset as an indicator of bargaining failure. The World Court is designed as a court of last resort and it has been embedded in two institutions that actively promote peaceful dispute resolution: the League of Nations and the UN. These institutions view the use of military force as a failure of diplomacy, thus we think it is reasonable to treat states' use of violent force against other states as a failure of interstate bargaining.

We assembled a dyad-year dataset very similar to those employed in other interstate conflict studies (Russett and Oneal 2001), where we create a case for every pair of states as defined by the Correlates of War Project in each year of the states' existence.[10] We limit our analyses to politically relevant dyads, or those pairs of states that either border each other directly (on land or up to 250 miles of water) or contain a major power.[11] This decision is based on the logic that states must have some opportunity for conflict, with neighboring states being more proximate and major powers having greater global military reach.[12] In each dyad-year, we code a dichotomous variable for the onset of a militarized interstate dispute (MID). The source of the conflict data is Version 3 of the Correlates of War Project's MID dataset (Ghosn et al. 2004). A MID is defined as the threat, display, or use of military force by one state against another. From 1920 to 2001, we identified a total of 70,511 politically relevant dyads, with new disputes occurring in 2.36 percent of the dyads.

To capture successful interstate bargaining outcomes, we analyze the outcomes of negotiations over territorial, maritime, and river claims in

[10] For a description of the criteria used for system membership in the Correlates of War Project, see Small and Singer (1982).
[11] For definitions of major power status, see the Correlates of War homepage at http://correlatesofwar.org.
[12] For a discussion of why contiguous states fight each other more frequently than noncontiguous states, see Vasquez (1995).

the Western Hemisphere, Europe, and the Middle East, as coded by the ICOW Project (Hensel *et al.* 2008). These issues reflect the type of coordination games we described in Chapter 3, because there are often multiple solutions possible for drawing borders or managing joint resources. In these situations, an adjudicator can help the parties converge on particular equilibrium solutions. We examine whether negotiations over contentious issues produce agreements between the disputants, whether the parties comply with agreements reached, and whether agreements that are struck end the overall contentious issues at stake. These analyses more directly capture the out-of-court effects of the PCIJ/ICJ because we are able to determine if agreements are struck more frequently in the shadow of the World Court. In other words, these analyses capture the more passive role that the Court plays in helping parties to bargain more efficiently on their own.

To date, the ICOW Project has completed data collection on three types of issues: territorial claims (Western Hemisphere and Western Europe from 1816 to 2001), maritime claims (Western Hemisphere and Europe from 1900 to 2001), and river claims (Western Hemisphere, Western Europe, and the Middle East from 1900 to 2001). Territorial claims involve questions of sovereignty over a specific piece of land (including islands), and maritime claims occur when states disagree about the ownership or usage of a maritime area, while river claims arise over the usage and/or navigation of a river that crosses state boundaries. Issue claims are identified where there is sufficient evidence of contention involving official representatives of two or more nation-states over the issue type in question (Hensel *et al.* 2008). A complete list of issue claims is available on the ICOW website,[13] as well as all of the data employed in our analyses below.

To identify cases of bargaining success, we focus on peaceful settlement attempts, such as mediation efforts or bilateral talks to resolve a territorial claim. For example, there have been several dozen attempts to resolve the territorial dispute between the United Kingdom and Argentina over ownership of the Falkland Islands. We limit our analyses to years in which the World Court has been in existence, starting with the formation of the PCIJ in 1920 and ending in 2001, the last year of the ICOW dataset. From 1920 to 2001, there were a total of 1,136 peaceful attempts to settle issue claims in the Western Hemisphere, Europe, and the Middle East.

We utilize three ICOW variables to capture bargaining success in a given negotiation round. Our first indicator captures whether or not the parties

---

[13] See www.paulhensel.org/icow.html.

reach an agreement over the contentious issue at stake; 621 agreements (54.7%) were reached in the 1,136 settlement attempts between 1920 and 2001. Our second measure codes compliance with agreements, with compliance measured dichotomously as a one if the parties carry out the agreement within a five-year period or in the time period stipulated in the agreement (if longer), and zero otherwise. Both claimants complied with the terms of 513 of the 621 agreements reached, with an overall compliance rate of 82.6 percent. The final measure of bargaining success records whether or not the agreement ends the overall issue at stake. Some agreements are merely procedural, such as the parties agreeing to seek out the assistance of a mediator for future settlement. Other agreements are merely functional; they may resolve issues related to resource extraction or troop movements, but they do not resolve the issue in contention.[14] Functional and procedural agreements cannot end an issue claim by definition. Furthermore, there are cases where one or both parties renege on agreements that are struck, creating situations where the issue at stake is left unresolved. Agreements that end an issue claim are considered to be highly successful bargaining outcomes; 46 percent of the agreements reached in given negotiation rounds resolve the issue at stake.[15]

The ICOW Project also identifies militarized disputes that occur over the specific issues in contention. We conduct an analysis of MID onset using the claim dyad-year version of the ICOW dataset. This dataset records a dyadic case in each year that a claim is ongoing; for example, if a maritime claim between the United States and Canada existed between 1960 and 1984, this would add fifteen cases to the claim dyad-year data. There are a total of 6,097 claim dyad-years in the Western Hemisphere, Europe, and the Middle East from 1920 to 2001. We can compare the results of this more limited regional analysis to the overall results for politically relevant dyads globally.[16] The ICOW data allows us to measure bargaining failure over a specific issue, while the politically relevant dyadic data captures conflict onset in a global context over all possible contentious issues.

---

[14] For example, the United Kingdom and Argentina have reached several agreements over fishing and oil extraction rights around the Falklands, although they have not resolved the ultimate question of who owns the island.

[15] These analyses involve a smaller number of cases because we exclude the procedural and functional agreements.

[16] One important limitation in using the ICOW data for these analyses is the lack of Middle East cases to date. This creates a very small number of Islamic law dyads for analysis. However, we do have adequate data to compare the bargaining behavior of civil law and common law dyads.

Independent variables

The primary theoretical variables capture the domestic legal traditions of the states in each dyad. We use the same coding rules as described in Chapter 2, yet we aggregate this information about domestic legal traditions to the dyadic level. We create three dummy variables to capture the similarity of legal traditions: "Both civil law," "Both common law," and "Both Islamic law." The omitted category consists of dyads where the disputants have divergent legal systems or where both countries have mixed law traditions. In the dataset for all politically relevant dyads in the world (1920–2002), 31% of the dyads are both civil law, 7% of the dyads are both common law, while 3% of the dyads are both Islamic law. The remaining 57% of dyads have states with divergent and/or mixed legal traditions. In the ICOW claim dyad-year dataset, 42% of the dyads are both civil law, 10% of the dyads are both common law, while 1% of the dyads are both Islamic law. Given that the dataset is dominated by cases in the Western Hemisphere, it is not too surprising that civil law states are overrepresented relative to the global sample, while Islamic law states are underrepresented.[17] For the MID analyses, we also create interaction terms between domestic legal traditions and acceptance of PCIJ/ICJ compulsory jurisdiction, as described in Chapter 5.[18] These interactions are designed to test our theoretical conjectures about the interactive effects between domestic law and international courts. We expect the interactions to have a negative and significant effect on MID onset for civil law dyads where both states accept PCIJ/ICJ jurisdiction; this would indicate that civil law states are able to bargain more efficiently out of court in the shadow of the PCIJ/ICJ, avoiding militarization of their contentious issues.

Our control variables are very similar to those employed in previous chapters, although we convert them to a dyadic format. A dyad is considered to be democratic if both states score six or higher on the Polity IV democracy scale. In the politically relevant dyad sample, 15.5% of the dyads are jointly democratic. Those percentages are higher in the ICOW datasets, with 35.4% of the claim dyad-year cases and 40.4% of the settlement attempt cases being jointly democratic. Relative capabilities are measured as the challenger's CINC score divided by the total challenger-target capabilities in the dyad. The average in the claim dyad-year dataset

---

[17] A similar pattern holds for the ICOW settlement attempt data: 46% of dyads are both civil law, 8% of dyads are both common law, and 1% of dyads are both Islamic law.
[18] We do not have enough cases in the settlement attempt analyses to include interaction terms because there is a high degree of multicollinearity between the component and interaction terms.

is 0.474, while the average in the settlement attempt dataset is 0.452.[19] In the model with all politically relevant dyads, we use two additional variables that are employed by Russett and Oneal (2001): peace years and distance. Distance captures the miles between the capital cities, while the peace-years variable records the number of years since the last militarized dispute in the dyad; the mean dyadic distance is 3,418 miles. The average number of peace years is 25 years. All of these measures were generated using the Expected Utility Generation (EUGene) Program (Bennett and Stam 2000).

In the empirical models employing ICOW data, we use variables that are similar to other studies of MID onset over issue claims and the success of attempts to manage issue claims (Hensel 2001; Hensel et al. 2008). First, we employ the ICOW measure of issue salience, which ranges from zero to twelve for each issue claim, with higher values denoting issues of greater importance to both sides.[20] In the claim dyad-year dataset, the average salience is 6.5 with a standard deviation of 2.4; in the settlement attempt dataset, the average salience is 7.1 with a standard deviation of 2.3. We also control for functional and procedural attempts in the settlement dataset (e.g. fishing rights around the Falklands) because these attempts have a higher success rate than those intended to settle the overall issue at stake (e.g. who owns the Falklands Island). Forty percent of the total peaceful attempts to settle contentious issues were functional or procedural.

We also employ controls for dyadic democracy (described above), prior militarized conflict, and relative capabilities. We code relative capabilities as the share of the challenger's CINC score in the dyad. Since the challenger is the state challenging the status quo of an issue, it should be better able to achieve what it wants in negotiations as its relative power increases. We also include a measure of prior militarized conflict as one if the pair of states in the dyad experienced any militarized conflict over the specific issue in question over the past fifteen years, and zero otherwise. Previous ICOW analyses (e.g. Hensel 2001; Hensel et al. 2008) have shown increased militarization of an issue to make all forms of peaceful and militarized interaction more likely.

Empirical results

We begin with an examination of all politically relevant dyads. As noted above, the onset of a militarized dispute is treated as an instance of

---

[19] ICOW considers the challenger to be the state challenging the status quo on an issue.
[20] For more detail on the construction of the salience index, see Hensel et al. (2008).

Table 7.4 *The effect of PCIJ/ICJ jurisdictional acceptance on dyadic militarized conflict*

Variable	Model 1: without interactions, coefficient (S.E.)	Model 2: with interactions, coefficient (S.E.)
Both civil law	−0.27 (0.06)★★★	−0.19 (0.06)★★★
Both common law	−0.87 (0.15)★★★	−0.87 (0.15)★★★
Both Islamic law	0.07 (0.10)	0.08 (0.10)
Both PCIJ/ICJ	0.26 (0.08)★★★	0.50 (0.10)★★★
Civil law interaction	—	−0.71 (0.17)★★★
Common law interaction	—	0.22 (0.53)
Islamic law interaction	—	0.35 (0.45)
Democratic dyad	−0.94 (0.11)★★★	−0.94 (0.11)★★★
Relative capabilities	−0.11 (0.06)★	−0.12 (0.06)★★
Distance	−0.00 (0.00)★★★	−0.00 (0.00)★★★
Peace years	−0.05 (0.00)★★★	−0.05 (0.00)★★★
Constant	−2.07 (0.07)★★★	−2.09 (0.07)★★★
	N = 70,511	N = 70,511
	χ^2 = 606.95★★★	χ^2 = 649.68★★★

Entries are coefficients followed by robust standard errors: ★ $p < 0.10$; ★★$p < 0.05$; ★★★ $p < 0.01$.

bargaining failure. In Table 7.4, we present two logit models (with robust standard errors): Model 1 presents the results excluding the interaction terms between domestic legal traditions and PCIJ/ICJ jurisdictional acceptance, while Model 2 includes the interactions.

We can see that the results are very similar in the two models. The results support our theoretical argument, as pairs of civil law states in the World Court are better able to avoid militarized disputes than most other pairs of states. As we can see in Table 7.5, the combination of civil law and PCIJ/ICJ acceptance reduces the probability of MID onset from a 1.3 in 100 chance (the baseline) to an 8 in 1,000 chance.[21]

The only other pair of states with a lower probability of militarized conflict is a common law dyad outside of the World Court.[22] Furthermore, the interaction term is significant only for civil law dyads, which is consistent with our theoretical argument that the Court is able to correlate strategies, construct focal points, and provide information most effectively to civil law states because the PCIJ/ICJ embodies civil law principles. The control variables are consistent with findings reported by other dyadic

[21] The baseline probability is calculated by setting all variables at their mean or mode.
[22] In the monadic dataset, common law states have the highest average democracy scores, thus our findings in this model reflect to some degree the democratic peace.

Table 7.5 *Substantive effects, dyadic militarized conflict*

Variable	Prob. (change)
Dyadic legal system	
Mixed law, no PCIJ/ICJ	0.013 (baseline)
Mixed law, both PCIJ/ICJ	0.021 (+0.008)
Civil law, no PCIJ/ICJ	0.010 (−0.003)
Civil law, both PCIJ/ICJ	0.008 (−0.005)
Common law, no PCIJ/ICJ	0.005 (−0.008)
Common law, both PCIJ/ICJ	0.011 (−0.002)
Islamic law, no PCIJ/ICJ	0.014 (+0.001)
Islamic law, both PCIJ/ICJ	0.031 (+0.018)
Democratic dyad	
0 (min.)	0.013
1 (max.)	0.005 (−0.008)
Relative capabilities	
0 (min.)	0.013
1 (max.)	0.012 (−0.001)
Distance	
5 (min.)	0.030
11989 (max.)	0.001 (−0.029)
Peace years	
0 (min.)	0.045
185 (max.)	0.000 (−0.45)

conflict scholars, with militarized conflict being less likely in democratic, asymmetric, and distant dyads with a long history of peaceful relations (Russett and Oneal 2001).

We present a similar analysis in Table 7.6, looking at the onset of MIDs over contentious issues. As noted above, the ICOW data currently captures three regions: the Americas, Europe, and the Middle East. However, there is more data coded in the Western Hemisphere relative to the other two regions, with the Middle East having the smallest number of cases. The lack of Middle East cases makes it impossible to include a measure for "Both Islamic law," thus we limit our analyses to civil and common law dyads. Table 7.6 presents three different models of results: Model 1 presents estimates for all ICOW data, Model 2 presents estimates for the Americas region only, while Model 3 provides results for Europe. Model 1 does not provide support to the theoretical hypothesis because the coefficient for "Both civil law" is positive and insignificant, while the interaction term has the wrong sign (positive). When we divide the models into distinct regions, we can see why this pattern

Table 7.6 *The effect of PCIJ/ICJ jurisdictional acceptance on conflict over contentious issues*

Variable	Model 1: all regions, coefficient (S.E.)	Model 2: Americas, coefficient (S.E.)	Model 3: Europe, coefficient (S.E.)
Both civil law	0.06 (0.17)	0.36 (0.22)*	−1.71 (0.47)***
Both common law	−1.37 (0.73)*	−1.03 (0.74)	—
Both PCIJ/ICJ	−1.48 (0.53)***	−1.40 (0.62)***	−2.20 (1.04)**
Civil law interaction	1.49 (0.59)***	1.63 (0.69)**	1.60 (1.25)
Common law interaction	2.29 (1.06)**	2.12 (1.12)*	—
Democratic dyad	−0.23 (0.17)	−0.11 (0.22)	−0.03 (0.32)
Challenger's capabilities	0.44 (0.21)**	0.70 (0.26)***	−0.68 (0.54)
Issue salience	0.18 (0.03)***	0.19 (0.04)***	0.38 (0.10)***
Recent conflict	1.95 (0.15)***	2.06 (0.18)***	1.05 (0.36)***
Constant	−5.42 (0.31)***	−5.90 (0.38)***	−5.01 (0.87)***
	N = 6,021	N = 4,448	N = 1,150
	$\chi^2 = 215.51$***	$\chi^2 = 184.84$***	$\chi^2 = 42.03$***

Entries are coefficients followed by robust standard errors: * $p < 0.10$; **$p < 0.05$; *** $p < 0.01$.

emerges. In Europe, the coefficients for both civil law and both PCIJ/ICJ are negative and statistically significant; the interaction term is not significant. In the Americas, however, we see an opposite pattern, with the coefficients for civil law and the interaction term being positive and significant.

How are we to explain these disparate regional findings? As we noted in Chapter 5, the PCIJ was created primarily by European states. Many civil law countries in Europe were thus originator states and had more at stake in the success of the institution. We can see this pattern in the third column of Table 7.7, whereby the World Court provides an effective out-of-court option for European states; the probability of conflict drops to an 8 in 1,000 chance for militarized conflict from the baseline of a 7.5 in 100 chance.[23]

In contrast, civil law dyads in the Americas actually have a higher probability of conflict if they join the PCIJ/ICJ (0.021) relative to civil law dyads outside of the Court (0.017). This may simply reflect the endogenous relationship between international courts and interstate disputes. Countries that have no issue disagreements may have no need to join

---

[23] There are not enough common law dyads in Europe to estimate the effect of this legal tradition.

Table 7.7 *Substantive effects: conflict over contentious issues*

Variable	All regions, prob. (change)	Americas, prob. (change)	Europe, prob. (change)
Dyadic legal system			
Other, no PCIJ/ICJ	0.017 (baseline)	0.012 (baseline)	0.075 (baseline)
Other, both PCIJ/ICJ	0.004 (−0.013)	0.003 (−0.009)	0.009 (−0.066)
Civil law, no PCIJ/ICJ	0.018 (+0.001)	0.017 (+0.005)	0.014 (−0.061)
Civil law, both PCIJ/ICJ	0.018 (+0.001)	0.021 (+0.009)	0.008 (−0.067)
Common law, no PCIJ/ICJ	0.004 (−0.013)	0.004 (−0.008)	—
Common law, both PCIJ/ICJ	0.010 (−0.007)	0.009 (−0.003)	—
Democratic dyad			
0 (min.)	0.017	0.012	0.075
1 (max.)	0.014 (−0.003)	0.010 (−0.002)	0.073 (−0.002)
Challenger's capability share			
0 (min.)	0.014	0.009	0.105
0.99 (max.)	0.022 (+0.008)	0.017 (+0.008)	0.056 (−0.049)
Issue salience			
0 (min.)	0.005	0.004	0.012
12 (max.)	0.047 (+0.042)	0.035 (+0.031)	0.309 (+0.297)
Recent militarized conflict			
0 (min.)	0.017	0.012	0.075
1 (max.)	0.108 (+0.091)	0.084 (+0.072)	0.188 (+0.113)

international courts, whereas states with many border disputes may seek out an impartial adjudicator for conflict resolution assistance. The fact that every land border in the Western Hemisphere has been challenged at some point in the past two centuries certainly supports this conjecture (Hensel *et al.* 2008). The results for the control variables are similar to previous studies employing the ICOW data as well, with militarized conflict over issues being more likely as the challenger's capability share increases, as the issue becomes more salient to both sides, and when the parties have a history of prior conflict.

We turn our attention now to cases of successful interstate bargaining. Countries may experience conflicts over issues in world politics, yet they have many peaceful foreign policy tools at their disposal to resolve their disagreements. In Tables 7.8 and 7.9, we seek to determine if domestic legal traditions and acceptance of PCIJ/ICJ compulsory jurisdiction influence the success of negotiation attempts to resolve territorial, maritime, and river conflicts.

Two of the three measures, "reaching agreement" and "agreement ends claim," provide strong support for our theory. Civil law dyads have a significantly higher probability of reaching agreements in a given

Table 7.8 *The effect of PCIJ/ICJ jurisdictional acceptance on interstate bargaining outcomes*

Variable	Model 1: reach agreement, coefficient (S.E.)	Model 2: compliance, coefficient (S.E.)	Model 3: agreement ends claim,[a] coefficient (S.E.)
Both civil law	0.38 (0.13)***	−0.12 (0.24)	0.49 (0.26)*
Both common law	−0.25 (0.28)	−0.40 (0.45)	0.90 (0.56)
Both Islamic law[b]	—	0.29 (0.80)	1.12 (0.68)*
Both PCIJ/ICJ	0.69 (0.18)***	0.45 (0.28)	0.78 (0.30)***
Democratic dyad	−0.06 (0.14)	0.08 (0.26)	−0.33 (0.28)
Challenger's capabilities	−0.47 (0.20)**	0.12 (0.35)	0.59 (0.39)
Issue salience	−0.02 (0.03)	0.05 (0.05)	−0.03 (0.05)
Recent conflict	−0.25 (0.14)*	0.17 (0.26)	−0.22 (0.28)
Functional/procedural	1.06 (0.14)***	0.61 (0.24)***	—
Constant	−5.42 (0.31)***	0.75 (0.37)**	−0.62 (0.38)
	N = 1,110	N = 613	N = 303
	$\chi^2 = 82.13$***	$\chi^2 = 16.15$*	$\chi^2 = 14.10$*

Entries are coefficients followed by robust standard errors: * $p < 0.10$; ** $p < 0.05$; *** $p < 0.01$.
[a] This analysis excludes functional and procedural settlements, which cannot end issue claims by definition.
[b] All eleven cases of negotiations between two Islamic countries produced an agreement, which is why the variable is excluded from the model.

negotiation and these agreements are very likely to end the issue in contention. Mixed law dyads that do not recognize the compulsory jurisdiction of the PCIJ/ICJ have a 0.395 chance of reaching agreement in a given negotiation, while civil law dyads who bargain in the shadow of the Court have a 0.657 chance for reaching agreement (a 66 percent increase). Furthermore, we see that civil law dyads that work with the World Court are more successful than other dyads; the probability of agreement is highest for civil law dyads (0.657) compared to common law (0.505) and mixed law (0.566) dyads. We see a similar pattern for whether or not an agreement reached ends the overall issue at stake, although Islamic law dyads have the highest probability of success on this front, with a 0.796 probability of ending the issue at stake once an agreement is reached. This result fits with the strong norms of *pacta sunt servanda* in the Islamic law tradition.[24] More broadly, the analyses show

---

[24] In the compliance analyses, Islamic law states also exhibit the highest rates of agreement compliance among all dyads. Yet this effect is not statistically different from zero, and thus we cannot come to strong conclusions.

Table 7.9 *Substantive effects: bargaining outcomes*

Variable	Reach agreement, prob. (change)	Compliance, prob. (change)	Agreement ends claim, prob. (change)
Dyadic legal system			
Other law, no PCIJ/ICJ	0.395 (baseline)	0.767 (baseline)	0.369 (−0.119)
Other law, both PCIJ/ICJ	0.566 (+0.171)	0.838 (+0.071)	0.560 (+0.072)
Civil law, no PCIJ/ICJ	0.489 (+0.094)	0.745 (−0.022)	0.488 (baseline)
Civil law, both PCIJ/ICJ	0.657 (+0.262)	0.821 (+0.054)	0.675 (+0.187)
Common law, no PCIJ/ICJ	0.338 (−0.057)	0.688 (−0.079)	0.589 (+0.101)
Common law, both PCIJ/ICJ	0.505 (+0.110)	0.775 (+0.008)	0.757 (+0.269)
Islamic law, no PCIJ/ICJ	—	0.814 (+0.047)	0.642 (+0.154)
Islamic law, both PCIJ/ICJ	—	0.873 (+0.106)	0.796 (+0.308)
Democratic dyad			
0 (min.)	0.395	0.767	0.488
1 (max.)	0.380 (−0.015)	0.780 (+0.013)	0.406 (−0.082)
Challenger's capability share			
0 (min.)	0.448	0.758	0.424
0.99 (max.)	0.337 (−0.111)	0.779 (+0.021)	0.569 (+0.145)
Issue salience			
0 (min.)	0.432	0.691	0.533
12 (max.)	0.371 (−0.061)	0.811 (+0.120)	0.454 (−0.079)
Recent militarized conflict			
0 (min.)	0.395	0.767	0.488
1 (max.)	0.336 (−0.059)	0.796 (+0.029)	0.432 (−0.056)
Functional/procedural attempt			
0 (min.)	0.395	0.767	—
1 (max.)	0.653 (+0.258)	0.859 (+0.092)	—

that all dyads with states belonging to the World Court are able to bargain more effectively, as they have a significantly higher rate of reaching agreement than states outside of the Court, and a significantly higher chance of ending overall contention over an issue.

A good example of the out-of-court effect of the World Court on interstate bargaining occurred in a maritime dispute between Sweden and Denmark that began in the 1970s. Sweden insisted that the border should be divided between Sweden's mainland and Sjaelland of Denmark. Denmark argued that a middle line should be drawn between Hessel Island off Sjaelland and the Swedish mainland. Both states accepted the compulsory jurisdiction of the World Court since the inception of the PCIJ in 1921, thus adjudication was a real possibility for resolving this issue. Furthermore, both states have civil law traditions, a factor that increases the perceived fairness of the adjudicator in this instance, which should enhance the out-of-court bargaining effects. In August 1983, Sweden threatened to take the case to the ICJ. The issue was successfully resolved just two months later through bilateral negotiations, an impressive outcome considering the maritime dispute had been ongoing for more than a decade. This case shows the inherent difficulties in assessing the efficacy of international institutions in interstate bargaining by examining only cases where the institutions intervene as active conflict managers. Even if we consider this smaller set of cases where international institutions actively intervened, they have a strong record when employing binding tools of conflict management. For example, Mitchell and Hensel (2007) find that twenty-eight of the twenty-nine judgments rendered by the World Court to settle territorial, maritime, or river disputes have experienced full compliance by both parties.

The control variables have effects similar to those reported in other ICOW studies (e.g. Hensel 2001; Mitchell 2002; Hensel et al. 2008). Issues that are more salient produce fewer agreements and the parties are more likely to renege on any agreements reached. The challenger is less likely to make concessions as its relative capabilities in the dyad increase. Functional and procedural attempts to settle issues have higher success rates (more agreements with higher rates of compliance).

As in previous chapters, we also added a variable for the number of shared memberships in peace-promoting organizations, as coded by the MTOPS dataset. These organizations have explicit wording in their charters that calls for member states to resolve disputes peacefully. Thus, our expectation is that these organizations will help to promote successful bargaining over contentious issues. In the MID analyses, our reported effects for both civil law and both PCIJ/ICJ are unaltered by the inclusion of this variable. Interestingly, dyads that have more shared IOs have a higher propensity to experience militarized conflict. This effect holds in both the politically relevant dyad-year dataset (Table 7.4) and the ICOW claim dyad-year dataset (Table 7.6). This demonstrates that international courts bring something different to the bargaining table than IOs more broadly. Much like our findings earlier for the ICC show, an international court is able to achieve greater efficacy than other treaties or institutions in the same issue arena. In the settlement attempt analyses (Table 7.8), the addition of shared IOs does not alter our findings for reaching agreement. Furthermore, shared membership in peace-promoting organizations does not influence the likelihood of reaching agreement in a given negotiation. However, the significance of both civil law and both PCIJ/ICJ variables are somewhat reduced in the agreement ends claim model (Model 3), with p-values of 0.078 and

0.074, respectively. In that analysis, shared IO memberships increase the chances that agreements will end overall contention over the issue (p = 0.075). The overall conclusion from these robustness checks is clear, though, demonstrating that international courts are particularly effective conflict managers in world politics, even in comparison to other peace-promoting IOs.

Bilder's (1998) conjecture was indeed accurate: states do bargain more effectively in the shadow of the World Court. Yet the selection effect of some states supporting international courts more than others suggests that these out-of-court effects vary across states, courts, and time. Furthermore, we do not code the extent to which states limit their obligations to the World Court. The out-of-court effects should be strongest for those states that place the fewest restrictions on their optional clause declarations; the robust results for civil law dyads accords with this claim because these states place the fewest reservations on their optional clause declarations (Chapter 6). In the future, we hope to create an interval measure of the restrictions or reservations states place on their commitments to international courts. This will give us a better handle on how the rational design of legal commitments influences the efficacy of international courts.

Conclusion

In this chapter, we examine the consequences of state support for international courts. Skeptics identify a series of obstacles that international courts face in their efforts to foster interstate cooperation, including a lack of widespread state support, a plethora of reservations, a lack of major power support, and biases in judicial outcomes. Optimists have envisioned a more significant role for international courts in world politics: courts can induce more efficient interstate bargaining out of court and encourage certain types of behaviors, such as good human rights practices and peaceful conflict resolution. We show that neither of these diametrically opposed viewpoints is correct. International courts can influence member state behavior, although the effects are contingent on states' domestic legal traditions and the legal design of the courts. Courts can foster cooperation in some instances between some pairs of states, but fail to help other pairs of states resolve disagreements. In short, the rational design processes that lead the originators of new international courts to select particular legal design features influences subsequent decisions by joiners to recognize the jurisdiction of these courts. The rational legal design of the courts also conditions the efficacy as these adjudicators as well.

With respect to the ICC, we show that states that ratify the Rome Statute see significant improvements in their treatment of citizens in the form of fewer cases of torture, political imprisonment, and disappearances. However, signature of the ICC treaty alone has no effect on human rights practices (with the exception of torture), which suggests that some countries view the initial commitment to a new court as "window dressing"; it is only the significant legal act of ratification which enhances the consequences of state support for the court. Civil and common law countries are significantly more likely to ratify the Rome Statute, which in turn has a positive effect on human rights practices in those member states. Unlike other studies that find human rights treaties to have no effect on states' human rights practices, we show that the ICC is distinct; its autonomy and authority give it more leverage for altering the behavior of member states. There is certainly some endogeneity in this process because states with better human rights practices are more likely to ratify the Rome Statute. However, we are encouraged that the international court still has an effect on state behavior in the set of states that selected themselves into the legal institution. Whether or not the ICC will be an effective court in the human rights arena remains to be seen, especially as the contentious cases before the Court unfold.

Our findings for the World Court show that there are significant out-of-court effects on interstate bargaining processes. States who bargain in the shadow of the Court are better able to avoid militarized conflict, they can reach agreements more readily in a given negotiation round, and they are better able to strike accords that resolve the underlying issues at stake in negotiations. On the other hand, these effects are modified by states' domestic legal traditions and their relation to the legal design of the PCIJ/ICJ. Because these courts were designed according to civil legal principles, they have been more effective at managing conflicts between states with domestic civil law traditions. The adjudicator has more credibility in these dyads and can help the parties reach cooperative deals. The ability of states to credibly sue each other in the face of an impartial adjudicator creates a significant out-of-court effect as well, with states reaching successful agreements even when employing simple tools of bilateral negotiation. As studies of the GATT/WTO have suggested, adjudication may work best when threatened but not exercised (Hudec 1993; Busch and Reinhardt 2000; Reinhardt 2001).

One interesting implication of this relationship is that the proliferation of international courts could have positive benefits for successful interstate conflict management. The larger the number of international courts, the more likely it is that disputants can find an acceptable adjudicator on the international scene, which in turn would enhance the out-of-court effects on bargaining. However, the proliferation of courts could also threaten the development of international law as a whole, a topic we consider more fully in the final chapter.

8   Conclusion

In his book *How International Law Works: A Rational Choice Theory*, Andrew T. Guzman writes:

The study of international law is undergoing a transformation from a discipline focused on practice and doctrine into one putting greater emphasis on theory and social science methodology. International law scholars are rapidly adopting more sophisticated analytical techniques and applying these tools to study how states use law to promote cooperation in our anarchic international system. (Guzman 2008, 211)

The goal of this book is to contribute to both aspects of this transformation – theory and social science methodology. We develop a rational legal design theory of international adjudication, which attempts to explain an important part of cooperation in the international system: the creation and expansion of international courts. In particular, we ask why states create new international courts and why states join pre-existing international courts. We argue that an interesting intersection of domestic and international law occurs when international courts are formed. After accepting a basic premise that states can benefit from bargaining with the potential assistance of an adjudicator, we contend that not all adjudicators are created equal. Different courts are created to suit the interests of a particular group of states. States have incentives to create international courts in their own legal image to reduce uncertainty in future bargaining situations. Thus, the initial negotiators of new courts, who we call the "originators," design institutions in ways that are optimal from both a political and legal standpoint. Similarly, states that join standing international courts, the "joiners," look to the court's rules and procedures in order to assess the ability of the court to be capable, fair, and unbiased.

We argue that domestic legal traditions influence the decisions of both originator and joiner states. We demonstrate that the characteristics of civil law, common law, and Islamic law influence states' acceptance of the jurisdiction of international courts, the durability of states' commitments to international courts, and the design of states' commitments to the courts. These design choices influence the efficacy of international courts as well, as states bargain most effectively in the shadow of an international court that operates according to familiar legal principles and rules. In short, our theory posits that we can understand the influence of international courts more clearly by focusing on their rational legal design.

The empirical chapters are designed to contribute to the second aspect of recent transformation of international law scholarship – using social science methodology and analytical techniques to answer questions pertaining to international law. In Chapters 4 through 7, we test our theoretical arguments on two international courts: the ICC and the World Court. Our empirical results provide insights into several important aspects of international adjudication. Our arguments about the originators of an international court are tested in Chapter 4, where we empirically examine international negotiations in Rome in 1998, which led to the creation of the ICC, a hybrid of civil and common law principles. Chapter 5 focuses on the potential joiners to a standing international court, the World Court, an embodiment of civil law principles. Chapter 6 examines another crucial aspect of international adjudication: the design of states' commitments to the World Court. The final empirical segment of our project, Chapter 7, looks at the consequences of state support for the ICC and the World Court. We show that international courts can influence member state behavior, although their effects are contingent on states' domestic legal traditions and the legal design of the courts.

The empirical results provide strong support for our theoretical conjectures. We show that states that design new international courts and states that join pre-existing international courts are influenced in their decision processes by their domestic legal traditions. Originators embed characteristics of their own domestic laws into international courts because they want to create an optimal adjudicator, one that they can view in the future as unbiased and fair. Joiners of pre-existing international adjudicative bodies engage in forum shopping with the goal of finding a court that best suits their interest, one that operates according to rules embedded in their own domestic legal traditions. Generally speaking, familiarity with rules increases states' trust in an international court, because in states' eyes, familiarity with legal rules employed in a court's proceedings increases the predictability of an outcome. Our results also demonstrate that states design their commitments to international courts by using the rules of contract formation embedded in their own domestic legal traditions. Therefore, our rational legal design theory is able to elucidate not only our understanding of courts' institutional design; it also sheds light on another aspect of design: the design of states' commitments to international adjudicative bodies, such as the number and types of reservations that states place on their declarations to international courts. In both of these processes, the rules of domestic legal traditions are purposively carried over into the international arena.

Taken together, our results show that the international system should not be perceived as a domain that is occupied only by international law; domestic laws infiltrate relations between states in numerous and important ways. As we show, the impact of domestic legal traditions does not stop with the creation, expansion, and design of international courts. It continues to play an important role in the functioning of these bodies, as international courts have significant out-of-court effects on interstate bargaining processes. As demonstrated empirically in Chapter 7, ratification of the Rome Statute positively influences states' human rights practices. With respect to the World Court, we find that states who bargain in the shadow of the PCIJ/ICJ are better able to avoid militarized conflict, they can reach interstate agreements more readily in a given negotiation round, and they are better able to strike accords that resolve the underlying issues at stake in negotiations. Courts do a lot more than adjudicate; they have broad effects on member states' behavior in ways that are missed when we focus only on those cases that actually come before the courts. We cannot assess the efficacy of international courts without considering their broader context, considering how the cases that could have come before the court but didn't tell us something interesting about the institution as well. Furthermore, we show that the legal design put into place by the originators of a new court influences the level of state support the court will receive, as well as its perceived abilities as a qualified adjudicator.

Our rational legal design theory and empirical findings relate well to a broader research agenda on IOs, cooperation, and international law. For example, the international law and comparative law literatures have long recognized that states' views of international law, including international treaties, depend largely on their domestic legal systems. In general, civil lawyers approach drafting and interpretation of multinational agreements as they would a civil code (Koch 2003). Similarly, common law lawyers promote designing international agreements in the spirit of their domestic legal tradition (Jouannet 2006). Islamic law scholars see international law through the lenses of the Koran: "Muslim jurists view the Islamic law of nations as derived from the eternal truth and justice that God had bequeathed to humanity through His messenger" (Bsoul 2008, 2–3). Our results provide support for Zartner-Falstrom's assertion that "contemporary attitudes towards the authority of existing international law can best be seen as a function of a state's historical legal tradition" (2006, 344). Domestic legal systems indeed influence the way that states approach international treaties and IOs. A state's internal laws determine to a large extent how states negotiate, draft, and interpret international agreements.

Our theory could be generalized to understand the design of state commitments in other arenas, such as the forging of new security agreements or trade pacts. For example, in the context of military alliances, Powell (2010) shows that civil law states' alliances are straightforward and have relatively few contingencies. In contrast, common law states place a higher number of contingencies on their alliances, resembling the "all-inclusive" approach of domestic common law contracts. These include clauses relating to the specific target of the alliance, the geographical scope of the alliance, and the level of military commitment in the event of conflict. Islamic law states are extremely careful in signing international contracts, as representatives of these states take particular care in designing thorough interstate contracts in line with the Koran.[1] These findings on military alliances mesh very closely with the findings presented in Chapter 6, as we show that common law countries place the highest number of reservations on their optional clause declarations to the World Court, with Islamic law states having a moderate number of reservations and civil law states having the fewest number of reservations. Powell's (2010) similar findings for the design of military alliances provide additional support for the rational legal design theory of adjudication presented in this book.

Similarly, studying territorial disputes, Powell and Wiegand (2010) show that in order to increase familiarity with rules of peaceful resolution, states use their domestic legal systems to provide them with clues about the most trustworthy ways to settle disputes. They find that an important relationship exists between domestic law and interstate conflict management strategies. For example, civil law dyads, following a more formal character of civil law, prefer more legalized dispute resolution methods compared to common law dyads. Pairs of Islamic law states embrace the informal character of Islamic adjudication and are most likely to use non-binding third-party methods, while common law dyads tend to resolve their territorial disputes through bilateral negotiations. Thus domestic law influences not only the willingness of states to

---

[1] Powell and Rickard (2010) examine the relationship between domestic legal traditions and bilateral trade flows, another important form of interstate cooperation. Their analyses show that levels of bilateral trade are lowest among Islamic law dyads in comparison to civil law or common law dyads.

utilize legalized dispute resolution mechanisms in world politics, but also delineates the strategies that states will be most comfortable employing on the international scene.

Powell and Wiegand's (2010) study meshes well with recent work on international institutions and conflict management. The design of international institutions is an important feature influencing their efficacy as conflict managers. Hansen *et al.* (2008) find that IOs are more likely to help disputing states reach agreements to resolve geopolitical disputes if they are highly institutionalized, if they have more democratic state members, and if the states in the international institution share more similar foreign policy preferences. Mitchell and Hensel (2007) find that the tools employed by international institutions vary in their effectiveness, with binding tools of adjudication or arbitration significantly outperforming other forms of conflict management, such as mediation, good offices, and inquiry (see also Huth and Allee 2002). Our study suggests that the legal design of international institutions is also a significant factor influencing conflict management success. International courts are better equipped to help states resolve interstate disputes if they share legal principles. This idea could be expanded to the legal design of other institutions, such as regional or global trade agreements, military alliances, and environmental accords. We might also compare the effectiveness of more limited, regional organizations that are populated by states with similar legal traditions in comparison to global organizations that bring together states with diverse legal traditions.

Our study also adds interesting insights to the rational institutional design literature by showing that international courts are becoming increasingly institutionalized, which is somewhat at odds with the design of interstate cooperation in other issue areas. The move away from flexibility in international adjudication is quite interesting in a broader theoretical sense, given recent work in political science on institutional design. Koremenos (2005), for example, shows that in situations of uncertainty and risk aversion, states prefer to sign agreements with renegotiation provisions. And yet, in the arena of international adjudication, less flexibility in the design of new courts is resulting in broader state support for many international courts, as the burgeoning support for the ICC and WTO illustrates. This trend reinforces our arguments about the inherent legal nature of international courts. Although created by states just like other IOs, international courts are distinct in their ability to impact international law by shaping interpretation of its principles and rules. As history shows, international adjudicative bodies have the ability to impact the very nature of the environment in which all states co-exist by molding the understanding of notions of right and wrong in the international system. It is international courts that have filled in the loop holes of international law, sometimes in ways contrary to states' interests. International courts, therefore, constitute a vivid example of international institutions that are able to become increasingly independent from their originators, more so than other IOs. In fact, the whole idea of giving an international court its own jurisdictional authority (*compétence de la compétence*) is a norm that is lacking in the creation of other international institutions. Strong, independent authority by an IO, such as the UN, is often seen as pathological behavior (Barnett and Finnemore 1999). Perhaps only the EU embodies this process of increasing legalization and authority that we have seen endowed to international courts.

Sometimes, because delivering judgments and rendering advisory opinions involves interpretation of the law, a slight evolution of international law can take place, as the courts interpret the law in ways that states never intended, filling in the law "where rules are vague" (Alter 2006, 322). As the adjudicator chooses a particular interpretation of a norm over others, normative innovation takes place, and the normative structure is reshaped, expanded, and reenacted (Stone Sweet 1999). For example, although the ICJ cannot formally create law, scholars of international law agree that the judgments and advisory opinions of the ICJ and its predecessor, the PCIJ, have played a crucial part in the continued evolution of international law (Shaw 2003, 1005). This is another reason why there is a lot at stake for the originators seeking to establish a new international court. To the extent that the court's rules mesh well with member states' domestic law, this can lend some predictability to the path by which the court will evolve and the types of decisions it will render.

In the early stages of international adjudication, states were more likely to grant international courts substantial levels of independence as far as the power to determine their own jurisdiction and the rules of procedure. For example, the Advisory Committee of Jurists while drafting the PCIJ Statute decided to adopt only a few general rules pertaining to the procedure, giving the Court considerable freedom in developing its own rules (Brown 2007, 38–39). Similarly, while developing the ICTY and ICTR, "[t]he Security Council left to the tribunal judges development of the tribunals' rules of procedure and evidence" (Schiff 2008, 45). As intended by the originators, however, these courts evolved in a certain direction. Even if the original procedures of a court are to some extent ambiguous, they evolve along a certain trajectory, so that expanded rules can be easily integrated with the existing rules.[2] The PCIJ/ICJ remained

---

[2] Compatibility of new norms with the pre-existing normative structure enhances the legal coherence of international regimes.

anchored in the civil law tradition, and the two *ad hoc* tribunals operated mostly according to common law rules of procedure.[3]

However, courts established as successors of the PCIJ, ICTY, and ICTR were much more institutionalized and meticulously drafted. For example, the ICJ, as the successor of the PCIJ, includes an injunction that "the parties to a dispute may jointly propose modifications to the rules," which "gives the parties some degree of control over the rules, should they require this" (Brown 2007, 39). The ICC constitutes an even more acute example of how international courts have become more formalized over time. The Rome negotiators, the originators of the ICC, "spelled out Court procedures in much greater detail than did the tribunal statutes and shifted rule-making responsibility to the ICC's quasi-legislative organ, the Assembly of States Parties to the Treaty, rather than leaving it (as in the tribunals) to the judges" (Schiff 2008, 45).

We believe that two separate phenomena can explain the fact that international courts have become increasingly institutionalized. First, states have become progressively more aware of the fact that the courts' inherently legal nature may have important consequences. For example, the prerogative to interpret international law gives courts a substantial amount of power. This explains why over time states are more apt to regulate courts' rules and procedures in the inception stages. It is simply beneficial for states to meticulously describe a court's underlying rules and procedures before the court engages in adjudication. It is also less risky to clearly delineate the court's jurisdiction up front. States have learned that international courts, if given free range, may evolve into more powerful and, to a large extent, more self-sufficient international institutions. The ECJ constitutes a great example, as the Court established important principles such as direct effect and supremacy through its judicial decisions. Having learned from experience, states increasingly design more institutionalized courts. Consider the Rome Statute, which devoted one third of the entire Statute to the Court's procedures. The originators of the Court diligently drafted the ICC's rules of proceedings, leaving less independence for the judges or the Court itself. The ICC judges can interpret those rules; they cannot, however, make them.

Second, states take much greater care in carefully designing courts that can potentially affect their direct interests. The ICTY and ICTR were engaged in retrospective justice in the context of conflicts in the former Yugoslavia and Rwanda (Schiff 2008, 43). The potential impact of the ICC, on the other hand, is much greater. The principle of

---

[3] Over time, several civil law elements of procedure were embedded in their structure as well.

complementarity may not necessarily protect any state from the Court's investigations. If the ICC establishes that a state "is unwilling or unable genuinely to carry out the investigation or prosecution," a case may be admissible in the Court (Article 17(1)(a)). The lesson here is that states have become more aware of the fact that the payoffs of designing a flexible court may not be worth the risks.

An immediate implication of our theory is that there exists a reciprocal relationship between domestic legal traditions, states' attitudes towards international courts, and the proliferation of courts. As we demonstrate, domestic legal traditions influence states' willingness to both create and join pre-existing international courts. However, the relationship between domestic law and international law does not stop here. The design of a court, or its legal set-up, influences the way that this court will view and interpret international law. In turn, states prefer international courts that interpret international law in a way that satisfies their preferences. As we noted in Chapter 3, different international adjudicative bodies often interpret international law differently, which increases states' uncertainty about the outcome of the settlement (Charney 1998; Spelliscy 2001). The resulting diversity in application of international law raises concerns about the quality of the international legal framework (Koskenniemi and Leino 2002, 554).

First, states can become confused with the international legal framework as a whole. Second, states can take advantage of the multiplicity of available adjudicative bodies by choosing a court that will best suit their interests through adapting a specific interpretation of international law. There are several principles in international law that limit to some extent the process of forum shopping, such as the doctrine of *lis alibi pendens*, which prohibits states "to commence another set of competing proceedings concerning the same dispute before another judicial body" (Shany 2003, 22–23). Another principle restricting forum shopping is the *res judicata* rule, also known as the "doctrine of finality," which states that "the final judgment of a competent judicial forum is binding upon the parties" and therefore cannot be relitigated (Shany 2003, 22–23). These two rules, however, do not curb states' ability to forum shop before making a final decision about which judicial forum to select. States can *a priori* examine the up-to-date jurisprudence of a court and its legal rules and procedures and then make their decisions.

In the international system, there is a lot of jurisdictional overlap between the general courts such as the ICJ, and specialized courts such as the ITLOS, the WTO, or the ICC. This reality may create "the risk of a 'race to the court house' between the parties to the dispute," a phenomenon ever-present in the domestic courts (Shany 2003, 79–80). Thus, although proliferation of international courts may lead to a more peaceful world, at the same time it may weaken the uniformity of the international legal system, causing inconsistency of judicial decisions and doctrinal problems. "Various judicial bodies operating under the guise of international law generally act as independent entities and do not share unifying characteristics which could transform them into a coherent judicial system" (Shany 2003, 104). Therefore, it is possible that the proliferation of international courts, while giving states more opportunity for peaceful resolution of disputes, may increase uncertainty that states face with regards to international adjudication. Different courts generate different expectations, just as different rules of procedure may lead to diverging interpretation of international law. Forum shopping is "perceived as a threat to legal certainty, as it deprives parties of foreknowledge as to which set of substantive and procedural laws (which might conflict with each other) will eventually govern their conduct" (Shany 2003, 131).[4]

As with any empirical study of a complex phenomenon, our study relies on several simplifying classifications and measurements. One of the most important issues that we believe should be addressed here is our choice of classification of domestic legal traditions. In this study, we have adopted the definition of the major legal system provided by Gamal Moursi Badr (1978, 187): major legal systems are only those legal systems "whose application extended far beyond the confines of their original birth places and whose influence, through reception of their principles, techniques or specific provisions has been both widespread in space and enduring in time." We argue in Chapter 2 that if we use this definition, only three legal traditions can be granted the name of a major legal tradition: civil law, common law, and Islamic law. In legal scholarship, however, there are several other classifications of legal systems that go beyond the substantive and procedural differences between legal traditions, and take into consideration the unique bond that can exist between a legal system and a political regime of a state. For example, Opolot (1980) distinguishes a socialist legal tradition in addition to the civil, common, and Islamic legal systems. He argues that "[i]n studying the law of a socialist country, as in any other type of law, one must

---

[4] See also Picker (2008, 1113), who argues that "even as international adjudicatory bodies remain specialized and independent, there is some indication of a move toward centralization in some fields of international law. For example, in the international criminal law context, the creation of the ICC may eventually result in the demise of many tribunals. Similarly, many international courts have begun to move beyond their original areas of competence toward a more general jurisdiction – the WTO's Dispute Settlement Body (DSB) now handles environmental issues along with their trade-related effects." This is similar to Brown's (2007) claim that there is a common law of international adjudication that connects the activities of all international courts.

consider legal matters against their political background" (Opolot 1980, 51). Although socialist domestic legal systems possess several character-istics of one of the three major legal families (civil law), they also have several unique features. The main traits that distinguish socialist law from civil, common, and Islamic legal traditions are inherently bound to the socialist political regime. Principles related to the very nature of Man, God, the dominant class, and the special courts, such as comrades' and people's courts, constitute unique ideas of socialism that permeated from the political system into the domestic legal framework of several socialist states.

Because our argument focuses on the substantive and procedural characteristics of domestic legal systems, such as the doctrine of the precedent, good faith, and appeal, we believe that the link between law and politics does not justify introducing a separate category of domes-tic legal systems. *De jure* differences present in socialist legal systems are not substantial enough to classify socialist law as one of the major legal systems (Powell 2006a). The domestic legal framework of Cuba, a con-temporary communist state, provides a very informative example. The concepts that underlie Cuba's legal system reflect the island's history as a Spanish colony, a satellite of the United States, and a centrally planned communist state. According to Michalowski (2002, 398), "Cuba's his-tory as a Spanish colony left the island with deep civil law traditions. Even after the 1959 revolutionary victory, the Cuban legal system con-tinued to emphasize written codes rather than court-based precedent as the source of law." Although this state's post-revolutionary communist regime has impacted the underlying concept of the written letter of law, the fundamental features of the civil legal tradition remain firmly planted in its procedural and substantive law. Thus, socialist institutions, such as a formal legal framework through which the government can manage economic production, have not fundamentally changed the basic civil structure of Cuba's domestic legal system.

Domestic legal systems are very complex because they vary accord-ing to numerous substantive and procedural characteristics, several of which we discussed in Chapter 2. A possible and interesting extension of research presented in this book would be to perform empirical analyses on the level of these differences. The presence or absence of the doctrines of the precedent and good faith lend themselves naturally to a more fine-grained categorization of domestic legal systems. Some common law countries adhere to a greater degree to the strict doctrine of judicial pre-cedent, while others significantly limit its application. Additionally, an important temporal variation exists in the way that common law states have approached *stare decisis*. Historically, *stare decisis* has had a more firm position in the United Kingdom than in the United States. Over time, however, *stare decisis* has softened also in the United Kingdom, especially after 1966, when the Practice Statement of the House of Lords established that previous decisions of the House are treated by it "as normally binding," but this is subject to a right "to depart from a previous decision when it appears right to do so" (Shahabuddeen 1996, 106–107). In our future research, we also plan to elaborate on the crucial distinction between *de jure* and *de facto stare decisis*. As we mentioned in Chapter 2, over time this doctrine has been mitigated in the common law tradition. Furthermore, de facto *stare decisis* has become a relatively common phenomenon in several civil law states, especially in the adjudication of highest level courts. Additionally, the process of European integration, in particular the activity of the ECJ, has increased the importance of judge-made law in all European states. At the same time, the greater significance of the written letter of law in the EU has led to a noticeable boost in the output of enacted law in the United Kingdom. Similarly to *bona fides*, this more detailed coding of legal characteristics would allow us to observe variation within each legal system, and also capture patterns of changes over time.

In the context of *bona fides*, it is important to note that, although this principle has a much stronger position in the civil legal family vs. the common law tradition, there exists considerable variation of the strength of this principle in the civil law world. In addition, several common law states have granted *bona fides* a relatively firm position in their legal system. For example, the United States Uniform Commercial Code in section 1–304, stipulates that: "Every contract or duty within this act imposes an obligation of good faith in its performance." In addition, the US Restatement (Second) of Contracts adopted by the American Law Institute in 1979 provides that individuals have non-waivable duties of good faith. In the same way, the United Kingdom had to improve the protection of contracts due to this country's membership in the EU. The European Consumer Protection Directive of 1994 transplanted *bona fides* into British contract law (Powell and Mitchell 2007).

We believe that capturing the variation of good faith within each legal tradition as well as over time would allow us to better understand states' willingness to uphold international commitments. If the strength of *bona fides* varies not only between the legal families but also within them and over time, this level of coding would help us link in a more direct way characteristics of domestic legal traditions and states' choices on the international arena. Also, the process of civil and common legal systems coming together could be better described theoretically and measured empirically. How would we construct such a measure of the strength of *bona fides*? Such an undertaking would require an in-depth analysis of legal texts and documents that deal with contractual relations. Taking insights from Kegley and Raymond (1990), one possibility would be to perform a content analysis of major domestic legal texts regulating contractual relations.[5] For civil law states, this task would be somewhat easier since *bona fides* is included in civil codes as one of the underlying principles governing contracts. In common law states with statutory contractual law, similar analyses could be performed, and in common law systems where contracts are still governed by case law, analysis of main stream cases would be required. Alternatively, we could code whether good faith is included as one of the major overarching legal principles in the legal system or whether it pertains only to a select group of contracts. A similar approach could be adapted in the context of the *pacta sunt servanda* principle.

One of the differences between domestic legal traditions that we talked about in Chapter 2 relates to divergent sources and the nature of law. We argued that the two Western legal traditions, civil law and common law, constitute secular legal systems. Islamic law, on the other hand, draws directly from religious sources, such as the Koran or the Sunna. However, law and religion are not connected in the same way in all Islamic law states. In fact, in several Islamic law states, Islamic law and faith are fused in their entirety, while in other states there exists a partial separation between them. A more fine-grained coding of Islamic law could specify the degree of secularization of law. Generally speaking, the application of *Shari'a* varies by state. A significant number of Arab states refer to the state as an independent sovereign Arab state, which "recognizes Islam as the state religion and Arabic the official language" (Roach 2005, 145). Other Islamic law states such as Saudi Arabia, Bahrain, Kuwait, Oman, and Yemen declare themselves as "Arab Islamic states." This term, as described in Chapter 3, implies direct incorporation of *Shari'a* into a state's political affairs. Key provisions of constitutions of such states very often identify God as the highest source of law. In practice, this means that *Shari'a* is set above all men-made laws, including international law.

[5] Kegley and Raymond (1990) perform their analysis using the 1816–1974 time frame, delineating periods in which the norm *pacta sunt servanda* or the norm that pacts can be unilaterally terminated (*clausula rebus sic stantibus*) predominated: "[E]ach text's interpretation was classified in terms of whether *pacta sunt servanda* or a broad interpretation of *rebus sic stantibus* was seen by the author as the dominant norm governing obligations between parties to agreement in general and alliance treaties in particular during the period of history being described" (Kegley and Raymond 1990, 96–97).

For example, Article 4 of Iran's constitution states that: "All civil, penal, financial, economic, administrative, cultural, military, political and other laws and regulations must be based on Islamic criteria. This principle applies absolutely and generally to all articles of the Constitution as well as to all other laws and regulations and the wise persons of the Guardian Council are judges in this matter."[6] Several states limit the use of *Shari'a* only to commercial or family matters. Others use it in the area of criminal law. The degree of *Shari'a*'s application varies, therefore, not only across states but also across substantive law. Saudi Arabia, for example, uses criminal procedures of *Shari'a* in an exclusive manner (Kelly 2010, 16). A slightly less rigid approach has been adapted by Malaysia's highest court, which has decided that "legal cases involving non-Muslims cannot be decided by *Shari'a* courts" (Kelly 2010, 16). Also in the United Arab Emirates, *Shari'a* courts, which hear cases involving civil matters between Muslims, operate side by side with civil and criminal courts. Variation in adherence to *Shari'a* exists also within several states. Nigeria, for example, endows its states with the power to enact their own criminal legal system (Kelly 2010, 18).

Few states where Islamic religion constitutes the main religion of the citizenry have successfully managed to separate religion from law. Turkey constitutes the most obvious example. Its secular constitution stipulates in Article 2 that "[t]he Republic of Turkey is a democratic, secular, and social state governed by the rule of law." Furthermore, Article 13 of the Constitution explains that "[f]undamental rights and freedoms may be restricted only by law and in conformity with the reasons mentioned in the relevant articles of the Constitution without infringing upon their essence." This article essentially implies that Islamic law does not reign supreme over promulgated secular laws. In future work, we would like to capture this variation within the Islamic legal family and provide a more detailed coding of the degree of interconnectivity between Islamic law and Islamic faith. As with above-described differences, variation in the degree of secularization within the Islamic legal family would allow us to capture not only cross-sectional variation but also over-time patterns of change.

Since this book focuses on only two international courts, the ICJ and the ICC, we would like to apply our theoretical framework to other international courts, such as the ITLOS. This court constitutes an independent judicial body that was established by the UNCLOS to hear disputes arising out of the Convention. A theoretical and empirical extension of our work to the ITLOS would require an in-depth

---

[6] Also quoted in Kelly (2010).

analysis of the proceedings and legal set-up of the Court. Just like the ICJ, the ITLOS does not formally uphold the doctrine of the precedent, as Article 33(2) of the Statute stipulates that "[t]he decision shall have no binding force except between the parties in respect of that particular dispute." As such, in this aspect, the ITLOS resembles the civil law system.

We would also like to extend our analysis to the IICJ, which constitutes the most important international institution (still in the planning stage) that would actually apply Islamic law on the international scene. The Statute of the IICJ, finally adopted in 1987, stipulates in Article 27 that *Shari'a* is to be the fundamental law of the Court. The set up of this Court embraces the fundamental premises of the Islamic legal tradition. For example, the decisions of the IICJ are to be binding, final, and without appeal. Furthermore, the members of the Court are to be elected from the Muslims of the Member States of the Islamic Conference Organization.

Within the broad theme of the relationship between Islamic law and international law, several interesting questions remain unexplored. First, can the attitude of Islamic law states towards international courts be changed to a more positive one? In Chapters 4 and 5, we demonstrated that Islamic law states are least likely to join the ICC and the ICJ. They view both of these courts as embodiments of the Western legal tradition. Participation of Islamic judges in the functioning of international courts is also very low. For example, the ICTY and the ICTR have two judges trained in Islamic law: Judge Mehmet Güney from Turkey and Judge Khalida Rachid Khan from Pakistan. Both of these judges, however, come from secularized Islamic law traditions, where the influence of Western legal thought is quite strong (Kelly 2010). How can the international community encourage a wider participation of traditional Islamic law states in the international legal system? Since the survival rates of commitments of these states to international courts are relatively high, Islamic law states could prove in the future to constitute firm supporters of the international legal framework. The establishment of a successful IICJ may well prove to be successful in helping Islamic states resolve disputes, as our analyses of the ICJ demonstrate, yet this success may come at a broader cost of weakening the coherence of international law as a whole.

A better understanding of the interconnection between domestic legal systems and international law helps us see international adjudication in a different light and gives us a better sense of its strengths and shortcomings. Our empirical models provide interesting insights into when and how states choose to support international adjudicators and how international courts affect state behavior in the international arena. We hope that this book will spurn further work on the domestic–international law nexus and expand ideas about the rational design of international institutions in new and promising directions.

References

Abbott, Kenneth W. and Duncan Snidal. 1998. "Why States Act through Formal International Organizations." *Journal of Conflict Resolution* 42(1): 3–32.

Abdal-Haqq, Irshad. 2002. "Islamic Law: An Overview of its Origin and Elements." *The Journal of Islamic Law and Culture* 7: 27–81.

Abtahi, Hirad. 2005. "The Islamic Republic of Iran and the ICC." *Journal of International Criminal Justice* 3: 635–648.

Al-Azmeh, Aziz. 1988. *Islamic Law: Social and Historical Contexts.* New York, NY: Routledge.

Al-Buraey, Muhammad A. 1985. *Administrative Development; An Islamic Perspective.* London, UK: Routledge and Kegan Paul.

Alexandrov, S. A. 1995. *Reservations in Unilateral Declarations Accepting the Compulsory Jurisdiction of the International Court of Justice.* The Netherlands: Martinus Nijhoff Publishers.

Allain, Jean. 2000. *A Century of International Adjudication: The Rule of Law and its Limits.* The Hague: T.M.C. Asser Press.

Al-Mutairi, Hezam Mater O. 2002. "Ethics of Administration and Development in Islam: A Comparative Perspective." *Journal of King Saud University,* Admin. Sci 14(1): 49–64.

Alter, Karen J. 1998. "Who Are the 'Masters of the Treaty'? European Governments and the European Court of Justice." *International Organization* 52(1): 121–147.

2003. "Do International Courts Enhance Compliance with International Law?" *Review of Asian and Pacific Studies* 25(1): 51–78.

2006. "Screening Power: International Organizations as Informative Agents," in Darren G. Hawkins, David A. Lake, Daniel L. Nielson, and Michael J. Tierney (eds.), *Delegation and Agency in International Organizations,* New York, NY: Cambridge University Press, pp. 312–338.

2008. "Delegating to International Courts: Self-Binding vs. Other-Binding Delegation." *Law and Contemporary Problems* 71(1): 37–76.

Alvarez, José E. 2005. *International Organizations as Law-makers.* New York, NY: Oxford University Press.

Arabi, Oussama. 1998. "Contract Stipulations (Shurut) in Islamic law: The Ottoman Majalla and Ibn Taymiyya." *International Journal of Middle East Studies* 30(1): 29–50.

238

Armstrong, David, Theo Farrell, and Helene Lambert. 2007. *International Law and International Relations*. New York, NY: Cambridge University Press.

Arsanjani, Mahnoush H. and W. Michael Reisman. 2005. "The Law-in-Action of the International Criminal Court." *The American Journal of International Law* 99(2): 385–403.

Aust, Anthony. 2007. *Modern Treaty Law and Practice*. Cambridge, UK: Cambridge University Press.

Badr, Gamal Moursi. 1978. "Islamic Law: Its Relation to Other Legal Systems." *The American Journal of Comparative Law* 26(2): 187–198.

Baird, Douglas G., Robert H. Gertner, and Randal C. Picker. 1994. *Game Theory and the Law*. Cambridge, MA: Harvard University Press.

Barnett, Michael N. and Martha Finnemore. 1999. "The Politics, Power, and Pathologies of International Organizations." *International Organization* 53(4): 699–732.

Bassiouni, M. Cherif. 1982. "Sources of Islamic Law, and the Protection of Human Rights in the Islamic Criminal Justice System," in M. Cherif Bassiouni (ed.), *The Islamic Criminal Justice System*. London, UK: Oceana Publications.

1996. *The Law of the International Criminal Tribunal for the Former Yugoslavia*. Boston, MA: Martinus Nijhoff Publishers.

2006. "The ICC – *Quo Vadis?*" *Journal of International Criminal Justice* 4(3): 421–427.

Bederman, David J. 2001. *International Law Frameworks*. New York, NY: Foundation Press.

Behrens, Hans-Jörg. 1999. "The Trial Proceedings," in Roy S. Lee (ed.), *The International Criminal Court: The Making of the Rome Statute*. The Hague: Kluwer Law International, pp. 238–246.

Bennett, D. Scott and Allan C. Stam. 2000. "Eugene: A Conceptual Manual." *International Interactions* 26(2): 179–204.

Bilder, Richard B. 1981. *Managing the Risks of International Agreement*. Madison, WI: University of Wisconsin Press.

1998. "International Dispute Settlement and the Role of International Adjudication," in Charlotte Ku and Paul F. Diehl (eds.), *International Law: Classic and Contemporary Readings*. Boulder, CO: Lynne Rienner, pp. 233–256.

Bochmer, Charles, Erik Gartzke, and Timothy Nordstrom. 2004. "Do Intergovernmental Organizations Promote Peace?" *World Politics* 57(1): 1–38.

Bojarski, Wladyslaw. 1994. *Prawo Rzymskie*. Torun: TNOIK.

Bolton, John R. 2001. "The Risks and Weaknesses of the International Criminal Court from America's Perspective." *Law and Contemporary Problems* 64(1): 167–180.

Bosly, Henri-D. 2004. "Admission of Guilt before the ICC and in Continental Systems." *Journal of International Criminal Justice* 2(4): 1040–1049.

Brewster, Rachel. 2006. "Rule-Based Dispute Resolution in International Trade Law." *Virginia Law Review* 92: 251–288.

Bridge. Michael G. 1984. "Does Anglo-Canadian Contract Law Need a Doctrine of Good Faith?" *Canadian Business Law Journal* 9(4): 385–426.

Brierly, James L. 1963. *The Law of Nations: An Introduction to the International Law of Peace.* Oxford, UK: Oxford University Press.

Briggs, H. W. 1958. "Reservations to the Acceptance of Compulsory Jurisdiction of the International Court of Justice." *Recueil des Cours* 93(I): 223–367.

Brower, Charles N. and Jeremy K. Sharpe. 2003. "International Arbitration and the Islamic World: The Third Phase." *American Journal of International Law* 97(3): 643–656.

Brown, Chester. 2007. *A Common Law of International Adjudication.* Oxford, UK: Oxford University Press.

Brownlie, Ian. 2003. *Principles of Public International Law,* 6th edn. Oxford, UK: Oxford University Press.

Bsoul, Labeeb Ahmed. 2008. "International Treaties (Mu'ahadat) in Islamic Practice in the Light of Islamic International Law (Siyar)." Lanham, MD: University Press of America.

Bull, Hedley. 1977. *The Anarchical Society: A Study of Order in World Politics.* New York, NY: Columbia University Press.

Burley, Anne-Marie and Walter Mattli. 1993. "Europe before the Court: A Political Theory of Legal Integration." *International Organization* 47(1): 41–76.

Busch, Marc L. and Eric Reinhardt. 2000. "Bargaining in the Shadow of the Law: Early Settlement in GATT/WTO Disputes." *Fordham International Law Journal* 24(1): 158–172.

Calabresi, Guido. 1985. *A Common Law for the Age of Statutes.* Cambridge, MA: Harvard University Press.

Carey, Henry F. 2002. "Adversarial Systems," in Herbert M. Kritzer (ed.), *Legal Systems of the World: A Political, Social, and Cultural Encyclopedia.* Santa Barbara, CA: ABC-CLIO, pp. 6–9.

Cassese, Antonio. 2005. *International Criminal Law,* 1st edn. Oxford, UK: Oxford University Press.

　　2008. *International Criminal Law,* 2nd edn. Oxford, UK: Oxford University Press.

Central Intelligence Agency. 2007. *CIA World Factbook,* available at www.cia.gov/library/publications/the-world-factbook.

Charney, Jonathan I. 1998. "Third Party Dispute Settlement and International Law." *Columbia Journal of Transnational Law* 36(1): 65–89.

Chayes, Abram and Antonia Handler Chayes. 1993. "On Compliance." *International Organization* 47(2): 175–205.

Christensen, Robert. 2002. "Getting to Peace by Reconciling Notions of Justice: The Importance of Considering Discrepancies between Civil and Common Legal Systems in the Formation of the International Criminal Court." *UCLA Journal of International Law and Foreign Affairs* 6(2): 391–395.

Cichowski, Rachel A. 2007. *The European Court and Civil Society: Litigation, Mobilization and Governance.* New York, NY: Cambridge University Press.

Cingranelli, David L. and David L. Richards. 2008. "The Cingranelli-Richards (CIRI) Human Rights Dataset Version 2008.03.12," available at www.humanrightsdata.org.

Crawford, James. 1995. "The ILC Adopts a Statute for an International Criminal Court." *The American Journal of International Law* 89(2): 404–416.

Crawford, Vincent P. and Joel Sobel. 1982. "Strategic Information Transmission." *Econometrica* 50(6): 1413–1451.

Cryer, Robert, Håkan Friman, Darryl Robinson, and Elizabeth Wilmshurt. 2007. *International Criminal Law and Procedure*. New York, NY: Cambridge University Press.

Damaska, Mirjan. 1986. *The Faces of Justice and State Authority*. New Haven, CT: Yale University Press.

Danner, Allison Marston. 2003. "Enhancing the Legitimacy and Accountability of Prosecutorial Discretion at the International Criminal Court." *The American Journal of International Law* 97(3): 510–552.

Darbyshire, Penny. 2001. *Eddey on the English Legal System*, 7th edn. London, UK: Sweet and Maxwell.

Davenport, Christian. 1995. "Multi-Dimensional Threat Perception and State Repression: An Inquiry into Why States Apply Negative Sanctions." *American Journal of Political Science* 39(3): 683–713.

David, Rene and John E. Brierly. 1985. *Major Legal Systems in the World Today*. London, UK: Stevens.

De Groot, Gerard-Renè. 1992. "European Education in the 21st Century," in B. De Witte and C. Forder (eds.), *The Common Law of Europe and the Future of Legal Education*. Deventer, The Netherlands: Kluwer Law and Taxation Publishers.

Dicey, Albert. 1959. *Introduction to the Study of the Law of the Constitution*, 10th edn. London, UK: Macmillan.

Dillard, Hardy Cross. 1978. "The World Court: Reflections of a Professor Turned Judge." *American University Law Review* 27(2): 205–250.

Dinan, Desmond. 2005. *Ever Closer Union: An Introduction to European Integration*. Boulder, CO: Lynne Rienner Publishers.

Dixon, William J. 1994. "Democracy and the Peaceful Settlement of International Conflict." *American Political Science Review* 88(1): 14–32.

Djankov, Simeon, Rafael La Porta, Florencio Lopez-de-Silanes, and Andrei Shleifer. 2002. "Courts: The Lex Mundi Project." NBER Working Paper Series 8890.

Duffy, John F. 1998. "Administrative Common Law in Judicial Review." *Texas Law Review* 77: 114–214.

El-Hassan, Abd El-Wahab Ahmed. 1985. "Freedom of Contract, the Doctrine of Frustration, and Sanctity of Contracts in Sudan Law and Islamic Law." *Arab Law Quarterly* 1(1): 51–59.

Elkind, Jerome B. 1984. *Non-Appearance before the International Court of Justice: Functional and Comparative Analysis*. The Netherlands: Martinus Nijhoff Publishers.

Eyffinger, Arthur. 1996. *The International Court of Justice, 1946–1996*. The Hague: Kluwer Law International.

Farnsworth, E. Allan. 1995. "Duties of Good Faith and Fair Dealing under the Unidroit Principles, Relevant International Conventions, and National Laws." *Tulane Journal of International and Comparative Law* 3(1): 47–63.

Farrell, Joseph. 1987. "Cheap Talk, Coordination and Entry." *RAND Journal of Economics* 18(1): 34–39.

Farrell, Joseph and Robert Gibbons. 1989. "Cheap Talk with Two Audiences." *American Economic Review* 95(5): 1214–1223.

Farrell, Joseph and Matthew Rabin. 1996. "Cheap Talk." *Journal of Economic Perspectives* 10(3): 103–118.

Fearon, James D. 1994. "Domestic Political Audiences and the Escalation of International Disputes." *American Political Science Review* 88(3): 577–592.

1995. "Rationalist Explanations for War." *International Organization* 49(3): 379–414.

1998. "Bargaining, Enforcement, and International Cooperation." *International Organization* 52(2): 269–305.

Fernández de Gurmendi, Silvia A. 1999. "The Process of Negotiations," in Raj S. Lee (ed.), *The International Criminal Court: The Making of the Rome Statute*. The Hague: Kluwer Law International.

Fischer, Dana, D. 1982. "Decisions to Use the International Court of Justice: Four Recent Cases." *International Studies Quarterly* 26(2): 251–277.

Ford, Christopher A. 1995. "Siyar-ization and its Discontents: International Law and Islam's Constitutional Crisis." *Texas International Law Journal* 30: 499–533.

Funken, Katja. 2003. "The Best of Both Worlds: The Trend towards Convergence of the Civil Law and the Common Law System." University of Munich School of Law Working Paper. SSRN Working Papers Series, available to http://search.ssrn.com/sol3/papers.cfm?abstract_id= 476461.

Gamble, John King Jr. 1980. "Reservations to Multilateral Treaties: A Macroscopic View of State Practice." *American Journal of International Law* 74(2): 372–394.

Gamble, John King Jr. and Dana D. Fischer. 1976. *The International Court of Justice: An Analysis of a Failure*. Lexington, MA: Lexington Books.

Garrett, Geoffrey and Barry R. Weingast. 1993. "Ideas, Interests, and Institutions: Constructing the European Community's Internal Market," in Judith Goldstein and Robert O. Keohane (eds.), *Ideas and Foreign Policy: Beliefs, Institutions, and Political Change*. Ithaca, NY: Cornell University Press, pp. 173–206.

Garrett, Geoffrey, R. Daniel Kelemen, and Heiner Schulz. 1998. "The European Court of Justice, National Governments, and Legal Integration in the European Union." *International Organization* 52(1): 149–176.

Gaubatz, Kurt T. 1996. "Democratic States and Commitment in International Relations." *International Organization* 50(1): 109–139.

Ghosn, Faten, Glenn Palmer, and Stuart A. Bremer. 2004. "The MID3 Data Set, 1993–2001: Procedures, Coding Rules, and Description." *Conflict Management and Peace Science* 21(2): 133–154.

Gill, Terry D., Harm Dotinga, Erik Jaap Molenaar, and Alex Oude Elferink. 2003. *Rosenne's the World Court: What it Is and How it Works*. Boston, MA: Martinus Nijhoff Publishers.

Gilpin, Robert. 1981. *War and Change in World Politics*. New York, NY: Cambridge University Press.

Ginsburg, Tom and Richard H. McAdams. 2004. "Adjudicating in Anarchy: An Expressive Theory of International Dispute Resolution." *William and Mary Law Review* 45(4): 1229–1339.

Glendon, Mare A., Michael W. Gordon, and Christopher Osakwe. 1994. *Comparative Legal Traditions: Text, Materials and Cases on the Civil and Common Law Traditions, with Special Reference to French, German, English and European Law*. St. Paul, MN: West Publishing Company.

Glenn, H. Patrick. 1993. "La Civilization de la Common Law." *Revue Internationale de Droit Comparè* 45(3): 549–575.

2001. "Are Legal Traditions Incommensurable?" *The American Journal of Comparative Law* 49(1): 133–145.

2007. *Legal Traditions of the World: Sustainable Diversity in Law*. Oxford, UK: Oxford University Press.

Goldsmith, Jack L. and Eric A. Posner. 2005. *The Limits of International Law*. Oxford, UK: Oxford University Press.

Goldstein, L. Judith, Miles Kahler, Robert O. Keohane, and Anne-Marie Slaughter (eds.), 2001. *Legalization and World Politics*. Cambridge, MA: MIT Press.

Goodliffe, Jay and Darren Hawkins. 2009. "A Funny Thing Happened on the Way to Rome: Explaining International Criminal Court Negotiations." *The Journal of Politics* 71(3): 977–997.

Goodman, Ryan and Derek Jinks. 2003. "Measuring the Effects of Human Rights Treaties." *European Journal of International Law* 14(1): 171–183.

Gordon, Michael Wallace. 2002. "Common Law," in Herbert M. Kritzer (ed.), *Legal Systems of the World: A Political, Social, and Cultural Encyclopedia*. Santa Barbara, CA: ABC-CLIO, pp. 322–324.

Gross, Leo. 1987. "Compulsory Jurisdiction under the Optional Clause: History and Practice," in Lori F. Damrosch (ed.), *The International Court of Justice at a Crossroads*. Dobbs Ferry, NY: Transnational Publishers, Inc., pp. 19–57.

Gruber, Lloyd. 2000. *Ruling the World: Power Politics and the Rise of Supranational Institutions*. Princeton, NJ: Princeton University Press.

Guariglia, Fabricio. 1999. "Investigation and Prosecution," in Roy S. Lee (ed.), *The International Criminal Court: The Making of the Rome Statute*. The Hague: Kluwer Law International, pp. 227–237.

Guzman, Andrew T. 2008. *How International Law Works: A Rational Choice Theory*. Oxford, UK: Oxford University Press.

Habachy, Saba. 1962. "Property, Right, and Contract in Muslim Law." *Columbia Law Review* 62(3): 450–473.

Hadfield, Brigid and Maurice Sunkin. 2002. "United Kingdom," in Herbert M. Kritzer (ed.), *Legal Systems of the World: A Political, Social, and Cultural Encyclopedia*. Santa Barbara, CA: ABC CLIO, pp. 1695–1700.

Hafner-Burton, Emilie M. 2005. "Trading Human Rights: How Preferential Trade Agreements Influence Government Repression." *International Organization* 59(3): 593–629.

Hafner-Burton, Emilie M. and Kiyoteru Tsutsui. 2005. "Human Rights in a Globalizing World: The Paradox of Empty Promises." *The American Journal of Sociology* 110(5): 1373–1411.

Hafner-Burton, Emilie M., Jana von Stein and Erik Gartzke. 2008. "International Organizations Count." *Journal of Conflict Resolution* 52(2): 175–188.

Hallaq, Wael B. 2005. *The Origins and Evolution of Islamic Law*. New York, NY: Cambridge University Press.

Hansen, Holley E., Sara McLaughlin Mitchell, and Stephen C. Nemeth. 2008. "IO Mediation of Interstate Conflicts: Moving beyond the Global versus Regional Dichotomy." *Journal of Conflict Resolution* 52(2): 295–325.

Harlow, Carol. 2006. "Global Administrative Law: The Quest for Principles and Values." *The European Journal of International Law* 17: 187–214.

Hathaway, Oona. A. 2002. "Do Human Rights Treaties Make a Difference?" *Yale Law Journal* 111(8): 1935–2042.

Hawkins, Darren and Wade Jacoby. 2008. "Agent Permeability, Principal Delegation, and the European Court of Human Rights." *Review of International Organization* 3(1): 1–28.

Helfer, Laurence R. and Anne-Marie Slaughter. 2005. "Why States Create International Tribunals: A Response to Professors Posner and Yoo." *California Law Review* 93(3): 901–956.

Henderson, Conway W. 1993. "Population Pressures and Political Repression." *Social Science Quarterly* 74(2): 322–333.

Hensel, Paul R. 2001. "Contentious Issues and World Politics: The Management of Territorial Claims in the Americas, 1816–1992." *International Studies Quarterly* 45(1): 81–109.

Hensel, Paul R., Sara McLaughlin Mitchell, Thomas E. Sowers II, and Clayton L. Thyne. 2008. "Bones of Contention: Comparing Territorial, Maritime, and River Issues." *Journal of Conflict Resolution* 52(1): 117–143.

Hudec, Robert E. 1993. *Enforcing International Trade Law: The Evolution of the Modern GATT Legal System*. Salem, NH: Butterworth Legal Publishers.

Hudson, Manley O. 1957. "The Succession of the International Court of Justice to the Permanent Court of International Justice." *The American Journal of International Law* 51(3): 569–573.

Hunt, David. 2004. "The International Criminal Court." *Journal of International Criminal Justice* 2(1): 56–70.

Huth, Paul K. and Todd L. Allee. 2002. *The Democratic Peace and Territorial Conflict in the Twentieth Century*. New York, NY: Cambridge University Press.

Ikenberry, John. 2001. *After Victory: Institutions, Strategic Restraint, and the Rebuilding of Order after Major Wars*. Princeton, NJ: Princeton University Press.

Imber, Colin. 1997. *Ebu's-su'ud: The Islamic Legal Tradition*. Edinburgh, UK: Edinburgh University Press.

International Peace Research Institute. 2009. Armed Conflict Dataset Website, available at www.prio.no/CSCW/Datasets/Armed-Conflict/UCDP-PRIO.

Iqbal, Walid. 2001. "Courts, Lawyering, and *ADR*: Glimpses into the Islamic Tradition." *Fordham Urban Law Journal* 28(4): 1035–1045.

Irani, George E. and Nathan C. Funk. 1998. "Rituals of Reconciliation: Arab-Islamic Perspectives." *Arab Studies Quarterly* 20(4): 53–73.

Jacobson, Harold K., William M. Reisinger, and Todd Mathers. 1986. "National Entanglements in International Governmental Organizations." *American Political Science Review* 80(1): 141–159.

Jaggers, Keith and Ted R. Gurr. 1995. "Tracking Democracy's Third Wave with the Polity III Data." *Journal of Peace Research* 32(4): 469–482.

Janis, Mark W. 2003. *An Introduction to International Law*. New York, NY: Aspen Publishers.

Jennings, Sir Robert and Sir Arthur Watts (eds.), 1992. *Oppenheim's International Law*. Essex, UK: Longman.

Joireman, Sandra F. 2001. "Inherited Legal Systems and Effective Rule of Law." *Journal of Modern African Studies* 39(4): 571–596.

2004. "Colonization and the Rule of Law: Comparing the Effectiveness of Common Law and Civil Law Countries." *Constitutional Political Economy* 15(4): 315–338.

Jolowicz, J. A. 2003. "Adversarial and Inquisitorial Models of Civil Procedure." *International and Comparative Law Quarterly* 52(2): 281–291.

Jouannet, Emmanuelle. 2006. "French and American Perspectives on International Law: Legal Cultures and International Law." *Maine Law Review* 58(2): 293–336.

Kegley, Charles W. Jr. and Gregory A. Raymond. 1990. *When Trust Breaks Down: Alliance Norms and World Politics*. Columbia, SC: University of South Carolina Press.

Keith, Linda Camp. 1999. "The United Nations International Covenant on Civil and Political Rights: Does it Make a Difference in Human Rights Behavior?" *Journal of Peace Research* 36(1): 95–118.

Keleman, R. Daniel and Eric C. Sibbitt. 2004. "The Globalization of American Law." *International Organization* 58(1): 103–136.

Kelley, Judith. 2007. "Who Keeps International Commitments and Why? The International Criminal Court and Bilateral Nonsurrender Agreements." *American Political Science Review* 1901(3): 573–589.

Kelly, Michael J. 2010. "Islam and International Criminal Law: A Brief (In) Compatibility Study." *Creighton University School of Law, Pace International Law Review Online Companion* 1(8): 1–31, available at http://digitalcommons. pace.edu/cgi/viewcontent.cgi?article=1007+context=pilronline.

Keohane, Robert O. 1984. *After Hegemony: Cooperation and Discord in the World Political Economy*. Princeton, NJ: Princeton University Press.

Keohane, Robert O., Andrew Moravcsik, and Anne-Marie Slaughter. 2000. "Legalized Dispute Resolution: Interstate and Transnational." *International Organization* 54(3): 457–488.

Khadduri, Majid. 1956. "Islam and the Modern Law of Nations." *American Journal of International Law* 50(2): 358–372.

Kim, Jeong-You. 1996. "Cheap Talk and Reputation in Repeated Pretrial Negotiation." *RAND Journal of Economics* 27(4). 787–802.

King, Gary, Michael Tomz, and Jason Wittenberg. 2000. "Making the Most of Statistical Analyses: Improving Interpretation and Presentation." *American Journal of Political Science* 44(2): 347–361.

Kingsbury, Benedict, Nico Krisch, and Richard B. Stewart. 2005. "The Emergence of Global Administrative Law." *Law and Contemporary Problems* 68: 15–61.

Koch, Charles H. 2003. "Envisioning a Global Legal Culture." *Michigan Journal of International Law* 25(1): 1–77.

Koh, Harold Hongjn. 1997. "Why Do Nations Obey International Law?" *The Yale Law Journal* 106(8): 2599–2659.

Kolanczyk, Kazimierz. 1997. *Prawo Rzymskie*, 5th edn. Warszawa: Wydawnictwa Prawnicze PWN.

Kolb, Robert. 2006. "Principles as Sources of International Law (with Special Reference to Good Faith)." *Netherlands International Law Review* 53(1): 1–36.

Koremenos, Barbara. 2005. "Contracting around International Uncertainty." *American Political Science Review* 99(4): 549–565.

Koremenos, Barbara, Charles Lipson, and Duncan Snidal. 2001. "The Rational Design of International Institutions." *International Organization* 55(4): 761–799.

Koskenniemi, Martti and Päivi Leino. 2002. "Fragmentation of International Law? Postmodern Anxieties." *Leiden Journal of International Law* 15(3): 553–579.

Kress, Claus. 2003. "Symposium – The Procedural Law of the International Criminal Court in Outline: Anatomy of a Unique Compromise." *Journal of International Criminal Justice* 1(3): 603–617.

Krisch, Nico. 2005. "International Law in Times of Hegemony: Unequal Power and the Shaping of the International Legal Order." *European Journal of International Law* 16(3): 369–408.

Krisch, Nico and Benedict Kingsbury. 2006. "Introduction: Global Governance and Global Administrative Law in the International Legal Order." *The European Journal of International Law* 17: 1–13.

Kritzer, Herbert M. (ed.), 2002. *Legal Systems of the World: A Political, Social, and Cultural Encyclopedia*. Santa Barbara, CA: ABC-CLIO.

Ku, Charlotte, Paul F. Diehl, Beth A. Simmons, Dorinda G. Dallmeyer, and Harold K. Jacobson. 2001. "Exploring International Law: Opportunities and Challenges for Political Science Research." *International Studies Review* 3(1): 3–23.

Kuran, Timur. 1995. "Islamic Economics and the Islamic Subeconomy." *Journal of Economic Perspectives* 9(4): 155–173.

Kydd, Andrew. 2003. "Which Side are You On? Bias, Credibility, and Mediation." *American Journal of Political Science* 47(4): 597–611.

Landman, Todd. 2005. "The Political Science of Human Rights." British Journal of Political Science 35(3): 549–572.

Langbein, John H. 1987. "Comparative Civil Procedure and the Style of Complex Contracts." *The American Journal of Comparative Law* 35(2): 381–394.

La Porta, Rafael, Florencio Lopez-de-Silanes, Andrei Schleifer, and Robert Vishny. 1999. "The Quality of Government." *Journal of Law, Economics, and Organization* 15(1): 222–279.

Lee, Roy S. 1999. *The International Criminal Court: The Making of the Rome Statute*. The Hague: Kluwer Law International.

Leeds, Brett Ashley. 1999. "Domestic Political Institutions, Credible Commitments, and International Cooperation." *American Journal of Political Science* 43(4): 979–1002.

Legrand, Pierre. 1996. "European Legal Systems Are Not Converging." *The International and Comparative Law Quarterly* 45(1): 52–81.

Lemke, Douglas. 2002. *Regions of War and Peace.* New York, NY: Cambridge University Press.

Leonard, Eric K. 2005. *The Onset of Global Governance: International Relations Theory and the International Criminal Court.* Burlington, VT: Ashgate.

Lippman, Matthew, Sean McConville, and Mordechai Yerushalmi. 1988. *Islamic Criminal Law and Procedure.* New York, NY: Praeger.

Lipson, Charles. 2003. *Reliable Partners: How Democracies have Made a Separate Peace.* Princeton, NJ: Princeton University Press.

Lloyd, Lorna. 1985. "'A Springboard for the Future': A Historical Examination of Britain's Role in Shaping the Optional Clause of the Permanent Court of International Justice." *The American Journal of International Law* 79(1): 28–51.

——— 1997. *Peace Through Law : Britain and the International Court in the 1920s.* Rochester, NY: Boydell Press.

Lombardini, Michele. 2001. "International Islamic Court of Justice: Towards an International Islamic Legal System?" *Leiden Journal of International Law* 14(3): 665–680.

Long, J. Scott. 1997. *Regression Models for Categorical and Limited Dependent Variables.* Thousand Oaks, CA: Sage.

Lukashuk. I. I. 1989. "The Principle *Pacta Sunt Servanda* and the Nature of Obligation Under International Law." *The American Journal of International Law* 83(3): 513–518.

Lundmark, Thomas. 2001. "Verbose Contracts." *The American Journal of Comparative Law* 49(1): 121–130.

Lutz, Eleen L. and Kathryn Sikkink. 2000. "International Human Rights Law and Practice in Latin America." *International Organization* 54(3): 633–659.

MacCarrick, Gwynn. 2005. "The Right to a Fair Trial in International Criminal Law (Rules of Procedure and Evidence in Transition from Nuremberg to East Timor)." Paper presented at the nineteenth International Conference of the International Society for the Reform of Criminal Law, Edinburgh, Scotland, available at www.isrcl.org.

Mann, F. A. 1973. *Studies in International Law.* Oxford, UK: Oxford University Press.

Markesinis, Basil S. 2000. *The Coming Together of the Common Law and the Civil Law.* Oxford, UK: Hart Publishing.

Mattei, Ugo. 1997a. "Three Patterns of Law: Taxonomy and Change in the World's Legal Systems." *The American Journal of Comparative Law* 45(1): 5–44.

——— 1997b. *Comparative Law and Economics.* Ann Arbor, MI: University of Michigan Press.

Matthews, Steven A. 1989. "Veto Threats: Rhetoric in a Bargaining Game." *Quarterly Journal of Economics* 104(2): 347–369.

McAdams, Richard H. 2005. "The Expressive Power of Adjudication." *University of Illinois Law Review* 5(5): 1043–1121.

Mearsheimer, John J. 1994/1995. "The False Promise of International Institutions." *International Security* 19(3): 5–49.

Merrills, J. G. 2005. *International Dispute Settlement.* New York, NY: Cambridge University Press.

Merryman, John Henry. 1985. *The Civil Law Tradition*. Stanford, CA: Stanford University Press.

Merryman, John Henry, David S. Clark, and John O. Haley. 1994. *The Civil Law Tradition: Europe, Latin America, and East Asia*. Charlottesville, VI: The Michie Company Law Publishers.

Michalowski, Raymond. 2002. "Cuba," in Herbert M. Kritzer (ed.), *Legal Systems of the World: A Political, Social, and Cultural Encyclopedia*. Santa Barbara, CA: ABC-CLIO, pp. 396–401.

Mitchell, Ronald. 1994. "Regime Design Matters: Intentional Oil Pollution and Treaty Compliance." *International Organization* 48(3): 425–458.

Mitchell, Sara McLaughlin. 2002. "A Kantian System? Democracy and Third-Party Conflict Resolution." *American Journal of Political Science* 46(4): 749–759.

Mitchell, Sara McLaughlin and Paul R. Hensel. 2007. "International Institutions and Compliance with Agreements." *American Journal of Political Science* 51(4): 721–737.

Mitchell, Sara McLaughlin and Emilia Justyna Powell. 2009. "Legal Systems and Variance in the Design of Commitments to the International Court of Justice." *Conflict Management and Peace Science* 26(2): 164–190.

Mitchell, Sara McLaughlin, Kelly M. Kadera, and Mark J. C. Crescenzi. 2009. "Practicing Democratic Community Norms: Third-Party Conflict Management and Successful Settlements," in Jacob Bercovitch and Scott Sigmund Gartner (eds.), *International Conflict Mediation: New Approaches and Findings*. New York, NY: Routledge, pp. 243–264.

Mohammed, Noor. 1988. "Principles of Islamic Contract Law." *Journal of Law and Religion* 6(1): 115–130.

Moore, Kathleen. 2002. "Islamic Law," in Herbert M. Kritzer (ed.), *Legal Systems of the World: A Political, Social, and Cultural Encyclopedia*. Santa Barbara, CA: ABC-CLIO, pp. 752–755.

Morag-Levine, Noga. 2007. "Common Law, Civil Law and the Administrative State: From Coke to Lochner." *Constitutional Commentary* 24(3): 601–661.

Moravcsik, Andrew. 1997. "Taking Preferences Seriously: A Liberal Theory of International Politics." *International Organization* 51(4): 513–553.

  2000. "The Origins of Human Rights Regimes: Democratic Delegation in Postwar Europe." *International Organization* 54(2): 217–252.

Morgenthau, Hans. 1948. *Politics among Nations: The Struggle for Power and Peace*. New York, NY: Knopf.

Morrow, James. 2007. "When Do States Follow the Laws of War?" *American Political Science Review* 1901(3): 559–572.

Moss, Giuditta Cordero. 2007a. "International Contracts between Common Law and Civil Law: Is Non-state Law to be Preferred? The Difficulty of Interpreting Legal Standards such as Good Faith." *Global Jurist* 7(1): 1–38.

  2007b. "Harmonised Contract Clauses in Different Business Cultures," in T. Wilhelmsson, E. Paunio, and A. Poholainen (eds.), *Private Law and the Many Cultures of Europe*. The Hague: Kluwer Law International.

Mushkat, Roda. 2008. "Hong Kong and Succession of Treaties." *International and Comparative Law Quarterly* 46(1): 181–201.

Nassar, Nagla. 1995. *Sanctity of Contracts Revisited: A Study in the Theory and Practice of Long-Term International Commercial Transactions.* Dordrecht: Martinus Nijhoff Publishers.

Neumayer, Eric. 2005. "Do International Human Rights Treaties Improve Respect for Human Rights?" *Journal of Conflict Resolution* 49(6): 925–953.

O'Connor. J. F. 1991. *Good Faith in International Law.* Brookfield, VT: Dartmouth Publishing Company.

Oduntan, Gbenga. 1999. *The Law and Practice of the International Court of Justice (1946–1996).* Enugu, Nigeria: Fourth Dimension Publishers.

Opolot, James S. E. 1980. *An Analysis of World Legal Traditions.* Jonesboro, TN: Pilgrimage Press.

Organski, A. F. K. and Jacek Kugler. 1980. *The War Ledger.* Chicago, IL: University of Chicago Press.

Owsia, Parviz. 1991. "Sources of Law under English, French, Islamic and Iranian Law: A Comparative Review of Legal Techniques." *Arab Law Quarterly* 6(1): 33–67.

Pair, Lara M. 2001. "NOTE and COMMENT: Judicial Activism in the ICJ Charter Interpretation." *ILSA Journal of International and Comparative Law* 8: 181–221.

Palmeter David and Petros Mavroidis. 1998. "The WTO Legal System: Sources of Law." *The American Journal of International Law* 92(3): 398–413.

Peczenik, Aleksander. 1997. "The Binding Force of Precedents," in D. Neil MacCormick and Robert S. Summers (eds.), *Interpreting Precedents: A Comparative Study.* Aldershot, UK: Ashgate Publishing.

Pejovic, Caslav. 2001. "Civil Law and Common Law: Two Different Paths Leading to the Same Goal." *Victoria University Wellington Law Review* 32(3): 817–841.

Phillimore, Walter George. 1922–1923. "An International Criminal Court and the Resolutions of the Committee of Jurists." *British Yearbook of International Law* 3(1): 79–86.

Picker, Colin B. 2008. "International Law's Mixed Heritage: A Common/Civil Law Jurisdiction." *Vanderbilt Journal of Transnational Law* 41: 1085–1140.

Poe, Steven C. and C. Neal Tate. 1994. "Repression of Human Rights to Personal Integrity in the 1980s: A Global Analysis." *American Political Science Review* 88(4): 853–872.

Poe, Steven C., C. Neal Tate, and Linda Camp Keith. 1999. "Repression of the Human Right to Personal Integrity Revisited: A Global Cross-National Study Covering the Years 1976–1993." *International Studies Quarterly* 43(2): 291–313.

Politi, Mauro and Federica Gioia. 2006. "The Criminal Procedure before the International Criminal Court: Main Features." *The Law and Practice of International Courts and Tribunals* 5(1): 103–123.

Posner, Eric A. 2004. "The Decline of the International Court of Justice." John M. Olin Law and Economics Working Paper No. 233; Public Law and Legal Theory Working Paper No. 81.

Posner, Eric A. and Miguel de Figueiredo. 2004. "Is the International Court of Justice Biased?" John M. Olin Law and Economics Working Paper No. 234.

Posner, Eric A. and John C. Yoo. 2005. "Judicial Independence in International Tribunals." *California Law Review* 93(1): 1–74.

Powell, Emilia Justyna. 2006a. "Conflict, Cooperation, and the Legal Systems of the World." Doctoral Dissertation. The Florida State University.

2006b. "The Dynamics of Support for the European Court of Justice." Working Paper.

2010. "Negotiating Military Alliances: Legal Systems and Alliance Formation." *International Interactions* 36(1): 28–59.

Powell, Emilia Justyna and Sara McLaughlin Mitchell. 2007. "The International Court of Justice and the World's Three Legal Systems." *Journal of Politics* 69(2): 397–415.

Powell, Emilia Justyna and Stephanie Rickard. 2010. "International Trade and Domestic Legal Systems: Examining the Impact of Islamic Law on Bilateral Trade Flows." Forthcoming in *International Interactions* 36(4).

Powell, Emilia Justyna and Jeffrey K. Staton. 2009. "Domestic Judicial Institutions and Human Rights Treaty Violation." *International Studies Quarterly* 53(1): 149–174.

Powell, Emilia Justyna and Krista E. Wiegand. 2010. "Legal Systems and Peaceful Attempts to Resolve Territorial Disputes." *Conflict Management and Peace Science* 27(2): 129–151.

Powers, David S. 1992. "On Judicial Review in Islamic Law." *Law and Society Review* 26(2): 315–341.

Powers, Kathy and Gary Goertz. 2009. "The Evolution of Regional Economic Institutions (REI) into Security Institutions or the Demise of Realist Military Alliances?" Working Paper, available at http://ducis.jhfc.duke.edu/wp-content/uploads/archive/documents/GoertzBackgroundReading.pdf.

Putnam, Robert D. 1988. "Diplomacy and Domestic Politics: The Logic of Two-Level Games." *International Organization* 42(3): 427–460.

Randazzo, Kirk A. and Reginald Sheehan. 2002. "Appellate Courts," in Herbert M. Kritzer (ed.), *Legal Systems of the World: A Political, Social, and Cultural Encyclopedia*. Santa Barbara, CA: ABC-CLIO, pp. 59–61.

Raymond, Gregory A. 1994. "Democracies, Disputes, and Third-Party Intermediaries." *Journal of Conflict Resolution* 38(1): 24–42.

2004. "International Adjudication and Conflict Management," in H. M. Hensel (ed.), *Sovereignty and the Global Community: The Quest for Order in the International System*. Aldershot, UK: Ashgate, pp. 221–248.

Rayner S. E. 1991. *The Theory of Contracts in Islamic Law: A Comparative Analysis with Particular Reference to the Modern Legislation in Kuwait, Bahrain and The United Arab Emirates*. Boston, MA: Graham & Trotman Ltd.

Reichel, Philip L. 2008. *Comparative Criminal Justice Systems*. Upper Saddle River, NJ: Prentice Hall.

Reinhardt, Eric. 2001. "Adjudication Without Enforcement in GATT Disputes." *Journal of Conflict Resolution* 45(2): 174–195.

Reus-Smit, Christian (ed.), 2004. *The Politics of International Law*. New York, NY: Cambridge University Press.

Ring, Jonathan, Sara McLaughlin Mitchell, and Mary K. Spellman. 2009. "What Did They Leave Behind? Legal Systems, Colonial Legacies, and Human Rights Practices." Working Paper, University of Iowa.

Roach, Steven C. 2005. "Arab States and the Role of Islam in the International Criminal Court." *Political Studies* 53(1): 143–161.

Rogowski, Ralf. 2002. "Civil Law," in Herbert M. Kritzer (ed.), *Legal Systems of the World: A Political, Social, and Cultural Encyclopedia*. Santa Barbara, CA: ABC-CLIO, pp. 304–310.

Rosen, Lawrence. 2000. *The Justice of Islam*. Oxford, UK: Oxford University Press.

Rosenne, Shabtai. 1957/1962. *The International Court of Justice: What it is and How it Works*. New York, NY: Oceana Publications.

1963. *The International Court of Justice: An Essay in Political and Legal Theory*. Leyden: A. W. Sijthoff's Uitgeversmaatschappij N. V.

Rossetti, Carlo. 2002. "Inquisitorial Procedure," in Herbert M. Kritzer (ed.), *Legal Systems of the World: A Political, Social, and Cultural Encyclopedia*. Santa Barbara, CA: ABC-CLIO, pp. 710–714.

Russett, Bruce and John R. Oneal. 2001. *Triangulating Peace: Democracy, Interdependence, and International Organizations*. New York, NY: W. W. Norton & Company.

Russett, Bruce, John R. Oneal, and David R. Davis. 1998. "The Third Leg of the Kantian Tripod for Peace: International Organizations and Militarized Disputes." *International Organization* 52(3): 441–467.

Saleh, Nabil. 2001. "Freedom of Contract: What Does it Mean in the Context of Arab Laws?" *Arab Law Quarterly* 16(4): 346–357.

Salmi, Ralph H., Cesar Adib Majul, and George K. Tanham. 1998. *Islam and Conflict Resolution*. Lanham, MD: University Press of America.

Sartori, Anne E. 2005. *Deterrence by Diplomacy*. Princeton, NJ: Princeton University Press.

Sayen, George. 2003. "Arbitration, Conciliation, and the Islamic Legal Tradition in Saudi Arabia." *University of Pennsylvania Journal of International Economic Law* 24(4): 905–953.

Schabas, William A. 2004. *An Introduction to the International Criminal Court*, 2nd edn. New York, NY: Cambridge University Press.

2007. *An Introduction to the International Criminal Court*, 3rd edn. New York, NY: Cambridge University Press.

Scheffer, David J. 1999. "The United States and the International Criminal Court." *The American Journal of International Law* 93(1): 12–22.

Schiff, Benjamin. 2008. *Building the International Criminal Court*. New York, NY: Cambridge University Press.

Schlesinger, Rudolf, Hans Baade, Mirjan Damaska, and Peter Herzog. 1998. *Comparative Law: Case-Text-Materials*. New York, NY: The Foundation Press, Inc.

Schultz, Kenneth A. 2001. *Democracy and Coercive Diplomacy*. New York, NY: Cambridge University Press.

Scott, Gary L. and Craig L. Carr. 1987. "The ICJ and Compulsory Jurisdiction: The Case for Closing the Clause." *The American Journal of International Law* 81(1): 57–76.

Scott, Gary L. and Karen D. Csajko. 1988. "Compulsory Jurisdiction and Defiance in the World Court: A Comparison of the PCIJ and the ICJ." *Journal of International Law and Policy* 16(2–3): 377–392.

Seagle, William. 1946. *The History of Law*. New York, NY: Tudor Publishing Co.

Shahabuddeen, Mohamed. 1996. *Precedent in the World Court*. New York, NY: Cambridge University Press.

Shany, Yuval. 2003. *The Competing Jurisdictions of International Courts and Tribunals*. Oxford, UK: Oxford University Press.

2007. *Regulating Jurisdictional Relations between National and International Courts*. Oxford, UK: Oxford University Press.

Shapiro, Martin. 1980a. "Appeal." *Law and Society Review* 14(3): 629–661.

1980b. "Islam and Appeal." *California Law Review* 68(2): 350–381.

1986. *Courts: A Comparative and Political Analysis*. Chicago, IL: University of Chicago Press.

Shaw, Malcolm N. 2003. *International Law*, 5th edn. New York, NY: Cambridge University Press.

Shihata, Ibrahm F. I. 1965. "The Attitude of New States Toward the International Court of Justice." *International Organization* 19(2): 203–222.

Sikkink, Kathryn. 1993. "Human Rights, Principled Issue-Networks, and Sovereignty in Latin America." *International Organization* 47(3): 411–441.

Simmons, Beth A. 1998. "Compliance with International Agreements." *Annual Review of Political Science* 1: 75–93.

1999. "See You in 'Court'? The Appeal to Quasi-Judicial Legal Processes in the Settlement of Territorial Disputes," in Paul F. Diehl (ed.), *A Road Map to War: Territorial Dimensions of International Conflict*, Nashville, TN: Vanderbilt University Press, pp. 205–237.

2000. "International Law and State Behavior: Commitment and Compliance in International Monetary Affairs." *American Political Science Review* 94(4): 819–835.

2009. *Mobilizing for Human Rights: International Law in Domestic Politics*. New York, NY: Cambridge University Press.

Simmons, Beth A. and Allison Marston Danner. 2010. "Credible Commitments and the International Criminal Court." *International Organization* 64(2): 225–256.

Simmons, Beth A. and Richard H. Steinberg. 2007. *International Law and International Relations: An International Organization Reader*. New York, NY: Cambridge University Press.

Singer, J. David, Stuart A. Bremer, and John Stuckey. 1972. "Capability Distribution, Uncertainty, and Major Power War, 1820–1965," in Bruce Russett (ed.), *Peace, War, and Numbers*. Beverly Hills, CA: Sage, pp. 19–48.

Singh, Mahendra P. 2001. *German Administrative Law in Common Law Perspective*. Heidelberg, Germany: Springer Verlag.

Singh, Nagendra. 1989. *The Role and Record of the International Court of Justice*. The Netherlands: Martinus Nijhoff Publishers.

Slaughter, Anne-Marie. 1995. "International Law in a World of Liberal States." *European Journal of International Law* 6(4): 503–538.

Slaughter, Anne-Marie, Andrew S. Tulumello, and Stephan Wood. 1998. "International Law and International Relations Theory: A New

Generation of Interdisciplinary Scholarship." *The American Journal of International Law* 92(3): 367–397.

Small, Melvin and J. David Singer. 1982. *Resort to Arms: International and Civil Wars, 1816–1980*. Beverly Hills, CA: Sage.

Souryal, Sam S. 2004. *q*. Huntsville, TX: Office of International Criminal Justice.

Spelliscy, Shane. 2001. "The Proliferation of International Tribunals: A Chink in the Armor." *Columbia Journal of Transnational Law* 40(3): 143–175.

Stewart, Richard B. 2003. "Administrative Law in the Twenty-First Century." *New York University Law Review* 78: 437–460.

Stone Sweet, Alec. 1999. "Judicialization and the Construction of Governance." *Comparative Political Studies* 32(2): 147–184.

Struett, Michael J. 2008. *The Politics of Constructing the International Criminal Court: NGOs, Discourse, and Agency*. New York, NY: Palgrave Macmillan.

Struett, Michael J. and Steven A. Weldon. 2006. "Explaining State Decisions to Ratify the International Criminal Court Treaty." Paper presented at the Annual Conference of the American Political Science Association, Philadelphia, August 30–September 2.

Summerst, Robert S. 1982. "The General Duty of Good Faith: Its Recognition and Conceptualization in the New Restatement of Contracts." *Cornell Law Review* 67(4): 810–840.

Swaine, Edward. 2003. "Unsigning." *Stanford Law Review* 55(5): 2061–2089.

Szafarz, Renata. 1993. *The Compulsory Jurisdiction of the International Court of Justice*. The Netherlands: Martinus Nijhoff Publishers.

Tape, Thomas G. 2005. *Interpreting Diagnostic Tests*. University of Nebraska Medical Center, available at http://gim.unmc.edu/dxtests/Default.htm.

Teson, Fernando R. 1992. "The Kantian Theory of International Law." *Columbia Law Review* 92(1): 53–102.

Teubner, Gunther. 1998. "Legal Irritants: Good Faith in British Law or How Unifying Law Ends Up in New Divergences." *The Modern Law Review* 61(1): 11–32.

Tiba, Ferew Kebede. 2006. "What Caused the Multiplicity of International Courts and Tribunals?" *Gonzaga Journal of International Law* 10(2): 202–226.

Tochilovsky, Vladimir. 2002. "Proceedings in the International Criminal Court: Some Lessons to Learn from ICTY Experience." *European Journal of Crime, Criminal Law and Criminal Justice* 10(4): 268–275.

Van Hoecke, Mark and Mark Warrington. 1998. "Legal Cultures, Legal Paradigms and Legal Doctrine: Towards A New Model for Comparative Law." *The International and Comparative Law Quarterly* 47(3): 495–536.

Vago, Steven. 2000. *Law and Society*. Upper Saddle River, NJ: Prentice Hall.

Vasquez, John A. 1995. "Why Do Neighbors Fight? Proximity, Interaction, or Territoriality." *Journal of Peace Research* 32(3): 277–293.

Virally, Michael. 1983. "Review Essay: Good Faith in Public International Law." *The American Journal of International Law* 77(1): 130–134.

Vogiatzi, Maria. 2002. "The Historical Evolution of the Optional Clause." *Non-State Actors and International Law* 2(1): 41–88.

Von Glahn, Gerhard. 1996. *Law Among Nations*, 7th edn. Boston, MA: Allyn & Bacon.

Von Glahn, Gerhard and James Larry Taulbee. 2007. *Law Among Nations: An Introduction to Public International Law*. New York, NY: Pearson Education.

Von Stein, Jana. 2004. "Making Promises, Keeping Promises: Democracy, Ratification, and Compliance in International Human Rights Law." Working Paper, University of Michigan.

Watson, Alan. 1984. "The Evolution of Law: The Roman System of Contracts." *Law and History Review* 2(1): 1–20.

Wehberg, Hans. 1959. "Pacta Sunt Servanda." *The American Journal of International Law* 53(4): 775–786.

Weller, Marc. 2002. "Undoing the Global Constitution: UN Security Council Action on the International Criminal Court." *International Affairs* 78(4): 693–712.

Whincup, Michael H. 1992. *Contract Law and Practice: The English System and Continental Comparisons*. The Hague: Kluwer Law and Taxation Publishers.

Wiegand, Krista E. 2009. "Bahrain, Qatar, and the Hawar Islands: Resolution of a Gulf Territorial Dispute." Forthcoming in *MiddleEast Politics* Winter 2010.

Wiegand, Wolfgang. 1996. "Americanization of Law: Reception or Convergence?" in Lawrence Friedman and Harry Scheiber (eds.), *Legal Culture and the Legal Profession*. Boulder, CO: Westview Press, pp. 137–152.

Williams, Paul R. and Michael P. Scharf. 2002. *Peace with Justice? War Crimes and Accountability in the Former Yugoslavia*. Oxford, UK: Rowman & Littlefield Publishers.

Wippman, David. 2004. "The International Criminal Court," in Christian Reus-Smit (ed.), *The Politics of International Law*. New York, NY: Cambridge University Press, pp. 151–188.

Zahraa, Mahdi. 1998. "Negotiating Contracts in Islamic and Middle Eastern Laws." *Arab Law Quarterly* 13(3): 265–277.

Zartner-Falstrom, Dana. 2006. "Thought versus Action: The Influence of Legal Tradition on French and American Approaches to International Law." *Maine Law Review* 58(2): 338–376.

Zimmermann, Reinhard and Simon Whittaker. 2000. *Good Faith in European Contract Law*. New York, NY: Cambridge University Press.

Index

Abbott, Kenneth W., 73, 75, 97
ad hoc tribunals, 100, 104, 106, 128, 229
adjudication, 2, 6, 7, 8, 54, 68, 69, 70, 72,
     73–74, 75, 81, 82, 118, 131, 137, 139,
     146, 153, 154, 163, 181, 206, 221,
     227, 229, 233
  expressive theory of, 12, 74, 80, 81, 83,
     137
  rational legal design theory of, 67, 69,
     92, 93, 94, 129, 135, 223, 226
adjudicative bodies, 31, 34–35, 51, 52, 57,
     60, 62, 74, 84, 96, 97, 99, 100, 101,
     104, 105, 127, 224, 227, 230
adjudicator, 2, 7, 9, 10, 12, 49, 69–70,
     71–72, 79–80, 83–85, 92, 94, 128,
     129, 135, 137, 138, 139, 156, 162,
     171, 194, 207, 209, 219, 220, 221,
     223, 224, 225, 228
  impartial, 216, 221
  international, 6, 79, 82, 92, 237
  unbiased, 3, 12, 71, 73, 74, 137, 139,
     153
administrative law, 52–53, 54, 87
  administrative governance, 52–53
  civil law, 53
  common law, 52
  Islamic law, 44, 53
adversarial approach, 55–56, 64, 105,
     106–107, 108
  and ICC, 110
  civil law, 64
  common law, 29, 55, 61, 106, 107, 108,
     109
  Islamic law, 56
agreements, 9, 12, 14, 43–44, 47, 48, 71,
     82, 85, 86, 90–91, 124, 164, 173–174,
     175–176, 196, 208–210, 217, 221,
     227
  bilateral, 70, 175
  contractual, 23, 70
  international, 11, 46, 63, 76, 77, 89,
     116, 169, 225

reaching, 129, 137, 194–195, 216–218,
     219
Al-Azmeh, Aziz, 11, 36
Al-Buraey, Muhammad A., 53, 54
Alexandrov, S. A., 1, 15, 140, 166, 169,
     170, 177, 179, 206
Allain, Jean, 9, 68, 91, 131, 132
Allee, Todd L., 156, 161, 227
Alter, Karen J., 5, 6, 9, 54, 70, 73, 85, 86,
     97, 228
Alvarez, Jose E., 34, 35
analogical reasoning, 37–38
appeal, 9, 17, 31, 58–61, 88, 109, 232, 236
  and ICC, 60, 109
  civil law, 58–59
  common law, 58–59
  international courts, 60
  Islamic law, 59–60
  proceedings, 17, 59, 78, 107, 109, 111
Arabi, Oussama, 48, 90, 175
arbitration, 6, 8, 30, 44, 87, 118, 130–131,
     134, 146, 181, 227
  and PCA, 8
Aust, Anthony, 44, 46, 49

Badr, Gamal Moursi, 22, 27, 29, 30, 231
bargaining, 7, 10, 14, 17, 71, 74, 76, 82,
     83, 86, 104, 137, 145, 159, 161–162,
     166, 207–208, 217
  and World Court, 85, 92, 206, 209, 211,
     220, 225
  in the shadow of a court, 7, 14, 83, 94,
     194, 221
  interstate, 4, 71, 73, 84, 85, 92, 94,
     95, 117, 138, 162, 164, 171, 195,
     207–209
  out of court effects, 19, 91–92, 195, 209,
     218, 220, 221–222, 225
  uncertainty, 3, 6, 11, 12, 51, 62, 70,
     73–74, 76–77, 84, 86, 96–98, 112,
     122, 137
Bassiouni, M. Cherif, 104, 106

255

CPSIA information can be obtained
at www.ICGtesting.com
Printed in the USA
LVHW051012191221
706635LV00011B/1038

9 781107 661677